Spectacles of Reform

Spectacles of Reform

THEATER AND ACTIVISM IN NINETEENTH-CENTURY AMERICA

Amy E. Hughes

THE UNIVERSITY OF MICHIGAN PRESS
ANN ARBOR

First paperback edition 2014

Published in the United States of America by
The University of Michigan Press
Printed and bound by CPI Group (UK) Ltd, Croydon, CR0 4YY

2017 2016 2015 2014 5 4 3 2

A CIP catalog record for this book is available from the British Library.

Library of Congress Cataloging-in-Publication Data

Hughes, Amy E.
Spectacles of reform : theater and activism in nineteenth-century America / Amy E. Hughes.
p. cm.
Includes bibliographical references and index.
ISBN 978-0-472-11862-5 (cloth : alk. paper) — ISBN 978-0-472-02889-4 (e-book)
1. Theater—United States—History—19th century. 2. Theater—Social aspects—United States—History—19th century. 3. Theater and society—United States—History—19th century. 4. American drama—19th century—History and criticism. 5. Spectacular, The, in literature. 6. Spectacular, The—History—19th century. I. Title.
PN2256.H86 2012
792.0973'09034—dc23 2012033645

ISBN 978-0-472-03597-7 (paper : alk. paper)

Cover: *Escape of Eliza and Child on the Ice*, #3 of 10 magic lantern slides by C. W. Briggs Company, 1881, Joseph Boggs Beale. Digital ID #86858d. Collection of The New-York Historical Society.

For SD

Acknowledgments

It has been a pleasure and privilege to work with LeAnn Fields as well as Alexa Ducsay, Scott Ham, and everyone else at the University of Michigan Press. I have deeply appreciated LeAnn's advice and expertise, and this is a better book because of her. Insightful comments and provocative suggestions offered by the anonymous readers of my manuscript helped me considerably during the final stage of writing; I sincerely thank them as well.

While a doctoral student at City University of New York's Graduate Center, four mentors worked patiently and tirelessly with me as I developed many of the ideas that lie at the heart of this project. Marvin Carlson offered countless hours of conversation, inspiration, and support. I am tremendously grateful for his influence and direction. Daniel Gerould initially sparked my interest in nineteenth-century melodrama, and his vast knowledge about the subject, as well as his enthusiasm about my own scholarly interventions, was invaluable. The guidance and attention provided by Judith Milhous has benefited me immensely over the years, and I will always endeavor to emulate both her meticulous approach to historiography and her commitment to her students. Heather S. Nathans at the University of Maryland has played a central role in my development as an academic professional since the day we met; her generous advice, probing questions, and unflagging encouragement have left an indelible mark on this book and on me personally. I am also indebted to teacher-scholars at the City University of New York, Columbia University, and the New School for Social Research who, very early on, urged me to explore some of the theoretical and methodological strategies I employ in this book: Courtney Bender, Oz Frankel, Alison Griffiths, David Jaffee, James De Jongh, Kevin Murphy, David Savran, Pamela Sheingorn, Alisa Solomon, and Maurya Wickstrom.

Prior to beginning doctoral work, I was lucky to meet teachers who became long-term mentors. Two warrant special mention. Louis Scheeder profoundly impacted me as an undergraduate and compelled me to pursue a teaching career; he has remained a positive force in my life, to my great fortune. Tobie S. Stein has advised and guided me for more than a decade and continues to serve as a model in my ongoing attempts to be the best teacher-scholar I can be. I am grateful to them both.

Brief but pivotal conversations at conferences, archives, and other venues shaped my conception of and commitment to this project in crucial ways. For galvanizing and challenging me, I thank Thomas Augst, Georgia Barnhill, Robin Bernstein, Charlotte Canning, Ric Caric, Mark Carnes, Jonathan Chambers, James M. Cherry, Joanna Cohen, Mark Cosdon, Esra Çizmeci, Chrystyna Dail, Tracy C. Davis, Paul Erickson, John W. Frick, Vincent Golden, Ezra Greenspan, Jonathan Gross, Lauren Hewes, Megan Sanborn Jones, Baz Kershaw, Jaclyn Penny, Sally Pierce, Peter P. Reed, Rebecca Schneider, Mike Sell, Jason Shaffer, Samuel Shanks, and Laura Wasowicz, among many others. I also treasure the exchanges I have had with colleagues in the American Theatre and Drama Society (ATDS), a professional organization that for many years has served as my intellectual home.

Professors and students at Brooklyn College, where I have taught since 2006, have provided me with important support, both moral and practical. The enthusiasm of the Department of Theater's faculty and staff has been sincere and steadfast. Jeanette Aultz, Rose Burnett Bonczek, Thomas Bullard, Robert I. Cohen, Mary Beth Easley, Michael Hairston, Deborah Hertzberg, Christopher Hoyt, Kip Marsh, Ruth Picans, Helen E. Richardson, Jaclyn Smerling, Teresa Snider-Stein, Tobie S. Stein, Jeff Stiefel, Laura Tesman, Lynn M. Thomson, and Judylee Vivier: your dedication, wisdom, and talent inspire me every day, and your faith in me has been instrumental to my completing this book. I have benefited immeasurably from the creativity and energy of students in our MA and MFA in Theater programs, especially Michael Anderson, Charles Bales, Erica Bates, Shane Breaux, Elizabeth Coen, Neal Freeman, Siobhan Glennon, Barry Honold, Andrew Kircher, Allison Lyman, Michael Maiella, Liz Ostler, and Will Shuler. Their generosity of heart and time allowed me to focus more attention on this project than I would have been able to otherwise. Outside of my department, the community of Noor Alam, Andrew Arlig, Caroline Arnold, Carolina Bank Muñoz, Brett Branco, Samir Chopra, Tri Datta, James Davis, Christopher

Ebert, Joseph Entin, Louis Fishman, Mobina Hashmi, Michael Meagher, Stephanie Jensen-Moulton, Danielle Kellogg, Ted Levine, Martha Nadell, Jason Nu, Naomi Singer, Karl Steel, Jocelyn Wills, and Liv Yarrow has been a huge gift. Philip Gallagher, Jerry Mirotznik, Donna Wilson, and Niesha Ziehmke deserve special acknowledgment for nurturing my passion for teaching and reinforcing my commitment to research and scholarship in the process. I also thank Maria Ann Conelli, dean of the School of Visual, Media, and Performing Arts, for her leadership and support.

Patient experts at libraries and special collections made essential contributions to my research by showing me new and exciting paths to explore. I extend heartfelt thanks to the curators and staff of the American Antiquarian Society, Boston Athenaeum, Boston Public Library, Brooklyn College Library, California Historical Society, Free Library of Philadelphia, Harvard Theatre Collection/Houghton Library, Historical Society of Pennsylvania, Library Company of Philadelphia, Mina Rees Library (Graduate Center, CUNY), New-York Historical Society, New York Public Library, San Francisco Performing Arts Library and Museum, San Francisco Public Library, and Stanford University's Special Collections. I am much obliged to Greg Lam Pak Ng, Big Machine Records, Library Company of Philadelphia, New-York Historical Society, and especially the American Antiquarian Society for allowing me to include exemplary illustrations of the spectacles I study in this book.

I offer special thanks to individuals and institutions who saw promise in my work and facilitated it with fellowships and grants. A Mrs. Giles Whiting Foundation Fellowship for Outstanding Teaching in the Humanities, as well as reassigned time for new faculty negotiated by the Professional Staff Congress of CUNY (my mighty mighty union), gave me the time I needed to finish the manuscript. In addition, I was the fortunate beneficiary of a Jay T. and Deborah Last Fellowship (American Antiquarian Society), Mellon Seminar Fellowship (CUNY Center for the Humanities), Doctoral Student Research Fund Fellowship (CUNY Graduate Center), Leonard and Claire Tow Faculty Travel Fellowship (Brooklyn College), Andrew W. Mellon Foundation Fellowship (Library Company of Philadelphia/Historical Society of Pennsylvania), Martin S. Tackel American Theatre Research Fellowship (PhD Program in Theatre, CUNY Graduate Center), ASTR Brooks McNamara Publishing Subvention (American Society for Theatre Research), ATDS Publication Subvention Award (American Theatre and Drama Society), and a publication subvention from the School of

Visual, Media, and Performing Arts at Brooklyn College. Support for this project was also provided by a PSC-CUNY Research Award, jointly funded by the Professional Staff Congress and CUNY.

The editors of the *Journal of American Drama and Theatre* (in a special issue curated by ATDS) and *Performing Arts Resources* (published by the Theatre Library Association) supported my work by publishing it: "Spectacles of Insanity: The *Delirium Tremens* on the Antebellum Stage," *JADT* 22, no. 2 (Spring 2010): 7–24; and "John B. Gough's Afternoon at the Theatre; Or, The Tyranny of an Account Book," *A Tyranny of Documents: The Performing Arts Historian as Film Noir Detective. Essays Dedicated to Brooks McNamara,* ed. Stephen Johnson, *PAR* 28 (2011): 101–9. I appreciate their permission to include revised material from these articles in chapter 2.

When I think about the many friends who provided intellectual stimulation and excellent company while I labored on this project, I am mystified by my good fortune. In particular, Margaret Araneo, Alison Kinney, David Langkamp, Jen-Scott Mobley, Ken Nielsen, Kathleen Potts, Jill Stevenson, Jessica Tabor-Fritch, and Jennifer Worth went above and beyond the call of duty to sustain, cajole, and buoy me during different stages of the thinking-and-writing process. From afar, Sasha Leitman helped me maintain both a sense of soul and a sense of humor from start to finish. My life and work have been incredibly enriched by these friendships.

My parents, Stephen and Susan K. Hughes, and brother, Paul W. Hughes, have constantly loved and encouraged me as I have pursued my dreams (even the wild ones); they deserve more thanks than I could possibly give in a lifetime. For always asking and always listening, I also thank David and Maureen Hughes, Michael Hughes, David and Sharon Dexter, and Richard and Kathy Willis. I relied on Mya Willis for countless games of hide-and-seek, and for that I spectacularly owe her. Inevitably, the publication of this book makes me think about five people, all terribly important to me, who will never read it: Victor and Evelyn Hughes, William and Jane Korns, and Dr. Robert Korns. Their example, affection, and belief in my potential continue to play a fundamental role in all of my pursuits. Even in their absence, their influence is palpable.

Finally, there is Scott Dexter. Thank you for saying "Yes, and . . ." again and again, and for spurring me to do the same—in this book, and in life. Intellectual gadfly, eloquent wordsmith, stalwart activist, intrepid adventurer, waggish wit, creative genius: you are everything. This book, and everything, is for you.

Contents

Contents

Introduction

For many Americans, the word *melodrama* usually brings a specific image to mind. In it, a black-clad mustachioed villain is tying a woman to the railroad tracks, cackling as he secures his prey. Checking his work with a firm tug, he hisses something about the brilliance of his devilish plan (or, perhaps, the devilishness of his brilliant plan), then scurries away, disappearing into the woods. As the heroine wiggles prettily on the rails, a whistle wails thinly in the distance and the ground begins to shake: a train is approaching. Realizing she is in danger of imminent death, she calls out desperately for help. "Will no one aid me?" The tumult of the oncoming locomotive grows louder; so do her fearful cries. When it seems all hope is lost, a dashing young man appears. With a few quick movements of his dexterous hands, he unravels her bonds and removes her from harm's way, a slim second before the train rushes by in a satisfying cacophony of sound and smoke. Our heroine has been saved, in the nick of time, by the hero.

This sensational scene, firmly embedded in the collective imagination, has in many ways come to symbolize melodrama itself, exemplifying the decadence, extremity, and excess associated with the genre as a whole. Endlessly revised and reprised, it has appeared in an astonishing variety of contexts, ranging from early film serials and animated cartoons to product advertising and pop-music album art (fig. 0.1). Despite the passage of time, fluctuations in taste, and the transformation of melodrama from genre to joke, the railroad rescue has endured, serving as fecund fodder for artists, humorists, and corporate entities.

The notoriety and ubiquity of this image belie its complicated, convoluted history. The version circulating today actually constitutes a "flamboyant display of historical forgetfulness," as Nan Enstad notes.[1] Railroad sequences began appearing on stage and in fiction during the mid-nineteenth century, and the scenario we recognize today first became popular in the United States after the premiere of Augustin Daly's melodrama *Under the Gaslight* (1867).[2] Daly's "railroad sensation," which concludes the fourth act, features a man—a one-armed Civil War veteran named Snorkey—tied to the tracks, who is saved from an oncoming train by the play's heroine, Laura. A century and a half later, this spectacle seems progressive, even feminist, when compared to the "gender-correct" copy circulating today. What did nineteenth-century audiences see in this sensational scene? What politics shaped and informed it? Would the answers to such questions allow us to understand better what we see—and what we *need* to see—in the reformed representation that is instantly recognizable today?

Apparently, when nineteenth-century Americans thought about melodrama, specific images came to their minds, too. In the biography of his brother Augustin, Joseph Daly reminisces about his early theater experiences by describing some of the extraordinary scenes he has seen. As if sifting through a collection of dusty playbills, he muses,

> And how the inky blackness of the bills of the play is illumined by strange meteors that flashed for their brief moment and were gone! Here is the singular Hebrew star, Adah Isaacs Menken . . . who has left some memories of herself as Mazeppa bound to a trained steed. . . . Here the bills show fairyland—Niblo's Garden with the Ravel pantomimists—and here the Revolutionary drama, a favorite entertainment when our country was young, in which one Yankee easily whipped half a dozen Britishers, and George Washington always appeared with red fire, in a final tableau.[3]

What is striking about this passage is the way in which Daly remembers: he reports the spectacle he sees when looking at a particular bill. Outstanding performers, sequences, and tableaux emerge from the complex layers of his memory. The sensations evoked by spectacle serve as a technology of recollection, a mechanism by and through which Daly relays his personal version of theater history. Even more striking, Daly describes the bodies within each spectacle: the barely clad Menken on horseback; the dexterous Ravels populating a fairyland at Niblo's; the singular Yankee triumphing over the unfairly advantaged British; George Washington surrounded by flames. Each is a fleeting, sensational moment in performance that, by virtue of its power and palpability,

Figure 0.1: American country pop singer Taylor Swift poses on the railroad tracks for her song "Mean" on *Speak Now* (2010). Consumers purchased more than one million digital copies of the album during the first week of its release, setting a new world record. Photograph by Joseph Anthony Baker. Courtesy of Big Machine Records.

burns itself into memory. Daly's method of recall underscores the importance of the spectacular instant to nineteenth-century theater audiences.

Spectacle has been a defining characteristic of melodrama since the early work of René-Charles Guilbert de Pixérécourt (1773–1844), the French father of the genre.[4] Exciting effects and tableaux, which were eventually dubbed "sensation scenes," enjoyed widespread popularity in America as well. Sensational aesthetics were not the exclusive domain of the theater, however. Novelists, including Ned Buntline, Mary Denison, and George Lippard, published thrilling stories that attempted to be both titillating and morally educative. Orators like William Wells Brown and John B. Gough mesmerized audiences with colorful stories emphasizing the necessity of abolition and temperance. And P. T. Barnum, perhaps the century's most famous sensation-maker, transformed events like the arrival of opera singer Jenny Lind in New York City (1850) into public spectacles.

Yet this century also comprises America's great age of reform. While readers and spectators increasingly sought sensational entertainment, public officials and philanthropists established institutions (prisons, asylums, schools) designed to discipline American subjects. Activists in the temperance, abolition, and women's suffrage movements attempted to transform political and social practices. The word *normal* ("constituting or conforming to a type or standard; regular, usual, typical; ordinary, conventional") also entered common usage, suggesting that the cultural urgency to adopt a repertoire of socially acceptable behaviors is a nineteenth-century invention.[5] The simultaneous, rapid, and paradoxical promotion of both normalization and sensationalism signals important tensions in Western culture during this period. Some of these tensions were enacted on American stages: in the mid-1800s, thousands of theatergoers attended plays extolling the values promoted by reformers. Why were reform-minded theater managers and audiences attracted to the melodramatic mode—or, conversely, why were producers and consumers of melodrama attracted to these politics? How did the imagery and affect embedded in these plays extend beyond the theater's walls? How did spectacle participate in that transference?

Spectacles of Reform explores how and why spectacle is a crucial component of the reform apparatus and a defining characteristic of American activism in general, whether highly organized or quietly quotidian. It advocates for a consideration of spectacle as methodology: a unique system of communication, employed in myriad contexts, that rehearses and sustains conceptions of race, gender, and class in extremely powerful ways. Spectacle capitalizes on the sensational and the profane, embracing what is deliberately hidden or secretly imagined and giving it material form. In essence, it renders visible the invisible; it makes sensation seen. Consequently, spectacle plays an instrumental role in the public and private spheres because of its potential to destabilize, complicate, or sustain sedimented ideological beliefs. Living in a society newly dominated by averages and norms, nineteenth-century spectators perceived melodrama's sensationalism (startling stage effects, dexterous actors, moments of intense affectivity) as exceptional, perhaps even radical. These sequences were not only exemplars of crowd-pleasing stagecraft but also complex experiences with the potential to transform humans in the audience through the human figures on stage.

Baz Kershaw's assertion that spectacle can play a powerful role in contemporary activism has inspired me to investigate historical antecedents exhibiting the dynamics he describes. He argues that spectacle offers scholars a unique opportunity "to figure what [spectacle] might be *doing* to the participants' sense of the human," and this is one of my central objectives. At the same time, I wonder: where and how do activist spectacles appear before and beyond the theatrical encounter? This question centers on "performance remains," to employ Rebecca Schneider's phrase—both *what* remains, and *how* it remains. "An action repeated again and again and again, however fractured or partial or incomplete, has a kind of staying power—persists through time—and even, in a sense, serves as a fleshy kind of 'document' of its own recurrence," Schneider writes. Why is spectacle kept alive through reinvention, revision, and repetition long after the drama is over? How are these spectacular remains interred in various archives, both documentary (texts, pictures, objects) and bodily (memories, flesh, collective imaginations)? More complicatedly, what remnants exist before the spectacle even begins—the forebears that shape content and reception, defying our assumptions about the linearity of time?[6]

To explore these questions, I examine three of the most popular sensation scenes that first appeared during the nineteenth century: the *delirium tremens* episode in W. H. Smith's *The Drunkard* (1844), Eliza crossing the ice floes in stage adaptations of Harriet Beecher Stowe's novel *Uncle Tom's Cabin* (1852), and the aforementioned "railroad sensation" in Daly's protofeminist play *Under the Gaslight* (1867). These spectacles—the drunkard temporarily experiencing insanity, the fugitive slave mother dashing across a river, and the heroine saving a man tied to the railroad tracks—had legs, working in tandem with visual and material culture to convey, allay, and deny urgent concerns about the rights and responsibilities of US citizenship. In addition, while theaters were presenting "situations," "effects," and "tableaux" on stage, products ranging from lithographs to children's books to decorative ceramics deployed similar "scenes" through illustration and ornamentation. They harnessed many of the dramaturgical strategies we associate with theatrical performance, suggesting that the coup de théâtre played a role in American cultural production more generally. Often, these artifacts reveal elemental facets of political culture, hidden in plain sight. As peculiar intersections of spectacle and reform, they bring into focus the dueling desires for excess and normalcy that, arguably, continue to obsess and regulate individuals today.

Theater scholars have studied the mechanics of stage spectacle, and historians have traced the impact of US reform movements, but to date the two fields have not come together to question how and why sensation scenes capitalized on public iconography and national sentiment associated with various advocacy projects. *Spectacles of Reform* illuminates spectacle's particular significance during the nineteenth century while also addressing enduring questions about the cultural importance of performance more generally. In that way, it fills a noteworthy gap in current scholarship on US theater history. A number of scholars have studied how entertainment reflected public aspirations and anxieties during the long nineteenth century, and their work deeply informs my thinking: Rosemarie K. Bank, John W. Frick, Jeffrey D. Mason, Bruce A. McConachie, Heather S. Nathans, Peter P. Reed, Jeffrey H. Richards, and Jason Shaffer, among others.[7] Scholars who have examined production practices and theatrical figures through the lenses of gender, race, and sexuality, such as Robert C. Allen, Robin Bernstein, Faye E. Dudden, Barbara Wallace Grossman, Eric Lott, Kim Marra, Lisa Merrill, Elizabeth Reitz Mullenix, and Harvey Young, have provided me with essential insights as well.[8] However, Americans' obsession with spectacle—the desire to see sensation—has been relatively neglected. Michael Booth, Michael Diamond, Martin Meisel, and Lynn Voskuil have explored the use of spectacle and sensationalism in British melodrama, but to date, no one has investigated similar activity in the United States.[9]

Unfortunately, most research on American theater during the nineteenth century elides questions about spectacle and its applications. In *Melodrama Unveiled: American Theatre and Culture, 1800–1850* (1968), a landmark study exploring theater as art and industry, David Grimsted dedicates a chapter to production practices during the first half of the century but focuses mainly on the mechanics of stage effects and critics' negative reactions to their heavy use. Monographs examining intersections of spectacle and slavery in the United States, including those by Joseph Roach, Saidiya V. Hartman, and Daphne A. Brooks, serve as valuable models for my exploration of abolitionist drama; but performances geared to other social issues, such as temperance and women's suffrage, fall outside the scope of those studies. In contrast to Gay Gibson Cima, who illuminates how women employed methods of abstracted embodiment to participate in the public sphere, I imagine the materiality of performance and spectatorship in order to appraise the reciprocity between popular entertainment and extratheatrical political activity. Michael M. Chemers and Mark Cosdon have offered important genre studies of spectacular entertainment (freak shows and pantomime, respectively). Like them, I focus primarily on one genre (melodrama), but for me melodrama functions more as crucible than subject, offering a unique opportunity to consider spectacle's role in American culture.[10]

Furthermore, most scholarship on the history of US reform tends to focus on one political issue (temperance *or* abolition *or* suffrage), whereas I examine a communication strategy (spectacle) utilized in multiple reform movements. *Spectacles of Reform* acknowledges the porous boundaries of nineteenth-century activism by studying the dynamics of "reform culture" more generally.[11] During this period, many activists supported more than one cause. Abolitionists promoted the tenets of temperance in their propaganda materials, and women who developed advocacy skills in the temperance movement eventually worked for abolition and even women's suffrage. Although some moralistic writings from the period betray deep suspicions of sensationalism, reformers and entrepreneurs staged provocative events whose politics ranged from the conservative to the progressive. I offer contrasting case studies drawn from theatrical, oratorical, and material media in order to sample this political plurality.

Why are discussions of spectacle mostly absent in nineteenth-century American theater historiography? Twenty years ago, McConachie called on theater historians "to question the ideological assumptions underlying such innocent-sounding terms as 'entertainment,' 'style,' 'dramatic art,' and 'culture.'"[12] Yet spectacle has not attracted serious investigation. Perhaps it has been taken less seriously due to long-lived assumptions that its main purpose is to amuse or decorate rather than provoke. Also, spectacle tends to require presence (liveness) more than poetry (language). As Kershaw observes, the contempt for spectacle can be traced all the way back to Aristotle's hierarchical taxonomy of the six elements of tragedy in *The Poetics:* spectacle (*opsis*) lies at the bottom of the barrel, forever buried under the weightier, culturally privileged concerns of plot, character, thought, diction, and music.[13]

I have seen repeated manifestations of this subtle prejudice at work. For example, at one point in her book *Uncle Tom Mania: Slavery, Minstrelsy, and Transatlantic Culture in the 1850s,* Sarah Meer perpetuates the impression that spectacle had little to do with reform when she writes, "Despite their 'moral' emphasis, Aiken and Conway [two early adapters of Stowe's novel] were not averse to incorporating some of the excitements that characterized spectacular melodrama."[14] In this remark, she characterizes the "excitements" of melodrama as being at odds with George L. Aiken's and H. J. Conway's "'moral' emphasis." Whether intentionally or not, Meer suggests that sensationalism obviates ideological communication. I believe that sedimented assumptions about spectacle embedded in statements like this have hindered our understanding of nineteenth-century spectators' experiences and expectations.

A general distaste for excess itself may also help to explain the lack of scholarship on sensationalism in nineteenth-century US theater. Melodrama, by definition, is excessive and indulgent. Invocations of the word today tend to be pejorative. Jacky Bratton observes, "Melodrama is the play not disguised as literature; theater allowing its falsity and allure to show; the Devil's way."[15] The exuberant qualities of melodrama, the traits that Susan Harris Smith says marginalized American drama for so long within the academy, keenly interest me.[16] This is why I treat excess—both the expressive mode and the cultural taboo—as a theoretical problem in this study.

Placing an "emphasis on *embodied* subjectivity," to employ Stanton B. Garner's phrase, in the first chapter I build a critical foundation for my case studies by rehearsing a theory of the *spectacular instant:* a heightened, fleeting, and palpable moment in performance that captivates the spectator through multiple planes of engagement. Author and activist Francis H. Underwood, founder of the antislavery periodical *The Atlantic Monthly,* highlights the centrality of embodiment in nineteenth-century theater in his anecdote about Harriet Beecher Stowe witnessing a performance of *Uncle Tom's Cabin:* "It must have been for her a thrilling experience to see her thoughts *bodied upon the stage,* at a time when any dramatic representation must have been to her so vivid."[17] Transforming the body from noun to verb in the context of performance, Underwood's expression is both curious and significant. Certainly, the body is embedded in the 1860s phrase "sensation scene." The word *sensation* derives from the Latin *sensus:* "perception, feeling, faculty of perception, meaning." The simultaneous presence of both feeling and meaning in this root demands an investigation of how spectacle harnesses corporeal poetics and politics—why bodies are necessary to make sensation seen.[18]

To that end, I taxonomize how human beings participate in spectacular performance: bodies *as* the spectacle (freaks, lecturers, solo performers), bodies *in* the spectacle (actors in melodramas), and bodies *at* the spectacle (audience members). Drawing on concepts of normalcy developed by scholars working within the frameworks of feminist, queer, and disability studies, I theorize corporeal excess by mapping the mechanisms of spectacle and enfreakment. Because they emphasize electronic media, postmodernist theories of spectacle, like those of Guy Debord and Jean Baudrillard, cannot be applied wholesale to nineteenth-century culture (which was undeniably but differently mediated); however, these insights have helpfully informed my understanding of spectacle's dynamism, so periodically I turn to them for inspiration as well.[19]

Each of the remaining chapters focuses on a major American reform movement, with a particular sensation scene serving as a kind of analytic epicenter. Although innovations in stage technology during the 1880s and 1890s allowed producers to achieve ever-more-spectacular effects, I am most interested in the relationship between spectacle and reform; therefore, I focus on a three-decade period when temperance, abolition, and suffrage were all part of national discourse. Each of my three case studies refers to one of these social dilemmas or "questions" (the temperance question, the slavery question, the woman question). They differ in crucial ways—iconographically, scenographically, and ideologically. By highlighting the differences among these scenes, I question the assumption that "melodrama must satisfy its audience's expectations rather than present a confrontation with belief and value," as Mason has argued.[20] The messages conveyed by the *delirium tremens* scene are politically assertive, even strident, whereas the politics articulated by Eliza's flight across the ice floes are more ambiguous. On the surface, the railroad rescue contains only a hint of prosuffrage sentiment; but when carefully examined in light of its historical moment, its feminist ethos becomes clearer. I also attempt to account for multiple responses, since no theory of reception can be universal. Activism, then and now, varies by degree: the intentions and desires of a working-class theatergoer attending a performance of *Uncle Tom's Cabin* probably differed markedly from those of a middle-class patron at an abolitionist lecture. There is as much to be learned from the differences in these hypothetical spectators' investments as from their similarities.

That said, *Spectacles of Reform* is a springboard, not a survey. I examine scenes in depth rather than in breadth, employing a methodology that emphasizes local and temporal contexts. Like Kershaw, I believe that the intentions and impact of spectacle are utterly contingent on the time, place, and powers involved.[21] Occasionally, I point to other plays and performances in which a particular tableau reappears, but that is not my main purpose. By focusing on specific productions in two US cities (Boston and New York), I hope to show how sensation scenes are invaluable archives, crowded and crammed with important cultural resonances—thereby encouraging others to study similar moments in additional plays, audiences, geographic regions, and cultural contexts in order to enhance our understanding of sensationalism in US culture.[22]

The staged alcoholic (or "drunkard"), both in theaters and in lecture halls, is the subject of the second chapter. Scholars have paid considerable attention to temperance propaganda depicting dystopian visions of the drunkard's family, but performances of the *delirium tremens* (DTs) played an equally important role in shaping public perceptions about the dangers of drink. Unlike many sensation scenes, which relied heavily on scenic effects, an actor's portrayal of the DTs was an exclusively somatic spectacle. Because of the body's centrality, this scene offers unique insight into the relationship between sensationalism, embodiment, and reform on the nineteenth-century American stage. Dipsomania, both as medical disorder and theatrical spectacle, invoked prescriptions of normalcy and self-discipline that emerged in the United States during the antebellum period. Medical texts suggest that physicians considered the DTs to be, essentially, a temporary episode of insanity, and therefore a shocking departure from the norm. Alcoholic characters suffering from the syndrome—most notably Edward Middleton in W. H. Smith's *The Drunkard; or, The Fallen Saved* (1844), arguably America's most famous temperance drama—were meant to horrify spectators. In harnessing the grotesque power of the DTs, dramatists, performers, and activists implicitly reinforced the orderly and efficient body privileged by "respectable" individuals in eastern urban centers. I also look at public commentary about John B. Gough, a recovering alcoholic and temperance advocate whose meteoric rise to fame occurred in the Boston region immediately prior to and alongside of *The Drunkard*. He performed, in essence, one-man melodramatic sensation scenes: virtual tableaux that amused, saddened, and moved his spectators. Multiple dimensions of the Gough phenomenon—the anecdotal and the actual, the public and the private—help illuminate why the DTs played such a prominent role in temperance-reform culture during the 1840s.

The third chapter explores how and why fugitive slaves were spectacularized in theatrical, iconographic, and discursive contexts, analyzing how the runaway seizes agency in the process of breaking the law. The focal point is Eliza's crossing of the Ohio River in dramatic versions of Harriet Beecher Stowe's *Uncle Tom's Cabin; or, Life among the Lowly* (1852), including plays by C. W. Taylor, H. J. Conway, and George L. Aiken. In this scene—which became popular as a result of its realization on stage, even though it occupies a mere two paragraphs in Stowe's novel—a quadroon mother, holding tightly to her child, jumps onto a series of moving ice floes in order to flee the bounty hunters who pursue her. As Kershaw observes, in spectacle the threat of disaster is omnipresent; spectacle often endeavors "to eliminate the human, to reduce it to total insignificance in the grand scheme—or chaos—of things."[23] Eliza's escape exemplifies a tendency in sensation scenes to generate affect by endangering the body at its center.

Moreover, the appearance of Eliza's flight in diverse media (children's literature, illustrated sheet music, political cartoons, ceramics) suggests that many Americans embraced Eliza as an activist symbol. It certainly posed a striking counterpoint to other depictions of absconded slaves, such as the type ornament that was frequently included in newspaper ads for runaways. *Uncle Tom*'s heroine embodies a protest of the erasure of personhood demanded by the slavery system, and I assert that this reading—which has more to do with subjectivity than race—possibly preceded or even exceeded spectators' appraisal of Eliza's ethnicity. At the same time, her equivocal racial status and her circulation in domestic space suggest that the politics of the image are, ultimately, ambivalent.

The fourth chapter investigates the origins of the victim tied to the train tracks. Daly's *Under the Gaslight: A Totally Original and Picturesque Drama of Life and Love in These Times, in Five Acts* (1867) premiered in New York City at a time of heightened suffrage activity: one year after the founding of the American Equal Rights Association, and one year before the full ratification of the Fourteenth Amendment, which paved the way for voting rights for African American men but excluded women. After Laura rescues Snorkey from the railroad tracks, the latter proclaims, "And these are the women who ain't to have the vote!" To contextualize this loaded comment, I assess competing conceptions of "true womanhood" articulated by proponents and opponents of women's suffrage and analyze how Laura reflects or deflects these constructions of femininity. In addition, discursive and pictorial depictions of the Civil War citizen-soldier help to illuminate Snorkey's significance in the story. It is also noteworthy that during the scene Laura uses an axe to break her way out of a locked shed, because the American version of this tool (literally, the "American axe") came to be associated with a host of gendered, nativist values during the late eighteenth and early nineteenth centuries. Finally, I ponder how and why this melodramatic scenario transformed into a more "gender appropriate" image within the public mind. Aided by Baudrillard's concept of "a real without origin or reality," a phenomenon that occurs through the accrual of time and repetition, I reflect on how later permutations of the railroad rescue belie the idea of a stable, unequivocal progenitor.[24] The simulacrum's stamina and stickiness attest to the sensation scene's significance within American culture.

One important note, regarding structure: in an effort to honor the slippery and inexorable character of the sensation scenes I examine, each chapter ends with a dénouement. I appreciate the paradox embedded in *dénouement* as a critical term: etymologically, the word connotes "unknotting" or "unraveling";

and yet, in dramaturgical analysis it refers to the final moments in a play when all loose ends are tied. I treat the dénouement as an unraveled space in which I share speculative, rather than conclusive, meditations on the broader significance of my discussion. I believe this approach respects and reflects the capricious, wily, hard-to-capture (hard-to-tie) quality of my subjects: scenes seen across media and across time. Sometimes, the dénouement offers a deliberate unknotting of the argument advanced in the chapter, because the spectacles I examine often leave me with more questions than answers.

The afterword—which, in many respects, constitutes the most substantial, ambitious, experimental, and hypothetical dénouement of all—explores how spectacle continues to fascinate American audiences. In the early twentieth century, melodrama found another home in cinema, and the histories of these two entertainment forms (one live, the other recorded, but both equally obsessed with spectacle) are inextricably intertwined.[25] Television is also a part of this tangled history: the sensationalism associated with melodrama, freak shows, and minstrelsy now manifests there, particularly in "reality TV" and "human interest" news programs. The DTs, the fugitive slave, and the railroad rescue have endured, manifesting in Disney (*Mickey's Mellerdramer*, 1933), Mighty Mouse (*Eliza on the Ice*, 1944), and Dudley Do-Right (1959–70) cartoons as well as recent blockbuster films like *Titanic* (1997) and *Hancock* (2008). In addition, new media technologies often transform real people and events into public spectacles, many of which operate and circulate like melodramatic sensation scenes once did. Individuals who fascinate the public, such as Chesley B. Sullenberger III (of "Miracle on the Hudson" fame), Wesley Autrey (New York City's "Subway Hero"), and Nadya Suleman ("Octomom"), have become our heroes and our freaks.

During the nineteenth century, the mechanisms of the spectacular instant were adopted in myriad contexts and continue to be habitually employed today. The means of production and distribution have changed, but contemporary performance culture still harnesses the affective dynamism of sensation scenes to inspire and discipline US citizens. In other words, spectacle was—and remains—central to the dramaturgy of reform itself.

1

The Body as/in/at the Spectacle

The melodramatic body is a body seized by meaning.
—PETER BROOKS, "MELODRAMA, BODY, REVOLUTION"[1]

In his landmark study of nineteenth-century Victorian and European theater, Martin Meisel argues that the most innovative trait of melodrama was the close relationship between picture and story: "its *dramaturgy* was pictorial, not just its *mise en scène.*" He further asserts that "such pictorialism was strongest in what were regarded as its most 'dramatic' gestures." The most dramatic of melodrama's gestures was the *situation:* a spectacular, climatic scene depicting a pivotal moment within a play. Examining how such sequences worked in tandem with literary and visual culture beyond the theater's walls, Meisel shows how the situation became a foundational, defining characteristic of the new dramaturgy, functioning as "a site of a complex interplay of narrative and picture, rather than one member in a three-legged race to a synthesis." Situations variously comprised silent tableaux (often called "realizations," especially when a famous illustration or painting was re-created on stage) or technological triumphs (such as burning buildings, sinking ships, and the like). As Tom Gunning notes, by the 1860s critics and patrons began calling these elaborate effects "sensation scenes," a phrase alluding to the "particularly intense, even overwhelming experience" that they provided.[2]

However, Meisel's main objective is to illuminate connections between staged realizations and extratheatrical visualizations rather than to reveal spectacle's phenomenology. What made these scenes sensational, and why did audiences find them so appealing? Because spectators considered a great many things sensational, the matter is complicated. Some sensation scenes featured impressive scenery; others involved nothing more than an actor's body. Freak shows, panoramas, lectures, and world's fairs were also dubbed "sensational." In publications ranging from newspapers to almanacs to children's books, provocative stories and incendiary images competed fiercely for readers' attention and fostered an appetite for sensation. Despite their incredible diversity, these products and practices had qualities or characteristics in common that gave them the sense of the spectacular.

Clearly, *how* something is presented and perceived, rather than *what* is presented and perceived, constitutes spectacle. The sensational is, in a word, exceptional. Our sense of the spectacular springs from the cultural norms that are jarred, destabilized, and exceeded in the process of representation. Therefore, a theoretical conception of the spectacular instant must be based on relations rather than essentials. One way to approach this problem is through the body. As culture's most conspicuous target for normalization, the body often reveals the unique pressures and politics of a historical moment. Concerns about bodies lie at the heart of the three reform movements featured in this book: temperance advocates touted the advantages of bodily discipline; abolitionists declared the injustices of bodily possession; women suffragists challenged assumptions about bodily essentialism. The centrality of the body in both spectacle and reform is one reason why, I argue, spectacle functions as methodology in reform.

Spectacle is nimble; spectacle is quick. Whether as big as a house or as small as a postage stamp, it strikes and overwhelms us with surprising intensity. To assess this power and pliability, I examine how different individuals participate in performances of excess, whether *as* the spectacle (extraordinary bodies in freak shows), *in* the spectacle (actors in sensation scenes), or *at* the spectacle (people who witness performance). Each of these perspectives offers unique insights into spectacle's dynamics. When the body itself becomes a spectacle, as in the freak show, ideas about what is "normal"—how a human should look, act, and be—are promoted and reinforced at the expense of variety and difference. Because the norm perpetually haunts the aberrant body on display, I posit that the norm perpetually defines the spectacular. Meanwhile, for the body *in* the spectacle, the possibility of death is omnipresent. Actors on stage, especially those performing in melodramas, constantly flirt with disaster. Sensation scenes, in particular, aggressively highlight the body's vulnerability. This suggests that the body in extremity is another defining feature of spectacle. Finally, I analyze some of the interpretive practices that nineteenth-century bodies *at* the spectacle brought to the theatrical experience. Sensation scenes appeared not only on stage but also in other media. Books, newspapers, and illustrations frequently harnessed the scale, intensity, and excesses of spectacle. These assorted texts and objects promoted viewing habits—tactics of seeing—that influenced how Americans consumed and experienced the world. Routinely harnessed as a didactic tool, spectacle focused the reader's attention and served as a conduit for the communication of ideas.

The midcentury emergence of the expression "sensation scene" and the heavy use of the phrase in theatrical advertising suggest that audiences actively sought the bodily sensations—the thrills and chills—that melodrama offered. To explore the potential efficacy of the spectacular instant, in the dénouement I consider how the visual is visceral. How do the things we see influence what we feel? The connection between sight and sensation helps to explain the power, popularity, and persistence of spectacle in US culture.

Norm-Defying Acts: Theorizing the Spectacular Instant

What stimulates our sense of the spectacular? The *spec* in *spectacle* suggests that visuality is its defining feature: it is something we see, something we watch. But as Bernard Beckerman observes in his comparison of theatrical spectacles (mass pageants, melodramatic tableaux, performances of skill) and "nondramatic" spectacles (fireworks, parades, processions), "visual terms do not alone make the spectacle"; rather, spectacles are defined relationally, "tak[ing] their measure from human scale and capacity." Indeed, scale is, perhaps, the most obvious matrix by which we perceive spectacle—but scale is not the same thing as size. According to Beckerman, spectacle manifests "when scale and number exceed human proportion—that is, the proportion which spectators accept as the norm."[3] In other words, scale is conceivable only within a system of relations: in order to detect, describe, or analyze something in terms of scale, an explicit or implicit norm must be in mind. Exhibitions of skill, such as the extraordinary exertions of acrobats or the tours de force of actors, generate awe because such performers exceed the abilities of average people.

Intensity is another defining quality of spectacle, which, like scale, exists only in relation. An event or experience is described as *intense* when it exceeds the expected or the routine. Discussing melodramatic situations, Meisel observes that some provide "a culminating symbolic summary of represented events" while others "substitute an arrested situation for action and reaction." Either way, such scenes serve as caesurae within a fast-moving plot, presenting an opportunity for the intensity to peak. This intensity derives from "the greater pressure of the whole on the particular," to employ Charles Altieri's phrase. It invokes a larger narrative world, an entire moral universe. This occurs regardless of whether the scene is an elaborate, action-oriented sequence or a static, frozen tableau. Bert O. States, comparing theater and film, argues that the compression of live performance lends it an intensity that can only happen in the theater: "Theater is swift (even Chekhov is swift). This swiftness has nothing to do with clock time or the suspense of the plot, but only with the fact that *everything* happens through the actor. This is the swiftness of condensation, of life raised to an intense power of temporal and spatial density." The temporal and spatial density States associates with theater generally is taken to another level during the spectacular instant.[4]

Excess—a word invoking both superabundance and superfluity—is another of spectacle's characteristics. As Baz Kershaw writes, "Performance ecology usually thrives on excess—even the excess of subtraction, as in Beckett's aesthetic," and the spectacular instant embraces and celebrates this inherent propensity of the theatrical endeavor. Emotional excess, in particular, is often included among melodrama's trademark qualities, as Peter Brooks contends: "The emotions and conditions expressed are almost overwhelming in their instinctual purity; they taste too strong." In his view, melodrama's tendency toward excessive expression is at once compelling and alienating.

> If we can sense its appeal (as well as its evident limitations), it must be because we are attracted to (though perhaps simultaneously repulsed by) the imaginary possibility of a world where we are solicited to say everything, where manners, the fear of self-betrayal, and accommodations to the Other no longer exert a controlling force.[5]

Brooks's assertion underscores what Kershaw has described as our "curiosity and contempt" of spectacle. In a strange and paradoxical way, spectacle both attracts and repulses us.[6] If melodrama appeals to a repressed and abhorred desire for excess—a desire "to say everything"—what cultural and historical factors influenced or caused that repression?[7]

The trend toward normalization during the nineteenth century provides a provisional answer to this question. During this period, a variety of spaces emerged to control, contain, and hide abject bodies. These institutions coincided with new systems of bodily discipline, predicated on self-regulation, that were typically enacted through a repertory of acceptable behaviors. Lennard J. Davis has explored the "remarkable fact" that our modern definition of the word *normal* emerged in the mid-nineteenth century. Its earlier meaning was "perpendicular," referring to an object of measurement—the carpenter's square ("norm"). The word's etymology reveals that evaluation, comparison, and referentiality are deeply embedded in the notion of normality.[8]

The concept of the norm informed (perhaps even inspired) a number of scientific, philosophical, and practical trends. Phrenology, an important predecessor of psychology that gained increasing popularity in Europe and America through 1850, provides some of the earliest evidence of the ascendance of the norm-as-ideal. Phrenologists postulated that a person's innate character could be read in the bumps of the skull. Similarly, new fields like statistics and eugenics (the cataloging of humans according to race) relied on norms and averages to measure and analyze data. Michel Foucault notes that the quantitative sciences ascended alongside regulatory practices, such as the school examination, that assigned penalties and rewards based on rankings rather than privilege, "thus substituting for the individuality of the memorable man that of the calculable man." For example, as Rodney Hessinger as shown, the University of Pennsylvania successfully maintained order among its male undergraduates during the early 1800s by introducing procedures classifying students in terms of their relative achievements. By replacing professorial approval with peer approval, thereby emphasizing "horizontal" rather than "vertical" authority structures, the system encouraged young men to practice self-control and self-improvement. Even Marxist philosophy—yet another product of the nineteenth century—allies itself with the ideal of the norm, as Davis observes: "Marx is unimaginable without a tendency to contemplate average humans and think about their abstract relation to work, wages, and so on. In this sense, Marx is very much in step with the movement of normalizing the body and the individual." These novel ways of calculating and quantifying phenomena in the natural and social worlds helped to establish the norm as one of the most powerful mandates within Western culture.[9]

And yet, like spectacle, norms can only be defined within a system of relations. Deviance defines typicality; exceptions define rules. The norm is, first and foremost, a mode of measurement and a mechanism for comparison. It identifies and reconciles difference by establishing a common denominator for all. In the process, the norm simultaneously reveals and denies the realities of diversity. Moreover, it is based on a powerful fiction: anyone and everyone can conform to it. The triumph of the norm (a barometer) over the Platonic ideal (a principle) has enormous consequences for corporeality, signaling a paradigm shift regarding the body's potentials. According to Davis,

> The idea of a norm pushes the normal variation of the body through a stricter template guiding the way the body "should" be. . . . The new ideal of ranked order is powered by the imperative of the norm, and then is supplemented by the notion of progress, human perfectibility, and the elimination of deviance, to create a dominating, hegemonic vision of what the human body should be.[10]

In other words, the norm commands the subject to curtail and contain his or her own excesses—or else. When the norm is ascendant, a directive to be ordinary or commonplace replaces the more benign notion that humanity is and always will be inferior to the ideal. Because averages champion conventions rather than exceptions, atypical subjects are automatically excluded, stigmatized, marginalized.

In a culture that enforces normalcy, excess is automatically abject. Indeed, judgment and repudiation seem entrenched in the word itself, folded within its overindulgent consonants. Normalcy celebrates efficiency; excess epitomizes waste. Normalcy prescribes moderation; excess seizes abundance. Norms renounce, contain, and extinguish the abnormality that excess represents. To embrace excess, then, is to deny both the value and the power of discipline's operations. (By definition, excess is *un*disciplined.) This is why spectacles of excess—bold, un-self-conscious displays; bodies in extremity; demonstrations of extraordinary skill—are inherently radical. In this sense, excess is always already political, too.

The Body *as* Spectacle

A striking fact about nineteenth-century spectatorship is that patrons circulated in venues where freaks and plays were in close proximity. Our contemporary aversion to the freak show, both in theory and in practice, is a relatively recent invention. Freakery grew in popularity in the United States during this period and sometimes shared space (literally and conceptually) with theatrical, oratorical, and ethnographic performance.[11] Audiences did not delineate amusements by genre in the same way we do today. Meisel suggests that the complex relationship between images and texts collapsed traditional genre categories within the newly mediatized culture of the nineteenth century; he declares, "The crowning blow to the notion of genre as fixed, immutable, and finite fell in the nineteenth century, whose practice reveals a faith in the infinite variability and particularity of genre."[12] In other words, different modes of cultural production promiscuously borrowed from and referred to one another; they were neither independently constituted nor unilaterally perceived.

The most obvious point of overlap is the midcentury museum, exemplified by P. T. Barnum's American Museum in New York City and Moses Kimball's Boston Museum. Museums featured a stunning variety of curiosities, ranging from the theatrical to the archaeological. The superabundant objects attracted middle-class patrons interested in viewing scientific exhibits, freaks, panoramas, lectures, and melodramas in a single visit. Some marketing materials from the period suggest that human oddities were the museums' principal draw. Freaks unequivocally dominate an advertisement for Barnum's museum circa 1860; it announces that there are "three performances daily" (presumably in Barnum's lecture room, where melodramas were staged), but the words are nearly lost on the periphery, literally and figuratively sidelined by the aberrant bodies depicted in the placard (fig. 1.1). Similarly, in scrapbooks from this era that have survived, *cartes de visite* of famous freaks abut photographs of celebrated actors, just as they shared space in museums.[13]

These blurry boundaries between entertainments that we tend to view separately today warrant a serious consideration of the intertextual relationship between theater and freakery. I contend that freak shows affected nineteenth-century spectators' ways of seeing in important respects, influencing the manner in which Americans perceived bodies both on stage and off. Bluford Adams and Matthew Rebhorn have studied how specific exhibits interacted with melodramas presented in the same venue—for example, Barnum's "What Is It?" (an African American performer presented as a human-primate hybrid) and Dion Boucicault's *The Octoroon; or, Life in Louisiana,* which were presented simultaneously at the American Museum on the cusp of the Civil War. Such collisions provide important opportunities to reconstruct audiences' readings of particular plays.[14] But beyond specific instances of intertextuality, I argue that freak shows invited patrons to *look differently* in general. During the nineteenth century, displays of abnormal bodies fostered a methodology of viewing that

Figure 1.1: A sketch of the lecture hall where P. T. Barnum presented plays (proscenium arch, center) is barely visible among the myriad depictions of human curiosities. *Wonders of Barnum's Museum,* lithograph poster by Tom McIlroy, ca. 1860. Collection of The New-York Historical Society, negative #40586.

emphasized the human in all kinds of spectacle. Because the freak is an exemplary case of the body *as* spectacle, representational strategies employed in freak shows help to illuminate how spectators perceived, read, and experienced other forms of sensational entertainment.

As many scholars have observed, freaks are not born but rather made—a process David Hevey terms "enfreakment." Humans born with bodily or mental variances only become freaks when constructed, displayed, and viewed as such. Robert Bogdan argues that nineteenth-century entrepreneurs fashioned freaks using two modes of representation: the exotic, which emphasized "the culturally strange, the primitive, the bestial, the exotic" (African Bushmen, Circassian Beauties, Aztec Children, tattooed men and women, and "missing link" exhibits); and the aggrandized, which "emphasized how, with the exception of the particular physical, mental, or behavioral condition, the freak was an upstanding, high-status person with talents of a conventional and socially prestigious nature" (well-dressed giants, dwarves, bearded women, conjoined twins, living skeletons, and fat ladies). Some producers employed tactics and strategies from both modes, as did exceptionally skilled performers, such as acrobats, sword swallowers, snake charmers, and so forth, who took part in the show.[15]

The excesses embodied by these performers certainly lent them the sense of the spectacular.[16] In exhibitions of extraordinary bodies, strategies of juxtaposition were routinely employed to distinguish them from "normal" people. An advertising print from the 1860s for the American Museum exemplifies this practice. In it, Barnum juxtaposes his own body with those of the human curiosities at his museum (fig. 1.2). The freaks are presented in the aggrandized mode: nicely dressed and standing tall, they perform middle-class respectability. In many ways it is reminiscent of a family portrait—a humdrum affair. In this picture (as on the platform), it is Barnum who makes them extraordinary. In the absence of the showman's recognizable body, their variations in height and girth would be undetectable. As I discuss later, this strategy of comparison-and-contrast is elevated nearly to methodology in images generated by and within American reform movements: a normal, healthy, respectable body or scene is often presented next to a strange, startling, unappealing opposite. Such images argue for the superiority of one over the other; they render visible—indeed, spectacularize—hierarchical binaries. The tactic is used so frequently that it seems to have been part of the grammar of nineteenth-century visual literacy.

And yet, like spectacle generally, the defining features of the body-as-spectacle defy simple explanation. A case in point is William Tillman, whom Barnum presented at his museum in 1861 (fig. 1.3). In July 1861, Tillman, the black steward and cook of the schooner *S. J. Waring,* was captured along with two white men by the crew of the Confederate privateer *Jeff Davis.* According to popular accounts of the event, Tillman was so displeased by the idea of being sold into slavery in the South that he escaped his bonds, murdered several of his captors, and took command of the *Waring* with the aid of his fellow prisoners, ultimately sailing the ship back to New York City. Writer, orator, and fugitive slave William Wells Brown includes Tillman in his book *The Negro in the American Rebellion* (1867), a chronicle of African Americans' contributions to the Civil War. Brown champions Tillman as an exemplar of the integrity and

Figure 1.2: P. T. Barnum (third from left) among his freaks. *Barnum's Gallery of Wonders: Four Giants and Two Dwarfs*, lithograph poster by Currier & Ives, ca. 1860s. Collection of the New-York Historical Society, negative #43430.

courage of black men, also noting, "At Barnum's Museum [Tillman] was the centre of attractive gaze to daily increasing thousands." Brown observes that the public interest in the hero's story was so great that multiple "pictorials" of him were put into circulation, depicting Tillman as "an embodiment of black action of the sea, in contrast with some delinquent Federal officer as white inaction on land." Brown's explication of Tillman's story reveals (perhaps inadvertently) that audiences viewed the hero as atypical of his race: "Unstinted praise from all parties, even those who are usually awkward in any other vernacular than derision of the colored man, has been awarded to this colored man."[17]

The enfreakment of Tillman, both by Barnum and by the public at large, underscores the elasticity and latitude of nineteenth-century definitions of abnormality. It suggests that in the freak show, strange shapes and sizes were not the only kind of exceptionalism on display. Like Tom Thumb and "bearded lady" Madame Clofullia, Tillman was extraordinary; but it was his impressive actions that made him so. The excess he embodied was an excess of potential: he surpassed racist, culturally constructed expectations of his innate abilities and proclivities. It is tempting to wonder if Tillman's outdoing of racist expectations challenged the accuracy of those expectations—in other words, whether Tillman's outdoing was also an undoing, at least partially. Unfortunately, it seems more likely that, like other human curiosities displayed at Barnum's museum, he was presented as an exception that proved the rule. Like them, he affirmed, through his extraordinariness, the culturally constructed norm.

At the heart of enfreakment is the publicization of the body: the act of making it available for staring, appraising, judging, and consuming. Long before Barnum presented Tillman to audiences at his museum, African men and women were bodied forth in a wide range of public spaces. The enfreakment of Tillman occurred at a time when, as Carolyn Sorisio has argued, the black body was always already public: "More than any other body, the African American body was the one that was scrutinized, taxonomized, and chattelized. It was whipped, worked, sold, raped, and studied with a ferocity close to frenzy. Publicly accessible—through the slave auction or the medical examination table—the body of the African American was figuratively, and quite often literally, public."[18] In arenas of capital exchange, slave auctioneers made black bodies accessible and assessable for consumers and casual observers alike; but similar exposures occurred in abolitionist contexts. Reformers such as Theodore Dwight Weld harnessed the sensationalism associated with black bodies to support their cause. Weld, an early leader of the movement, endeavored to

Wm. TILLMAN, THE COLORED STEWARD,
of the Schooner S. J. WARING which was captured by the Piratical Brig JEFF DAVIS and recaptured by TILLMAN and Wm. STEDDING the German Sailor after having killed three of the Pirates in charge of her. He is receiving Visitors daily at
BARNUM'S MUSEUM, NEW YORK.

Figure 1.3: William Tillman, the African American steward who saved the *S. J. Waring* from Confederate pirates in 1861, depicted in a lithograph advertising P. T. Barnum's American Museum. *Wm. Tillman, the Colored Steward,* Currier & Ives, ca. 1861. Collection of the New-York Historical Society, negative #79100d.

render the black body visible in his treatise *American Slavery as It Is: Testimony of a Thousand Witnesses* (1839). The emphasis on witnessing in Weld's subtitle reveals how *seeing* the black body—transforming it into spectacle—was a prevalent strategy in abolitionist discourse. According to Stephen Browne, Weld's book was "the largest-selling anti-slavery tract in American history"; Harriet Beecher Stowe and Charles Dickens appropriated its graphic descriptions of slavery in *Uncle Tom's Cabin* and *American Notes* (1842), respectively. Reformers also published narratives and sponsored performances by "professional fugitives" (such as Frederick Douglass, William Wells Brown, Henry "Box" Brown, and Sojourner Truth, among many others) who shared their personal stories with the public. These texts and shows capitalized on the runaways' sensational experiences as well as their liminal, almost freakish, legal status.[19]

Extraordinary bodies violate rules, disrupt conventions, and defy expectations. "The strangely formed body has represented absolute Otherness in all times and all places since human history began," Leslie Fiedler observes. As the stigmatized antithesis of the norm, the freak serves as a lightning rod for corporeal anxiety by embodying undesirable variations of the white, male, heterosexual, able-bodied ordinary. She functions, in effect, as the über-barometer of digression. Rachel Adams identifies an important relationship between freaks and social prohibitions regarding excess: "Freaks remind us of the unbearable excess that has been shed to confer entry into the realm of normalcy. The figures of the half man–half woman, the dog-faced boy, or conjoined twins confront us with their refusal of the apparently primal distinctions between man and woman, human and animal, self and other." Public presentations of human curiosities were part of a larger cultural system obsessed with both sensationalism and discipline. For nineteenth-century audiences, freak shows defined and delineated what was normal, right, and proper; and through repetition and accretion, they canonized the evolving concept of the normal body.[20]

The viewer's complicated relationship with a human "on view" helps to explain the curiosity and contempt inspired by spectacle generally. In the epigraph that begins this chapter, Brooks suggests that the body is a highly charged site in melodrama, serving as the communicative epicenter of meaning. We may be able to understand better the corporeal dilemmas of a historical moment by examining how performers and characters deviate from or adhere to norms. In the next section, I apply this concept to bodies *within* spectacles in order to illuminate the paradoxical phenomena produced by the actor/character at the center of a sensation scene.

The Body *in* the Spectacle

A visceral conception of spectacle emphasizes the embodied nature of live performance—the essential fact that living beings enact and witness theater. The phenomenology of the live performance event, in which two realities exist concurrently, is one of the theater's pleasures; the action comprises "an event in the real world as well as an illusion of an unreal world," as States writes. More than any other component of the mise-en-scène, it is the actor who foregrounds this dynamic, because she embodies a form of excess: the actor exists doubly, both as character and person. In important respects, these multiple planes or presences are symbiotically linked. The actor reminds us of these plural realities whenever a slippage occurs between the actual and virtual—for example, during a literal "slip," when an actor breaks character—and, as States describes it, "the floor cracks open and we are startled, however pleasantly, by the upsurge of the real into the magic circle where the conventions of theatricality have assured us that the real has been subdued and transcended." In such a moment, the symbiosis achieves immanence, reminding participants of the excesses simultaneously allowed and disavowed in the actor-audience contract.[21]

Because the past always haunts the present, recollections, rumors, and urban legends accrue over time and are incorporated into what Hans Robert Jauss calls the "horizon of expectations": the cumulative knowledge that influences an audience's reading of a work of art.[22] Marvin Carlson has examined how a stunning variety of mementos "ghost" the actor's body, including previous parts she has played, details about her off-stage life, and other actors' performances of her role.[23] In addition, an actor's celebrity status sometimes collapses the distinction between actor and character; in extreme cases, her quirks and personality conflate with her character's. Bodily gestures or bits of dialogue escape the contextual confines of the play, and the audience perceives them through the lens of the historical moment.[24]

Such instances of rupture and convergence generate the sense of the spectacular. In September 1853, the *National Anti-Slavery Record* excerpted an article from New York's *Evening Post* that reported on just such a moment during a performance of James Sheridan Knowles's *Love, or the Countess and the Serf* (1839) at Barnum's museum. In the play, the serf Huon falls in love with a countess; when her father the Duke learns of this, he tries to force Huon to marry someone else, threatening him with death if he refuses. Huon then declares, "What is death compared to slavery?" The audience at the American Museum—watching the play at a time when tensions about slavery were steadily mounting—responded noisily to Huon's line. According to the newspaper account,

> The last word [*slavery*] was delivered with such emphasis that almost the entire audience began demonstrations of applause, while a few persons in the boxes, probably Southern gentlemen, hissed energetically. There was no allusion to Slavery in the South, and, as Mr. Clarke [playing Huon] enacted his part to the life, we could not divine the cause of their displeasure, unless the hated word, in any form, grates harshly upon their consciences.[25]

Instances like this not only offer a glimpse of how contemporary events ghost a performance, but also highlight the historical specificity of audience reception. Although it is a truism that spectators' understanding of themselves and their world contributes significantly to what they see, I suggest that it is during these moments that a relatively quotidian theatrical experience elevates into spectacle.

The simple fact that the performer *lives* contributes to our sense of the spectacular as well—after all, it is "the live actor who, living surrogate for the apparently dead, reminds us that, indeed, we very well may be able to meet the eyes of another," as Rebecca Schneider observes. Or, to invoke a frequently quoted phrase by Herbert Blau, "The actor out there, literally dying in front of your eyes, reveals the space that is never seen."[26] Our knowledge of the actor's vulnerability is central to the theater experience, because the performer's willingness to endanger himself underscores what States calls our "creatural bond with the actor." He elaborates, "Our sympathetic involvement with the characters is attended by a secondary, and largely subliminal, line of empathy born of the possibility that the illusion may at any moment be shattered by a mistake or accident. For the most part this is a low-risk investment, but it is a crucial aspect of the phenomenal quality of stage performance."[27] The actor is a biological being, and therefore susceptible to damage. Always for the actor, the threat of disaster looms: long-lived superstitions about certain utterances and actions, such as saying "Macbeth" or whistling in a performance space, reveal deep anxieties about injury and death within the theatrical community.[28]

Stage accidents may occur frequently or rarely, depending on the vocational context; but when they do happen, they are intricately woven into theatrical habits and histories—sometimes acquiring mythic status, as Jody Enders has shown. Disastrous precedents, both actual and apocryphal, ghost the performance as it unfolds, tugging at the spectator's memory and coloring her perception. Enders points out that, to a degree, the relative frequency of theatrical catastrophes is irrelevant, because "what matters is that each one of our stories transmits an eminently believable fear about the believable."[29] When they do occur, they are widely discussed and analyzed within different communities, ranging from small social circles to large publics, often facilitated by press coverage.[30]

The possibility of mishap was omnipresent during the nineteenth century. As David Grimsted notes, "failings in presentation ran through the tapestry of dramatic performances like a bright, untidy thread."[31] Such failings—past, present, and potential—enhanced spectators' pleasure, excitement, and fear. For sensation scenes in particular, the potential for injury was part of the thrill; it even informed their dramaturgy. Because they often involved elaborate effects and machinery, they aroused and intensified actors' and spectators' sense of vulnerability. Ben Singer, in his exploration of the "ten-twenty-thirty" melodramas that were popular at the turn of the twentieth century, relates a story told by the producer A. H. Woods, who once staged a dramatic rescue involving a burning building. Woods explains that at first, audiences were not impressed by the scene; but when the producers altered the actors' safety wires in such a way as to make them appear tenuous, spectators finally responded. Singer concludes, "The thrill only became truly a thrill when the producers were able to convince the audience there was in fact some real danger. . . . The effect was sensational not because it reproduced a convincing diegesis but, in a certain sense, precisely because it did not."[32]

Sometimes, nineteenth-century actors were harmed due to technical difficulties or unsafe conditions. The flaming ballet girl, for instance, became an icon of horror and erotica because of the many disfigurements and deaths suffered by female dancers who performed close to the footlights. Such occurrences were "reported in graphic detail in local papers and occasionally [became] the topic of titillating literature."[33] According to Mary Grace Swift, at least a dozen immolations occurred in American theaters between 1850 and 1870, but she suspects that there were many more: theater proprietors had an economic incentive to suppress these stories, given that a fear of fire might keep audiences away.[34] Despite managers' attempts to downplay the danger, stories about flaming ballet girls nevertheless found their way into print. In 1852, *Glea-*

son's Pictorial Drawing-Room Companion publicized the death of a female performer who caught fire on stage. The cover story, intended to introduce readers to Niblo's Garden in New York City, mentions a dancer who "approached too near the foot-light. Her thin gauze dress became lighted at once, and before it could be entirely extinguished by the promptness of her companions upon the stage, the poor girl received sufficient injury to cause her death but a few days subsequent." It is almost as if *Gleason's*, despite its self-declared status as a "Family Paper," could not divorce the specter of the flaming ballerina from the story of Niblo's Garden itself.[35]

Such anecdotes circulated in personal correspondence and daily conversation as well. In a letter to Moses Kimball regarding a backdrop commissioned for the Boston Museum, scene painter Sam Stockwell reports that he had recently witnessed a danseuse who "was nearly Burnt alive, but she will recover, being much better today. Imagine the scene[:] she rushed upon the stage in *flames*, the audience nearly jumped at her to put the fire out but every particle of clothing was consumed[,] exposing her to the crowd until covered and carried off. The rest of the spectators rushed out of the House *instantly*." By inviting Kimball to "imagine the scene," Stockwell underscores the incident's spectacular character: a naked ballerina, stripped of her costume by the flames, and a stampede of spectators fleeing for their lives.[36]

Dancers were not the only ones who courted physical danger on stage; all kinds of performers, including actors in melodramas, were vulnerable. A *New York Times* article from 1874, titled "Narrow Escape of Actors," reveals a general fascination with mechanical mishaps. It describes several theater accidents, including one involving a nearly fatal error made by a property man in Portland, Oregon. Reportedly, he mistakenly added poison to the faux whiskey used in a production of *Ten Nights in a Bar-Room*, causing one actor to sicken and exit while his scene partner fell to the stage in a seizure.[37] Other times, actors suffered grave consequences after a personal lapse in judgment or skill. An extreme case is the fatal misstep of Angelo Chiarini, an acrobat in the Martinetti circus troupe. In 1861, Chiarini fell from a tightrope during a performance in San Francisco and died the following day. One newspaper account detailed the tragedy moment by moment, focusing especially on how the performer's body signaled the crisis:

> As [Chiarini] started, he remarked that he feared he could not succeed. . . . He started slowly, halting every few steps, until arriving within fifteen paces of the

> Pavilion. On stopping at this point, the rope vibrated beneath his feet. The gymnast moved his pole quickly from side to side. The spectators became alarmed and excited, but he quickly recovered his equilibrium, and moved boldly forward. But just here he remarked, in a low voice, to those nearest him, "I'm gone," and almost instantaneously fell, clinging for a moment to the rope . . . and he fell to the ground, a mass of bleeding flesh and broken bones.[38]

The report's emphasis on how Chiarini grappled then ultimately succumbed reveals the critic's (and, presumably, the audience's) intense absorption in the performer's fall.

Although procedural missteps are by no means intentional, they result from the performer's voluntary assumption of risk; in such cases, the actor has only himself to blame. In contrast, actors sometimes become victims of physiological failure: incidents involving internal systems of the body over which they have no control. This is when the actor literally dies before our eyes. A famous instance of this sort of occurrence is the fatal hemorrhage suffered by Molière during a performance of *The Imaginary Invalid* in 1673; another is Edmund Kean's collapse on stage in 1833, when he was playing Othello to his son Charles's Iago. In neither case did the actor die instantly, but both events are usually included in historiographic inventories of deaths on stage.[39]

In addition, structural disasters—such as theater fires, collapsing walls or roofs, riots, and stampedes—can affect people on both sides of the curtain. Large-scale catastrophes like these are relatively rare today, but during the nineteenth century they were always within the realm of possibility. Alan Read points out that the average lifespan of a theater was only twenty-two years during the 1800s because of flame-operated stage lighting and flammable materials used in scenic design and theater architecture. He therefore asserts that the prevalence of fire deeply influenced the theatergoing experience: "It is the absence of fire from the contemporary theatre which marks it off from the past. . . . Now the fire chief is on hand to rectify matters, the omniscient fire chief who is trained to treat the theatre like a hotel. But are the contracts of attendance the same?"[40] Whenever they occurred, theater fires were widely publicized and discussed. For example, *Gleason's Pictorial* featured an elaborate illustration of the burning of Boston's National Theatre in 1852 (fig. 1.4). The accompanying article invokes the paradoxical sensations generated by the scene, stating, "It was most intense and beautiful, and lit the entire sky from horizon to horizon."[41]

In sum, show business was, quite simply, a dangerous endeavor.[42] An

Figure 1.4: A large crowd watches the National Theatre burn, suggesting that spectacular calamities inspired collective concern—and communal viewing. "Conflagration of the National Theatre," *Gleason's Pictorial Drawing-Room Companion* 2, no. 19 (1852): 296. Courtesy of the American Antiquarian Society.

acute, collective awareness of the possibility of disaster is evident not only in published texts from the period but also in mementos collected by theatergoers. A theatergoer's scrapbook from the 1870s provides evidence of how stage accidents played a role in one patron's memories of the theater. As would be expected in a scrapbook tracking an (unidentified) individual's theater experiences, it features a number of playbills and newspaper reviews of New York City productions, sometimes with notes and personal impressions scrawled in the margins. Materials related to theater accidents, fires, and deaths are also featured throughout. The theatergoer painstakingly chronicled the devastating destruction by fire of the Brooklyn Theatre in December 1876, in which more than 300 people died, documenting the disaster and its aftermath by culling articles from multiple newspapers.[43] The scrapbook also includes clippings related to two deadly incidents in 1865: a color illustration and article about the burning of Barnum's American Museum and a series of articles about the assassination of Abraham Lincoln at Ford's Theatre.[44]

Because of the dangers, large and small, that are part and parcel of the theatrical experience, I argue that the body in extremity is a defining feature of spectacle; or, to put it another way, the body in extremity is what makes a scene spectacular. The dazzle of visual effects, the cacophony of crisis, and the chaos of movement all contribute to the scale and intensity of the spectacular instant; but impressive stage technology is not enough. To be unequivocally sensational, a scene requires a virtual/actual body experiencing fictional/factual peril. Kershaw, describing a moment in the film *Steamboat Bill, Jr.* (1928) when Buster Keaton narrowly misses being hit by a falling wall, writes, "The utter vulnerability on display is heightened because the distance between Keaton and his character collapses with the wall. . . . In more general terms, human mortality immortalizes itself in the moment of spectacle, and the spectator sees this paradoxical process as it is happening."[45] In other words, the raging Ohio River in *Uncle Tom's Cabin* (1852), the burning building in Dion Boucicault's *The Poor of New York* (1857), and the rushing train in Augustin Daly's *Under the Gaslight* (1867) engage our interest; but Eliza teetering on the ice floes, the charred body of Badger dragged from the inferno, and Snorkey's close brush with death on the railroad tracks are what thrill our senses.

The Body *at* the Spectacle

Obviously, the sense of the spectacular ultimately resides in the spectator. During the nineteenth century, what aided spectators in their confrontation with spectacle? What do bodies *at* the spectacle bring to the sensational scenes they encounter on stage, in print, and in material artifacts? In short, how did Americans see? I argue that audiences acquired a spectacle-driven methodology of seeing through a variety of extratheatrical channels, including children's literature, newspapers, graphic arts, even city streets. They brought an assortment of interpretive practices to bear on what they saw—practices learned and refined while reading, working, walking, and living every day. Innovations in print production facilitated the wide distribution of images and established a close, almost symbiotic, connection between image and text. Because iconography played such a significant role in cultural communication, readers necessarily developed image-oriented reading practices—a kind of visual literacy—in order to engage with American cultural products, including performance.

Jonathan Crary has analyzed the unique "optical regime" that took shape in the early nineteenth century, a system that departed in significant ways from that of preceding centuries. Crary argues that, beginning in the 1820s and 1830s, there was a "repositioning of the observer," and "the imperatives of capitalist modernization . . . generated techniques for imposing visual attentiveness, rationalizing sensation, and managing perception." Whereas Crary focuses on devices and scientific advances that contributed to new ways of visually engaging the world, I assert that theatrical vocabularies and techniques also contributed to the "standardization of visual imagery in the nineteenth century," which was, as he argues, part of "a broader process of normalization and subjection of the observer."[46]

Pedagogical methods employed in nineteenth-century children's books suggest that, in many respects, the process of reading began as an exploration of images. As Patricia Crain observes in her study of early American alphabet books, "Learning to read means first and foremost learning how to look."[47] Texts like the *New England Primer* taught children both textual and iconographic vocabularies. The *Primer* was widely read and frequently reprinted; as a result, its symbols and pictures permeated the American visual vernacular.[48] Young readers were, in effect, trained in a repertoire of images at the same time they were trained in a repertoire of words. Other books—such as *Rollo Learning to Talk* (first published in 1835), part of the popular *Rollo* series by Jacob Abbott—used images to facilitate the development of verbal communication skills. A "Notice to Parents" at the beginning of the book provides instructions about using the illustrations to full effect: "When the child is interested, let him look at the picture *as long as he will.* He will ask you a question sometimes after a long pause, which will be exceedingly interesting. Let your object be to arouse and concentrate his powers, to awaken his curiosity, and to fix his attention. Let him in fact lead and guide the exercise."[49] These directions emphasize both the power and the utility of pictures in focusing, engaging, and educating young readers.

Some juvenile literature modeled a step-by-step process of assessing pictures, encouraging children to draw large conclusions from small details. Phrases like "Look at this picture" and "Do you see . . . ?" directed the child where to look, thereby teaching the art of seeing as well as reading. In *The Youth's Temperance Lecturer* (1840), which was reprinted more than a dozen times, temperance reformer Charles Jewett taught readers how to critically analyze an illustration in order to identify improper behaviors. A drawing of an inebriated man at the beginning of the book offers a tutorial in how to recognize a wretched drunkard (fig. 1.5). The accompanying text painstakingly instructs the young reader how to interpret and ultimately judge the subject.

> Little reader, look at this picture of a man, with his ragged clothes, worn-out shoes, and old slouched hat. What a sad plight he is in! One eye, you see, is shut up, and the other is but half open, while, with his bottle in his pocket, he is leaning on that large cask. It is the picture of a drunkard. He has spent his money for strong drink, so that he has none left to buy new clothes, new shoes, or a new hat. He has behaved so badly that his relations and friends do not love him as they did, and many of them will not have him in their company or in their houses.[50]

By cajoling the reader to examine the drunkard's face, eyes, complexion, clothing, posture, and props (the telltale bottle in his pocket, the cask upon which he leans), Jewett provides a methodology of seeing that the "little reader" can use in all manner of contexts.

The Youth's Temperance Lecturer belongs to a genre of texts that gave parents the opportunity to inculcate children with particular values by way of sensational scenes. As such, they constitute an intriguing overlap of spectacle and reform. But they also tutored young Americans in how to read bodies more generally. In Jewett's book, the reader not only learns how to recognize the visual cues and defining characteristics of a drunkard but also acquires an interpretive procedure she can apply to *all* bodies. By encouraging readers to critically analyze characters in illustrations, these texts extended an invitation to read every body—to enact "an interrogative gesture that asks what's going on and demands the story," as Rosemarie Garland-Thomson describes the act of staring.[51]

The frequent use of theatrical techniques in print and visual culture is another indication of spectacle's centrality in nineteenth-century American communication. Crain has noted the increasing prevalence of tableau presentation in primers from the mid-nineteenth century.[52] Some children's stories take the form of dramatic dialogue, complete with stage directions and character names preceding each person's "line." Others go so far as to invite physical enactment. In the preface to *Dialogues for the Amusement and Instruction*

A Drunkard.

LITTLE reader, look at this picture of a man, with his ragged clothes, worn-out shoes, and old slouched hat. What a sad plight he is in! One eye, you see, is shut up, and the other is but half open, while, with his bottle in his pocket, he is leaning on that large cask. It is the picture of a drunkard. He has spent his money for strong drink, so that he has none left to buy new clothes, new shoes, or a new hat. He has behaved so bad that his relations and friends do not love him as they did, and many of them will not have him in their company or in their houses.

Figure 1.5: The "little reader" is taught how to read the drunkard's body in Charles Jewett's *The Youth's Temperance Lecturer* (Boston: Whipple and Damrell, 1840), 6. Courtesy of the American Antiquarian Society.

of Young Persons (1856), Abbott suggests that the short dialogues therein are suited for performance in parlors or at school by children.[53] Abbott frequently declared in his prefaces his commitment to both educating and entertaining children—in essence, to teach and delight, as Horace recommends in *The Art of Poetry.* Perhaps his adoption of theatrical dramaturgy is one way he tried to accomplish that goal. The moral lessons in his stories reflect some of the key concerns promoted by contemporaneous reform movements. Abbott's *The Alcove* (1856), for instance, features a series of pictures portraying the decline of a man into drunkenness and, ultimately, incarceration. As in other illustrated books, the text guides the reader through a close reading of the images, aiding him in the process of visual interpretation.[54]

These technologies of seeing were not used exclusively in children's books, however; they were deployed in adult publications as well. They seem particularly prominent in reform literature. Like Jewett's *Youth's Temperance Lecturer,* Mason Locke Weems's book *The Drunkard's Looking Glass* (first published in 1812) also begins with a drawing of a drunkard. Weems mercilessly unpacks the image, piece by piece: "Every feature is a tell-tale; every grin and stare betrays him. Only look at his eyes, see how they twinkle!—his *cheeks,* how they swell and redden!—And Oh! That eternal chatter box his *tongue!*"[55] In some cases, this analytic procedure is enacted even in the *absence* of a picture. For example, when the antislavery newspaper *The Emancipator* ran an article about a fugitive slave in March 1844, it did not include an illustration but instead instructed the reader to imagine—and interpret—the fugitive's battered body.

> Before us sits one of the fugitives. His name is Justus Marshall. . . . The big scar-wreaths on his body, tell of the cruelty of a passionate, drunken, atheisticle master. He has received two hundred lashes at one time, and once in the madness of his agony from the scourge, he drew a razor across his throat to end his misery, and would have accomplished his design had it not been snatched from his hand. The mark there testifies to the truth of this.[56]

The reader is carefully led through the process of examining the runaway slave, scar by scar. Transforming the reader into a spectator, the article invites her to view the fugitive's body *as* spectacle, if only in her mind's eye.

Such instances suggest that sensational aesthetics played a prominent role in reform propaganda. Heather S. Nathans points out that antislavery plays and performances often urged the reader or spectator to identify sympathetically with the slave, combining "sympathy and sensation, pathos and professionalism" in order to affect audiences. *The Anti-Slavery Almanac* and *Anti-Slavery Record* tried to foster compassion for slaves by displaying their bodies: working, pleading, escaping, rescuing, suffering, dying. "Incendiary pictures"—images of Southern slave culture printed in antislavery publications—in many ways mimic sensation scenes. The first scenario depicted in the *Anti-Slavery Record* of April 1836, which exhibits a distinctly melodramatic sensibility, is a case in point. The illustration accompanies an article about William Peterson, a "heroic colored boy" who saved two white boys who fell through the ice while skating. According to the article, when Peterson succumbed to the frigid water, "no one would risk his life for him," and he drowned (fig. 1.6). Not unlike the presentation of William Tillman at Barnum's museum or Eliza's flight on the ice floes in *Uncle Tom's Cabin,* this vignette emphasizes the courage and moral purpose of a protagonist from an allegedly inferior race. Other pictures incite the reader's sympathy by showing horrific scenes of capital exchange. The *Anti-Slavery Almanac of 1838* includes an illustration of a slave mother, stripped naked to the waist and her hands chained, kneeling and calling after her two children as they are escorted away by a whip-wielding slave-driver (fig. 1.7). Despite the woman's nudity, the article addresses a juvenile reader and urges him or her to contribute to the moral-suasion effort: "Can you do anything to free the poor slave children, so they may not be torn from their mothers and sold? Yes; you can try to convince all your neighbors and playmates that it is wicked to rob the innocent of liberty. When every body believes this, there will be no slaves in the world." Both of these sensational images borrow tactics typically deployed in theaters: they illustrate the most intense and significant moment in the story; they are presented proscenium-style, focusing the reader's attention on the central characters; and they are rendered realistically, with an acute attention to detail.[57]

The *opsis*-centricity of US culture during this time reveals that Americans were attuned to images, to spectacle—to seeing sensation. This helps to explain the popularity, prevalence, and dramaturgical significance of sensation scenes not only in melodramas but also in pictorial and print media. It also affirms spectacle's utility in reform culture. Nineteenth-century America was a culture invested in, perhaps even driven by, spectacle. In many respects, it was a society of spectacle—not precisely in the way Guy Debord describes, of course.[58] But spectacle did operate as an essential mode of communication, if only because reading was as much about images as it was about words. The process

THE

ANTI-SLAVERY RECORD.

VOL. II. NO. IV. APRIL, 1836. WHOLE NO. 16.

WILLIAM PETERSON—THE HEROIC COLORED BOY.

THE MORAL CHARACTER OF THE AFRICO-AMERICANS.

IT will be remembered that in our last number we gave some facts to show that the despised colored people possess, in full measure, that *moral constitution*, which, far beyond any physical or intellectual excellencies, is the glory of man. It appeared that they had exhibited the highest degree of moral heroism—that they had denied themselves for the welfare of others—that they had overcome evil with good—that they had conquered by generosity. It is by no means useless to multiply such facts; for, how can any man fail to attack slavery with all his moral power, after he is brought to see the glorious image of his Creator on the brow of the slave? We make the following extracts from the interesting travels of E. S. Abdy, Esq., and vouch for the truth of his statements from our own personal knowledge.

I was once asked, with a sarcastic smile, by an American lady of Hibernian descent, if I had met with any interesting blacks in the

Figure 1.6: "William Peterson—The Heroic Colored Boy." *Anti-Slavery Record* 2, no. 4 (April 1836): 1. The spectacular nature of the episode and the proscenium-style presentation are reminiscent of a melodramatic sensation scene. Courtesy of the American Antiquarian Society.

1838.] **JUNE—SIXTH MONTH.** [30 days.

Ev'n her babes, so dear, so young,
And so treasured in her heart,
That the cords which round them clung,
Seemed its life, its dearest part;

These, ev'n these, were torn away!
These, that, when all else were gone,
Cheered the heart with one bright ray,
That still bade its pulse beat on!

D. M.	Positions of the Sun, Moon and Stars....Tides, Weather, &c.
1	Spica S. 8 40 a.
2	Arcturus S. 9. 26 a.
3	♅ □ ☉. *Fair and*
4	Mirac S. 9 48 a. *fine,*
5	♃ sets, 1 21 m. *with now*
6	♄ ☌ ☽. *and then a*
7	♄ S. 10 27 a. *shower.*
8	Spica S. 8 11 a.
9	Middling tides. *Windy.*
10	Arcturus S. 8 54 a.
11	Alphacca S. 10 9 a.
12	☿ greatest elong. W.
13	Mirac S. 9 11 a. *Change-*
14	☽ perigee. ♅ ☌ ☽. *able.*
15	♄ S. 9 52 a. *with consid-*
16	Arcturus S. 8 28 a. *erable*
17	♅ stationary. *rain.*
18	♀ ☌ ☽. ♃ sets 11 40 a.
19	♂ ☌ ☽. *Continues*
20	☿ ☌ ☽. *unsettled, with*
21	☉ enters ♋. Sum'r begins.
22	Middling tides. *rain occa-*
23	Alphacca S. 9 20 a. *sion-*
24	♂ ☊. ♃ sets 11 17 a. *ally,*
25	♄ S. 9 7 a. *and with but*
26	Antares S. 9 58 a. *a few*
27	♃ ☌ ☽. *fine days to the*
28	☽ apogee. *end of the*
29	Alphacca S. 8 55 a. *month.*
30	☉ farthest from the earth.

In Kentucky there lived a wicked woman, a slaveholder, and a member of the Presbyterian church. One of her slaves was the mother of two children, 7 and 9 years old. The woman sold the mother to another slaveholder, and did not let her know it. When she was seized, she shrieked and cried, and the children cried when they saw their mother torn from them, but the slaveholder did not regard their cries. He chained their mother, and drove her away, where she never saw her children again.

Can slaves be happy, when they are all the time exposed to such cruel separations? There are 600,000 children in the U. S. every moment liable to be torn from their mothers. Children, do you think slavery is right? What do thieves and robbers do? Who is a robber, if the man who takes children from their mothers and sells them is not a robber?

Children, pray for the wicked slaveholder, and for the heart-broken slave. Can you do anything to free the poor slave children, so they may not be torn from their mothers and sold? Yes; you can try to convince all your neighbors and playmates that it is wicked to rob the innocent of liberty. When every body believes this, there will be no slaves in the world.

Figure 1.7: A spectacle of suffering. Illustration in N. Southard, *Anti-Slavery Almanac for 1838* (Boston: D. K. Hitchcock, 1837), 7. Courtesy of the American Antiquarian Society.

of becoming linguistically literate was also a process of becoming visually literate. Citizens routinely employed this methodology of seeing when assessing, interpreting, and understanding other people and, by extension, themselves.

Dénouement: Affect and the Spectacular Instant

Why does the spectacular instant merit special consideration? Why depart from Aristotle's hierarchical taxonomy of theatrical elements in *The Poetics,* which champions plot and shuns spectacle? Presumably, the visual elements of excessive displays assault the *spec*tator more than other kinds of input. It is generally held that spectacle is distracting and absorbing, inhibiting our ability to think. Matthew S. Buckley has even suggested that melodrama's "sensational economy," in which spectacle plays an important part, may be roughly equivalent to an "addictive psychological drug." Brechtian theories and dramaturgies assume that a "distanced" spectator has more potential to think critically about what he sees and to take action in the world. The deemphasis of sight in Augusto Boal's conception of the spect*actor,* for example, suggests that the hypnotic hypervisuality of Western realism inhibits the audience's ability to socially and politically engage. But as Bruce McConachie observes, "By itself, the idea of the distanced spectator provides no magic key to unlocking the problem of audience response and political action." To some extent, critiques of spectacle have hindered discussion about its operations, impact, and potential.[59]

In contrast to many radical theater-makers and the scholars who affiliate with them, Kershaw argues that spectacle's tendency to foreground "a sense of the human" gives it a unique potential for activism: "Spectacle seems always to transform the human into something more, or less, than itself." But he also asserts that during the nineteenth century, the proscenium stage forced spectacle behind a frame and restricted its power to thrill. Allegedly, this act of enclosure, along with the advent of gas lighting and the new practice of darkening the auditorium, helped to transform the spectator from an active, unruly participant into a docile voyeur.[60] I would counter, however, that the visceral nature of performance narrows the gap between spectacle and subject. Theater is unpredictable, irrevocable, prone to accidents and mistakes; spectators are constantly aware of the actor's vulnerability. This was particularly true during the nineteenth century, when theater-making was fraught with risks, not only to producers and performers but also to audiences.

If we concede that our full experience of the theatrical event—everything we see, everything we sense—has the potential to influence how we feel, then we can approach a more nuanced understanding of sensationalism and its impact. Stanton B. Garner writes, "The embodied *I* of theatrical spectatorship is grounded, one might say, in an embodied *eye*"; so we must attend to every somatic aspect of reception.[61] The spectacular instant has a unique efficacy because of its rigorous stimulation of the senses; this is why nineteenth-century theater-makers and political reformers harnessed the power of spectacle again and again. They knew that spectacle is effective because it is *affective.*

One of the many legal battles over Augustin Daly's railroad rescue in *Under the Gaslight*—possibly the most famous and enduring sensation scene in American history—reveals that emotional potency is one of spectacle's most important, and valued, characteristics. Almost immediately after the premiere of Daly's play, others attempted to copy the railroad sequence. In the court case *Daly v. Palmer et al.* (1868), Daly sought an injunction against Henry D. Palmer and Henry C. Jarrett, who planned to present Dion Boucicault's *After Dark* (1868) at Niblo's Garden. Daly argued that the railroad rescue in Boucicault's play infringed on his copyright because it was nearly identical to the one in *Under the Gaslight.* The case was decided in Daly's favor and became a legal landmark, in that it extended copyright protection to recognizable mise-en-scène. Significantly, in his decision the presiding judge, Samuel Blatchford, considered not only the spectator's *visual* recognition of the scene, but also his *visceral* response.

> Such adaptation . . . is a piracy, if the appropriated series of events, when represented on the stage, although performed by new and different characters, using different language, is recognized by the spectator, *through any of the senses* to which the representation is addressed, as conveying substantially the same impressions to, and *exciting the same emotions* in, the mind, in the same sequence or order.

In other words, the feelings experienced by spectators during Daly's railroad rescue were part of its inherent value. Thus, Blatchford concluded that the sensations inspired by the scene, which were essential to its success, were protected by copyright. He considered Boucicault's copy to constitute plagiarism because the playwright attempted to elicit a similar effect—rather, a similar *a*ffect—in his spectators.[62]

Of course, *affect* is a highly contested term, one that theorists deploy in a remarkable variety of ways. Nevertheless, as Schneider asserts, "Thinking through affective engagement offers a radical shift in thinking about our mobilities in dealings with the binaried landscapes of social plots (such as gender, such as race), undoing the solidity of binaries in favor of mining the slip and slide of affect as negotiation."[63] Most conceptions of affect and emotion suggest that the two are extremely interdependent. Emphasizing the materiality of the body, Brian Massumi has argued that affect is, essentially, an involuntary and corporeal intensity that the subject translates into thought, action, or movement. Distinguishing affect from emotion, he claims that the latter is informed and circumscribed by culture, whereas the former is autonomous and raw. In a somewhat similar vein, Teresa Brennan conceives of affect as both energy and contagion, transmitted between and among bodies—in short, that "our emotions are not altogether our own." In marked contrast, Charles Altieri contends that affects (deliberately plural in his view) fall into four discrete categories: moods, emotions, passions, and feelings. Although his taxonomy highlights differences in intensity, Altieri tends to conflate affect and emotion, and culture's role in the production of feeling is not always clear. Sara Ahmed, on the other hand, has explored the "cultural politics" of emotion and the ways in which bodies are inexorably shaped by them, positing that "the distinction between sensation and emotion can only be analytic." In their assessment of affect, Eve Kosofsky Sedgwick and Adam Frank draw inspiration from Silvan Tomkins, a psychologist who theorized that several innate affects drive the motivational system. Offering an intriguing alternative to Freudian interpretations of human behavior, Tomkins challenged the assumption that bodily drives (breathing, thirst, hunger, and so forth) are the primary engines of human action, arguing instead that affects inform these routines at an even deeper level; it is the affective system's *interpretation* of needs that prompts action and reaction.[64]

For me, several ideas in these discussions stand out. First, affect is a vibrant, sensorial, palpable response to stimuli. Scholars and scientists continually debate about whether it is rooted in cognition, culture, or some combination of the two; but in many respects, that is a question of origin, and therefore a definitive answer will always elude us. More important, I think, is the fundamental assertion that affect is powerful due to its corporeal character. Whether transmitted between and among bodies, as Brennan argues, or contained within the individual, as Altieri seems to assert, affect is physically detectable, both as feeling (sorrow, fear, surprise) and expression (shrieks, applause, huzzahs). Second, the motivational character of affect lends it a unique kind of urgency. Affect is demanding, often trumping the considerations and aspirations with which it is in conflict. It is important to keep in mind that feeling—which has long been associated, frequently and condescendingly, with the feminine and the primitive—is usually on the losing end of the emotion/reason binary. As Ahmed observes, "The story of evolution is narrated not only as the triumph of reason, but of the ability to control emotions."[65] But just as spectacle's power derives in part from its intensity, speed, and chaos, so too does the power of affect. Third, if it is true that emotion succeeds rather than precedes affect—that emotion is interpreted through a multifaceted lens of personal and social values—then it is vitally important to take into account the historically specific pressures that might have shaped spectators' responses. By identifying the ways in which ideology influences "emotion," we can construct possible readings of performance in light of cultural conventions circulating during a particular moment.

The phenomenology of affect helps to explain why spectators sometimes experience a kind of palpable collectivity while watching a performance. Jill Dolan argues that when audiences share a collective feeling of hope at the theater—a moment that she calls a "utopian performative"—"audiences feel themselves allied with each other, and with a broader, more capacious sense of a public, in which social discourse articulates the possible, rather than the insurmountable obstacles to human potential." These experiences reveal "affective visions" of better worlds rooted in feeling rather than programs of action. States also touches upon this idea.

> Theater is the one place where society collects in order to look in upon itself as a third-personal other. Beneath all of the possible explanations of theater's usefulness as an image of man, there is this basic consubstantiality of form between its subject and its process. Theater . . . is a means of looking objectively at the subjective life of the race as something prepared for the community out of the substance of its own body.

Altieri notes that this is precisely why spectators report feeling *moved* (changed, renewed, transformed) during some artistic encounters: "We find ourselves invited to try out various attitudes toward valuing what we encounter, and, more important, we find some of those provisional identifications eliciting our own passionate investments and clarifying paths they might take beyond the work of art."[66]

These theorists convey a kind of optimism about the possibilities and promise of performance: we see our world and other humans in a different light, and what we see arouses our sympathy, our compassion, and our hope. But affect, in itself, does not necessarily warrant optimism. If affect is powerful but flexible, then it is efficacious but malleable. During the spectacular instant, the spectator interprets her somatic response through multiple layers—the situation, the moment, the culture of which she is a part—then transforms the feeling into one or more recognizable emotions that sustain, challenge, or complicate the values with which she previously identified. When imagining the plausible results of an affective encounter, these cultural factors must be accounted for. Furthermore, affect is not always effectual: we sometimes choose to repress, reject, or subvert what we feel. Indeed, Tomkins credits the affective system for "the extraordinary competence and freedom of the human organism." And yet, as Sedgwick and Frank (via Tomkins) reminds us, precisely because affect dominates the motivational system, affect tends to take priority. It has muscle and clout.[67]

The spectacular instant harbors a unique potential to generate affect because, I argue, the body as/in/at the spectacle serves as an epicenter of meaning. The intense and cumulative character of spectacle demands the viewer's attention and calls forth his affective response. Newspaper reports, personal accounts, and popular folklore about sensation scenes and the performers who enacted them provide evidence of this dynamic. Tom Gunning, discussing the gruesome Grand Guignol dramas of André de Lorde in late nineteenth-century France, seems to disagree with this contention, asserting that sensational displays elicit somatic reactions that inhibit understanding: "The sensation drama addresses itself directly to the body and senses. It is physical and emotional sensation rather than moral cognition that counts."[68] I advance an alternative view: the spectacular instant offered producers, reformers, audiences, and consumers a unique opportunity to articulate ideas. Viewing these moments through the complicated layers of history, I observe that some were progressive but others were not. The sentiments communicated during each spectacular onslaught were variously conformist, reformist, or somewhere in between.

This theoretical orientation informs my understanding of spectacle as methodology, a means of vibrantly reflecting or violently rejecting cultural ideology. For the historian, sensation scenes on stage and on the page provide intriguing insights into the beliefs that competed for attention during the age of reform. In the chapters that follow, I explore audiences' intense desire to consume spectacle—to see sensation—during pivotal moments in three major political movements, analyzing how certain images advanced or denied cultural paradigms vying for dominance. One scene, the *delirium tremens* episode in W. H. Smith's *The Drunkard* (1844), constitutes a significant paradox: it is a sensational, grotesque depiction that seems intended to canonize norms and make those norms compulsory. On the other hand, audiences witnessing the railroad rescue in Augustin Daly's *Under the Gaslight* (1867)—which, I argue, embraces a progressive vision of womanhood—probably perceived a challenge to widespread beliefs about gender. In contrast, the messages conveyed by images of Eliza's flight in adaptations of Harriet Beecher Stowe's *Uncle Tom's Cabin* (1852) are complicated and ambivalent. I imagine how these disparate spectacular scenes mobilized affect for conservative, progressive, or equivocal ends.

2

The Delirium Tremens

Spectacular Insanity in *The Drunkard*

Time would fail to enumerate the many habits that, acquired and indulged, mar the beauty and destroy the symmetry of the true man.

—JOHN B. GOUGH, *PLATFORM ECHOES*[1]

As intersections of activism and performance, moral reform melodramas—featuring implicit or explicit references to temperance, abolition, suffrage, and other issues—make up an intriguing subgenre. In them, sensationalism meets ideology; entertainment and politics collide. Crucially, at the heart of many such dramas is a spectacular instant: a sensational, affective representation that recycles, reiterates, and reimagines ideas in circulation. The *delirium tremens* scene in temperance melodrama, during which the protagonist experiences a psychotic episode as a result of overindulging in drink, is a case in point. The DTs (sometimes called *mania a potu* by early American physicians) was described and enacted in a wide variety of venues, ranging from theaters and lecture halls to reform publications and medical literature. Scholars have paid considerable attention to temperance propaganda depicting the drunkard's family and home, but performances of the DTs played an equally important role in shaping public perceptions about the dangers of drink. The display of the inebriate's out-of-control body, which posed a striking contrast to images centering on the drunkard's domestic situation, became ubiquitous in temperance melodramas in the wake of *The Drunkard; or, The Fallen Saved,* written by actor and reformed inebriate W. H. Smith and an anonymous collaborator (probably Rev. John Pierpont).[2] John W. Frick calls it "temperance melodrama's obligatory sensation scene," remarking that its "theatrical potential . . . proved irresistible to playwrights who sought spectacular effects that would frighten the intemperate into abstinence." Michael Booth includes the DTs in his sketch of temperance drama's typical formula; Judith N. McArthur describes it as a "standard" aspect of the genre; Jeffrey D. Mason asserts it was one of *The Drunkard*'s "principal attractions"; and Richard Moody, in his introduction to the play in a drama anthology, claims that sometimes "this shattering episode was given a solo exhibition."[3]

Playbills, advertisements, and actors' memoirs suggest that the scene fascinated nineteenth-century audiences. The preface to the 1847 acting edition of *The Drunkard* asserts,

> Mr. [W. H.] Smith's personation of Edward, evidently the result of accurate and laborious study, and deep knowledge of human frailty, was at times terribly real, particularly the scene of delirium tremens, which, though far short of the horrors of that dreadful malady, and appeared to those unacquainted with the disease to be overstepping the bounds of nature, was true to the letter, and universally acknowledged to be the most naturally effective acting ever seen in this city.

Reportedly, "it was no uncommon thing to see scores of men and women in the auditory weeping like children"—suggesting that the *The Drunkard* had an affective impact, both as melodrama and as morality tale.[4] Eventually, temperance plays came to be viewed as quaint and moralistic products of their time. In their 1938 biography of the nineteenth-century actor Harry Watkins, Maud and Otis Skinner describe *The Drunkard* as "one of those relics of other days filled with obvious moral lessons on the evils of drink, banal sentimentalism, crass comedy, melodrama, defiant heroism, villains, sob stuff, and *delirium tremens,* which moved audiences of the time to tears and thrills."[5] And yet, the authors implicitly acknowledge here that, at the height of its popularity, the DTs scene was widely considered a powerful spectacle.

One reason the DTs fascinated audiences is because alcoholics who made spectacles of themselves due to excessive drinking were more likely than ever to be sequestered in jails and asylums. Medical texts from the period indicate that physicians considered the disorder to be a temporary episode of insanity; and despite the relatively short duration of the illness, by the mid-nineteenth century, inebriates suffering from the DTs were often sent to asylums for treatment. Simultaneously, spectators embraced opportunities to see representations of the unruly drunkard's body on stage. They endeavored, in short, to see the sensation that was being hidden from public view. In essence, the DTs scene was a riveting and repulsive representation of a man gone mad. Yet the definition of dipsomania itself relied utterly (and unutterably) on prescriptions of normalcy and self-discipline that were emerging in the United States during the antebellum era.[6] By harnessing the grotesque power of this illness, dramatists, performers, and activists implicitly reinforced the orderly and efficient body privileged by "respectable" individuals in urban centers.

To assess the affective impact of the DTs within reform culture as well as audiences' reception of this spectacle, I analyze writings by the physicians Benjamin Rush, Pliny Earle, and Edward Jarvis, who conceive the disorder as a brief and curable affliction. Then, using *The Drunkard* as a case study, I explore how insanity is an ominous, omnipresent danger in American depictions of drunkenness. Originally produced by Moses Kimball at the Boston Museum in 1844, this popular "moral drama" became, in Bruce A. McConachie's words, "the model for most subsequent dramas of dipsomania" and inspired many imitations.[7] When P. T. Barnum presented the play at the American Museum in New York, it became the first ever to achieve an uninterrupted run of 100 performances. Madness materializes most vividly in the fourth act, when the character Edward Middleton suffers an attack of the DTs. But Middleton's breakdown is not an isolated spectacle: long before that, the threat of insanity is embodied by Agnes (the sister of Middleton's friend and confidant, William), who is designated "A Maniac" in the cast of characters. Despite Agnes's prominence in the story, theater historians who have studied *The Drunkard* generally ignore her presence and actions. This collective oversight has hindered a full and nuanced understanding of the drama and, perhaps, temperance entertainment generally.

Because my investigation centers not so much on *The Drunkard* as the *drunkard*—the stereotypical male inebriate who makes a spectacle of himself—I also examine the meteoric rise of John B. Gough, a temperance lecturer who (like Smith) was a former alcoholic and whose notoriety derived, in part, from his dramatic enactments of the DTs. Despite his great fame during his lifetime, Gough has received relatively little attention from historians.[8] A unique ability to conjure images while he spoke was one of Gough's most lauded talents. He performed, in essence, one-man sensation scenes: virtual tableaux that amused and horrified his spectators. His body, once gripped by ardent spirits, served as spectacular proof of the potential for redemption; and audiences were fascinated by the ways in which he personified reformation. He began performing in the Boston region immediately prior to and alongside of *The Drunkard,* indicating that Smith's drama did not emerge from a vacuum but probably reflected and interacted with Gough's solo performances.

I conclude by meditating on the curious relationship between sensationalism and reform that the *delirium tremens* sequence, in particular, foregrounds. I offer some thoughts about how the scene potentially illuminates a longstanding question in temperance historiography: was the reform movement conservative or progressive, traditionalist or visionary, disciplinary or sympathetic? To explore this question, I draw on psychologist Jonathan Haidt's theory regarding the "moral foundations" of decision making, which I believe offers a reading of temperance activism that is more careful and complex than the conservative/progressive binary can afford.

Historiography and *The Drunkard:* A Focus on the Family

Historians of the US temperance movement offer a variety of explanations for its emergence during the nineteenth century, including the greater availability of alcohol, especially hard liquor; the pressures of urbanization resulting from the growth of cities; changes in labor practices, such as the shift from an apprenticeship-based work environment to a more industrial model; and the religious spirit and optimism fueled by the Second Great Awakening, which emphasized the perfectibility of man and the nation. Such changes fostered anxieties about social order, respectability, and the stability of the traditional family unit.[9]

The prevalence of the drunkard's family in temperance illustrations, lithographs, and ephemera suggests that activists routinely used domestic images to advance their cause. Similar to the promotional materials touting extraordinary bodies in freak shows, discussed in chapter 1, many temperance products deployed strategies of juxtaposition, setting spectacles of indulgence alongside pictures of abstinence. *The Bottle* (1847), a graphic tale comprising eight plates by British artist George Cruikshank, is perhaps the most widely known nineteenth-century depiction of the inebriate's decline and its effect on the family. *The Bottle* operates through comparison and contrast: the first frame, picturing a tranquil and solvent middle-class home, functions as a barometer by which later scenes of depravity are measured. As the husband and wife's drinking habit worsens, the well-appointed room is raided and rendered bare

Figure 2.1: "The bottle has done its work—it has destroyed the infant and the mother, it has brought the son and the daughter to vice and to the streets, and has left the father a hopeless maniac." George Cruikshank, *The Bottle,* Plate VIII, 1847. Courtesy of the American Antiquarian Society.

by creditors. Eventually, every family member meets a horrible end. The youngest child dies from "cold, misery, and want"; shortly thereafter, the husband kills his wife in a drunken rage while their two remaining children watch. The spectacle of loss enacted in *The Bottle* hinges, in large part, on the illustration of normalcy rendered in the first plate. The markers of a happy and healthy household—comfortable furniture, decorative knick-knacks, respectable clothing, smiling faces—gradually disappear. Finally, the home itself disappears: the last scene is set not in the family's house but in an insane asylum, where the murderous and maniacal drunkard has been confined (fig. 2.1).

Prior to *The Bottle,* N. Currier—the New York City lithography firm that eventually transformed into Currier & Ives, a leading distributor of prints for the popular market—issued *The Drunkard's Progress: From the First Glass to the Grave* in 1846[10] (fig. 2.2). In it, a young man climbs a triangular staircase, enacting successive stages of dissipation on every step. Like *The Bottle,* this spectacle juxtaposes different degrees of intoxication as a way to encourage sobriety.

Figure 2.2: The drunkard, his states of dissipation, and his victims. *The Drunkard's Progress: From the First Glass to the Grave,* N. Currier, 1846. Courtesy of the American Antiquarian Society.

Although the focus in this print is clearly the drunkard, the family is nevertheless present: beneath the staircase, a forlorn woman and child (presumably, the family that the drunkard has abandoned) walk away from a dilapidated house toward an unknown destination.

Illuminated temperance pledge cards, such as the one issued by Rev. Theobald Mathew's Total Abstinence Society (TAS) during the early 1840s, allowed consumers literally to put a spectacle in their pockets (fig. 2.3). Signed by both recipient and administrator, the pledge card was a souvenir of oath-taking and of the eminent person who facilitated the act (in this case, Father Mathew, an internationally famous temperance activist). It also served as a material remnant of the temperance pledge, a performance of commitment that was distinctly embodied. The card, printed in 1844, predates *The Bottle* by several years but depicts scenarios that are nearly identical to Cruikshank's famous graphic melodrama. A tiny tableau in the bottom left corner illustrates "Intemperance": an irate drunkard holds a woman by the hair and threatens to hit her with

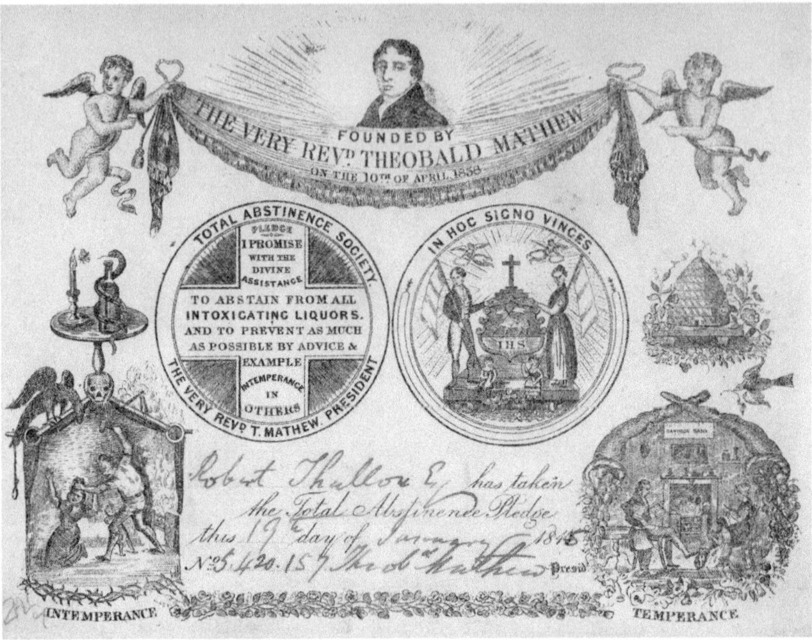

Figure 2.3: Temperance pledge card from the Total Abstinence Society, 1844. Collection of the New-York Historical Society, negative #85483d.

a mallet, while a child begs him to stop. An assembly of symbols—a skull, a noose, a predatory bird, and a bottle coddled by a serpent—hover above the scene. In the opposite corner, "Temperance" represents a normalized version of the same family. The man and woman sit calmly in a well-appointed parlor, accompanied by two attractively dressed children and a contented cat. Two overflowing cornucopias serve to frame the image, and a buzzing beehive—a popular nineteenth-century symbol representing the virtues of industry, honest labor, and wisdom—crowns the scene. These dramatic scenarios, one to be adored and the other abhorred, reminded the cardholder to adhere to the pledge in order to keep bedlam at bay.[11]

Reformers' anxieties about the impact of alcohol on the family, as illustrated in these artifacts, have deeply informed theater historiography. Most scholarship on temperance melodrama concentrates on the ways in which it depicts the home. Booth acknowledges that "the wretchedness of the drunkard" reinforced "the morality of temperance sentiments"; but he ultimately asserts that the "suffering of his wife and children" conveys the moral most strongly. McArthur focuses on the victimization of women and children in three pre–Civil War plays, including *The Drunkard.* McConachie argues that in moral reform melodramas "families are the victims"; he highlights how bourgeois values inform the characters, settings, and motifs of *The Drunkard* by focusing on the protagonist's wife and the material manifestations of the family's decline. And in the most comprehensive exploration of the genre published to date, Frick asserts that "fear for the integrity of the nuclear family was especially prominent on reformers' lists of concerns" and addresses that issue first and foremost in his analysis of themes embedded in temperance drama.[12] And indeed, the Middletons' worsening financial circumstance is an important focus in *The Drunkard.* Mary, Edward's wife, is forced to engage in menial labor when her husband abandons her and their daughter—a predicament that leads one character to declare, "O, she is low, degraded! She sank so far as to take in washing, to feed herself and child" (33). This state of affairs also makes Mary vulnerable to bodily violation. When she moves to Boston to search for her wayward husband, the villain of the drama, Lawyer Cribbs, visits her and attempts to take Middleton's place. He tries to convince her that her husband has been unfaithful, but Mary refuses to believe Cribbs, accusing him of slander. He retorts angrily, "Nay, then, proud beauty, you shall know my power—'tis late, you are unfriended, helpless, and thus: (*He seizes her, child screams*)"—at which point, William (Middleton's friend and confidant) enters, just in time to rescue her (37). Despite these trials and tribulations, including a suicide attempt by the protagonist, the fallen man is eventually saved and returns home. Like the TAS pledge card (fig. 2.3), in the closing tableau of *The Drunkard* everything is in its proper place: husband, wife, and child pray, sing, and engage in household activities together (50).

Because women and children appear so frequently in temperance imagery, many theater historians have studied the gendered, middle-class ideologies they champion. However, in my effort to supplement and perhaps complicate these observations, I suggest that the inebriate's depravity is most strongly signified by mental illness and the prospect of institutionalization. After all, the final scene of Cruikshank's graphic melodrama *The Bottle* depicts the protagonist suffering a permanent state of mania in an insane asylum (fig. 2.1). Therefore, I want to focus on this aspect of the drunkard's spectacular decline: insanity, widely considered to be the penultimate effect of alcohol abuse, and the harbinger of suicide. To date, scholarship on temperance melodrama has overlooked how medical discourse may have influenced widespread perceptions of the *delirium tremens.* As Joel Bernard has noted, medicine served as the "cornerstone" of nineteenth-century temperance ideology, and physicians took a keen interest in the relationship between habitual drinking, physical health, and antisocial behavior.[13] To understand the function of the DTs scene within temperance dramaturgy as well as audiences' fascination with this grotesque spectacle, we must take into account contemporaneous theories about the disorder's causes and cures.

Theories of Inebriation and Insanity in the Antebellum Era

During the first half of the nineteenth century, the number of institutions for the deviant and mentally ill rose markedly as concerns about alcohol consumption grew. In 1820, there were fewer than ten asylums in the United States; by 1860, one or more asylums could be found in nearly every state.[14] Sociologist Roger Bastide has argued that madness is a structural concept; it is defined and shaped by the community. Insanity, he asserts, "does not in fact exist as a natural entity, but only as a relationship. . . . a person is mad only in relation to a given society; social consensus defines the fluctuating boundary between the rational and the irrational."[15] Bastide's analysis suggests that the rapid increase in American insane asylums occurred due to revised notions of deviance as well as new "best practices" for the control and treatment of aberrant individuals.[16] The *delirium tremens,* as both diagnosis and cultural concept, seems to have played a role in the dissemination of these conventions. Although a detailed account of the medicalization of the DTs is beyond the scope of this study, I briefly chart some of the key ideas advanced by nineteenth-century medical practitioners who described alcohol-induced derangement.

Concerns about the impact of drink on the mind, morals, and body were pioneered in America by the physician Benjamin Rush, whose landmark essay *An Inquiry into the Effects of Ardent Spirits on the Human Body and Mind* (originally published in 1785) connected intemperance with ill health, criminal behavior, and madness. Rush's *Inquiry* constituted, according to Mark Edward Lender and James Kirby Martin, "a radical challenge to previous thinking; it assaulted the old dictum that alcohol was a positive good" (a necessity for health and healing). Rush's text was widely read: by 1850, nearly 200,000 copies had been printed. Because of its longevity, many scholars agree that Rush's *Inquiry* deeply informed the fundamental ideologies of the US temperance movement.[17]

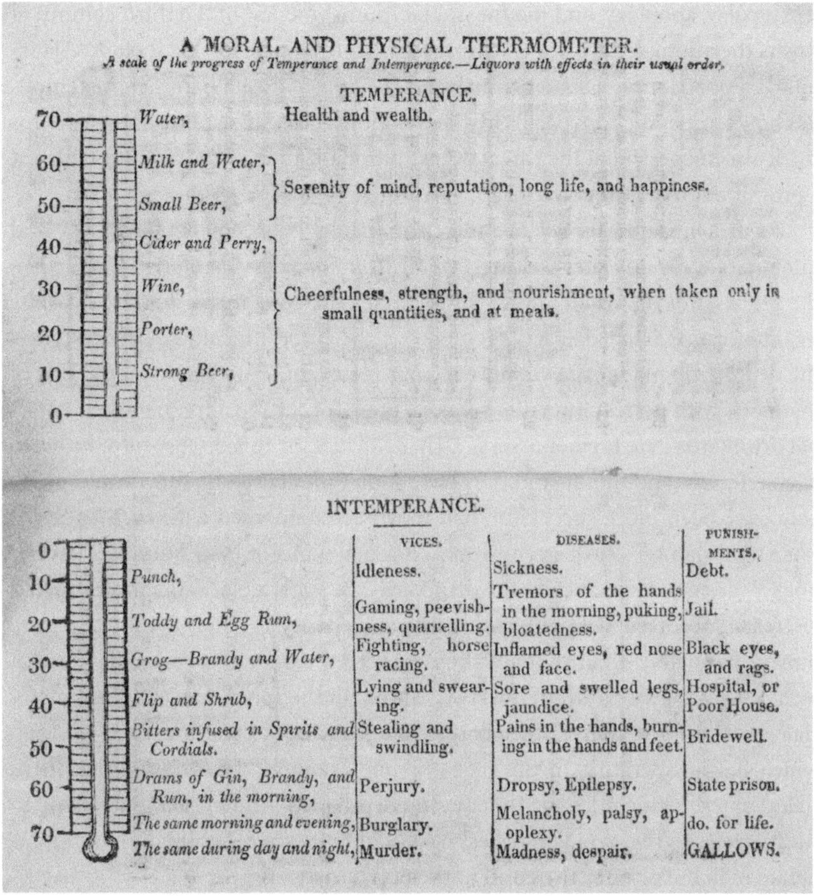
A MORAL AND PHYSICAL THERMOMETER.
A scale of the progress of Temperance and Intemperance.—Liquors with effects in their usual order.
TEMPERANCE.
70
60
50
40
30
20
10
0
Water,
Health and wealth.
Milk and Water,
Small Beer,
Serenity of mind, reputation, long life, and happiness.
Cider and Perry,
Wine,
Porter,
Strong Beer,
Cheerfulness, strength, and nourishment, when taken only in small quantities, and at meals.
INTEMPERANCE.
VICES.
DISEASES.
PUNISHMENTS.
Punch,
Idleness.
Sickness.
Debt.
Toddy and Egg Rum,
Gaming, peevishness, quarrelling.
Tremors of the hands in the morning, puking, bloatedness.
Jail.
Grog—Brandy and Water,
Fighting, horse racing.
Inflamed eyes, red nose and face.
Black eyes, and rags.
Flip and Shrub,
Lying and swearing.
Sore and swelled legs, jaundice.
Hospital, or Poor House.
Bitters infused in Spirits and Cordials.
Stealing and swindling.
Pains in the hands, burning in the hands and feet.
Bridewell.
Drams of Gin, Brandy, and Rum, in the morning,
Perjury.
Dropsy, Epilepsy.
State prison.
The same morning and evening,
Burglary.
Melancholy, palsy, apoplexy.
do. for life.
The same during day and night,
Murder.
Madness, despair.
GALLOWS.

Figure 2.4: "A Moral and Physical Thermometer: A Scale of the Progress of Temperance and Intemperance." Benjamin Rush, *An Inquiry into the Effects of Ardent Spirits upon the Human Body and Mind* (Boston: James Loring, 1823), 2–3. Courtesy of the American Antiquarian Society.

However, temperance historians generally overlook the fact that Rush also "made the first and most elaborate attempt [in the United States] to link the somatic and ethical dimensions of insanity," as Mary Ann Jimenez notes.[18] Later editions of the *Inquiry* included "A Moral and Physical Thermometer" charting the "diseases" and "punishments" inflicted by different types of alcohol (fig. 2.4). In the diagram, the habitual consumption of hard liquor results in vices like fighting, perjury, burglary, and murder, as well as physical ailments like epilepsy, palsy, apoplexy, and madness. The "punishments" in the third column of Rush's thermometer are, for the most part, destinations: the list includes "Hospital," "Poor House," "State prison," and "Gallows." Rush's barometer exemplifies how temperance advocates invoked notions of self-discipline in their rhetoric. It also suggests that the threat of institutionalization or incarceration played a prominent role in that rhetoric.

Rush continued to explore the connections between mental illness and intemperance in his later writings. In *Medical Inquiries and Observations upon the Diseases of the Mind* (1812), he reiterates his contention that ardent spirits often cause a "partial derangement" of the "moral faculties." He describes the drunkard's madness as temporary but recurrent: "Successive paroxysms of madness, with perfect intervals between them, occur most frequently in habitual drunkards." He further asserts, "The *remedies* for this disease have hitherto been religious and moral, and they have sometimes cured it. They would probably have been more successful, had they been combined with such as are of a physical nature." Rush even proposed a new kind of institution, the "sober house," designed specifically for drunkards. In such a place, inebriates would be treated as "objects of public humanity and charity. . . . They are indeed more hurtful to society, than most of the deranged patients of a common hospital would be, if they were set at liberty."[19] Although the sober house did not materialize until much later in the century (the New York State Inebriate Asylum, which began operating in the 1860s, is one example), his proposal seems to reflect an emerging mandate to sequester drunkards from the general public. In Rush's view, segregation was necessary not only for the rehabilitation of intemperate men but also for the good of the populace.

In 1813, T. M. D. Sutton, a British physician, published a pamphlet in which he coined the term *delirium tremens*—a phrase inspired by "the marked tremor of the hands caused by excessive drinking or as a result of sensitivity to alcohol in certain people."[20] Now, the disorder that eventually came to symbolize the drunkard's depravity had a name. This allowed scientific observers to distinguish alcohol-induced hallucinations from other kinds of mental disturbances. Medical practitioners quickly adopted the diagnostic term, and it entered popular culture through newspaper accounts, temperance narratives, and live entertainment.

Alcohol abuse soon became one of the most frequently cited reasons for sending individuals to lunatic asylums, second only to masturbation. According to Jimenez, medical practitioners described drunkenness as a kind of sensational excess—a manifestation of an individual's inability to adhere to social expectations. Cultural attitudes regarding self-control deeply informed the temperance movement and, as Ian R. Tyrrell notes, "helped to popularize the idea of self-improvement and strengthened the bourgeois ethic of frugality, sobriety, and industry in American society."[21] By the 1840s, temperance activists began to insist that drunkards could transform their lives if only they would take control of themselves through the total abstinence pledge.[22]

In 1848, Pliny Earle outlined the differences between *delirium tremens* and other forms of insanity in *History, Description and Statistics of the Bloomingdale Asylum for the Insane.* Earle, who was the asylum's head physician at the time, offered a statistical analysis of patients admitted there from 1821 to 1844 and also described the asylum's use of "moral treatment," in which caregivers tried to create an atmosphere of normalcy within the institutional setting.[23] In this phrase, *moral* seems to have a double meaning. First, it invokes the idea of compassionate care as opposed to punitive treatment. The increase in insane asylums was due, in part, to growing concerns regarding the catchall nature of prisons, which indiscriminately housed both the criminally deviant and the socially deviant. Institutions like Bloomingdale were designed to offer "asylum" to individuals whose abnormal behavior seemed involuntary rather than deliberate.[24] Second, in many respects "moral treatment" reflected the ideals and ardor of moral reform. As Robert H. Abzug and Steven Mintz argue, activists inspired by religious, millennialist views regarding the perfectibility of man and nation engaged in an extraordinary variety of political activities during the nineteenth century. According to Mintz, this period of time saw "the emergence of a cultural obsession with self-control, a preoccupation with suppressing animal instincts, disciplining the passions, controlling sensual appetites, distancing individuals from their bodily processes, and restraining impulsive behavior."[25] Although philanthropic in character, moral reform movements endeavored to eradicate aberrant behavior by promoting middle-class social norms. Similarly, moral treatment programs in insane asylums re-created middle-class life and routines in order to cure patients. In Earle's words, "The primary object is to treat the patients, so far as their condition will possibly admit, as if they were still in the enjoyment of their mental faculties. . . . The courtesies of civilized and social life are not to be forgotten, . . . operating, to no inconsiderable extent, as a means of effecting restoration to mental health." By mimicking the rituals of respectable society, inmates were supposed to relearn how to enact them.[26]

The *delirium tremens* is a central topic of discussion in Earle's *History*. In order to distinguish it from "insanity proper" (as he terms it), Earle devotes an entire chapter to the DTs. His description of the disorder is incredibly vivid—even theatrical. Like a melodrama punctuated by an elaborate sensation scene, his relatively dry and clinical prose explodes into a profusion of adjectives, imagery, and metaphors when he explicates a patient's experience of dipsomania.

> The walls of his apartment, mere mortar and whitewash to the view of other people, present to the patient pictures of every possible variety in character and composition. Animals of various kinds throng into his room, crouch before him with threatening gestures and grimaces the most frightful, creep beneath his bed, or crawl upon it with torturing menaces. Enemies in human form spring up to bind, to drag to prison, to the tribunal of justice, to the rack or to the place of execution, or, perchance to shoot or to slay with the sword; and, finally, the phantoms of the ideal world, specters with gorgon heads and bodies more hideous than those of the satyr or the fabled tenants of the lower regions, glower upon him with their eyes of fire, gnash their teeth in fiendish defiance, at length seize upon him, and he struggles with them in the full faith that he has encountered the devil incarnate.[27]

Earle's account incorporates many of the symptoms routinely embodied by performers who reenacted the DTs on various stages, including actors W. H. Smith and Harry Watkins and the most famous temperance lecturer of the nineteenth century, John B. Gough.

Earle insists that the *delirium tremens* differs from other kinds of mental imbalance and therefore should be treated differently. He observes that, although the symptoms can be severe, the illness is of relatively short duration. Because DTs sufferers exhibit normal behavior once their symptoms subside, he asserts that during treatment they are entitled to a certain autonomy that cannot be offered to the "properly insane." According to Earle, the vast majority of DTs patients at Bloomingdale recovered, although twenty died while institutionalized. Of the twenty deaths, he notes that three were the result of suicide. (Such data possibly buttressed widespread perceptions that drunkenness often led to suicide. Illustrations and melodramas usually incorporate self-harm in their depictions of the inebriate's decline: N. Currier's lithograph *The Drunkard's Progress* culminates in suicide, and Middleton, the protagonist in *The Drunkard,* is on the verge of drinking poison when Arden Rencelaw appears and convinces him to reform.)[28] Earle concludes that drunkards should be treated in institutions dedicated exclusively to them and their recovery—a proposal that seems to reflect a wider cultural trend to distinguish among the poor, the criminal, and the insane in order to manage each population more effectively.[29]

Earle's report on *delirium tremens* cases at Bloomingdale also reveals intriguing information about how gender and class figured into the treatment of drunkards. Of the 594 patients admitted from 1821 to 1844, 511 were male, suggesting that the disorder was much more prevalent in men—or, at least, that men were more likely to be sent to asylums. These statistics reflect the images that prevailed in temperance reform: drunkards were men, often husbands and fathers, whose vices caused them to victimize wives and children. Although female drunkards did exist, they rarely appeared in popular culture.[30] In addition, Earle's statistics suggest that the bulk of Bloomingdale's DTs patients hailed from the middle and upper classes. The patient's profession was recorded for roughly half of the cases; Earle observes that a slim majority were "merchants, traders, professional men, persons of leisure and young men without employment." He is careful to note that men from such classes were more likely to "resort to this institution when thus diseased. The great majority of persons whose pecuniary resources are limited are taken to places where the expenses are less."[31] The innovative programs of moral treatment at asylums like Bloomingdale attracted respectable families with financial resources. Rather than recovering at home—or, worse, being sent to a prison or poorhouse—such men could find refuge in the insane asylum.

Statistician and temperance advocate Edward Jarvis also explored the relationship between intemperance and madness in his book *Insanity and Idiocy in Massachusetts: Report of the Commission on Lunacy* (1855). Like Earle's *History,* Jarvis's *Report* attempts to reveal connections between alcohol, aberrant behavior, and insanity, reflecting what Robert A. Gross has termed "the fusion of morals and numbers" that permeated Jarvis's work. He charts the drunkard's trajectory from occasional errors in judgment to psychosis, asserting that mental derangement inevitably leads to "ill success and poverty" followed by "disorders of the nervous system and insanity, which, according to hospital records, find their most common origin in the exciting and exhausting effects of alcohol, especially among the poor." Although he discusses patients' family histories—gesturing toward a hereditary theory of mental illness—Jarvis strongly emphasizes self-discipline as the foundation of sound mental health.

This model, which privileged behavioral causes over biological ones, dominated most nineteenth-century discourse about insanity.[32]

These theories advanced by Rush, Earle, and Jarvis exhibit not only medical concerns but also moral ones. Respectable, middle-class behavior serves as the barometer by which the authors measure deviance. Rush, one of the earliest advocates of temperance in the United States, argued that immoderate drinking would lead to ruin; his Temperance Thermometer illustrated that habitual alcohol consumption would culminate in incarceration and death. Earle built on this claim by detailing the extraordinary number of *delirium tremens* cases at the Bloomingdale Asylum. And through a careful statistical analysis, Jarvis attempted to confirm the link between immoral behavior and insanity by proving that drunkenness was the leading cause of madness in Massachusetts. Although not all Americans would have been acquainted with these medical texts, the public did become familiar with their fundamental ideas and ideals by way of popular media: news reports, graphic representations, activist rhetoric, and performance.

Spectacular Indiscipline in *The Drunkard*

At the same time that insane asylums were sequestering drunkards from the general population, the *delirium tremens* increasingly appeared in entertainment culture. The theater and other amusements reinforced the idea that intemperate individuals would eventually run mad. In Smith's *The Drunkard*, the hero Edward Middleton endures a journey that seems structured, in many ways, like a medieval morality tale. His very name suggests he is a kind of middle-class Everyman, and other aspects of the text, including the subtitle, convey notions of salvation and transformation. Middleton's fall begins with a drastic change in his financial circumstances due to his drinking habit, which is effected in part through the devious machinations of the villain, Lawyer Cribbs. In the fourth act, he suffers from a spectacular bout of the *delirium tremens* and even attempts suicide.

Middleton's proclivities for pleasure and lightheartedness are highlighted from the outset. He is twenty-three when the play begins, and his age is cited as a reason why he is "giddy, wild and reckless" and a "dissipated collegian." In a conversation among Cribbs, Mary, and Mary's mother (Mrs. Wilson) in the first scene, Cribbs describes Middleton as "a gay young man" who is "fond of the world, given somewhat to excess, no doubt." Mrs. Wilson replies, "I understand you—very much unlike his father I would say," referring to Middleton's respected parent, who dies before the play begins. In other words, Middleton is a man on the cusp of success or failure: a push in one direction might decide his fate (8–9). When he begins drinking regularly several years after his marriage to Mary and the birth of their daughter Julia, the signs of decline become legible on his body. In the third scene of Act II, Middleton appears in a tavern in "rather shabby" dress (23) and, after a drunken fight with fellow patrons, becomes even shabbier when he begins bleeding from his forehead (25). Cribbs, who helped instigate the quarrel in the barroom, predicts, "He has tasted, and will not stop now short of madness or oblivion" (26). Later, as the drunkard contemplates returning home to his wife and daughter, he seems to be on the verge of *delirium tremens,* but by taking a swig from a bottle stashed away in a hiding place, he manages to delay it.

> Oh how my poor brain burns! My hand trembles! My knees shake beneath me! I cannot, will not appear before them thus; a little, a very little [drink] will strengthen me. No one sees; William must be there ere now, for my hiding place. Oh! The arch cunning of the drunkard! (*Goes to tree* R. H. [right-hand], *and from the hollow draws forth a bottle; looks round, and drinks. Cribbs behind exulting.*) So, so! It relieves! It strengthens! Oh, glorious liquor! Why did I rail against thee? Ha, ha! (26–27)

Imagining this moment in performance, it seems likely that for the audience—primed through advertising and word of mouth to expect a virtuosic rendition of the DTs in the play, but uncertain about preciously *when* it would occur—this monologue was a kind of tease, a titillating preview of the "real" DTs scene in Act IV. Spectators briefly glimpsed the behaviors (shaking hands, trembling knees) that the actor would enact more elaborately later, when he marshaled all of his energy and talent to conjure a grotesque spectacle of insanity. In this fashion, anticipation and tension build.

Middleton does return home, only to learn that Mary's mother has died because his drinking has impoverished the family. Blaming himself, he becomes frenzied; when Mary, Julia, and William (Middleton's friend and confidant) try to bar him from leaving, he calls out, "Unloose me; leave me; why fasten me down on fire? Madness is my strength: my brain is liquid flame!" (30). These comments pave the way for the play's long-awaited spectacular instant. Set outside a tavern on Hawley Street in Boston, the stage directions indicate that the disorderly drunkard is lying on the ground "without hat or coat, clothes torn, eyes sunk and haggard, appearance terrible, &c." (38). When he wakes, he calls for brandy and rum, and laments, "Pain! Dreadful pain! Heavens how I tremble. Brandy! Brandy? [*sinks down in agony.*]" (38). When the landlord of the tavern enters and denies the drunkard's appeals, Middleton tries to strangle him. Fortunately, William appears and stops him from committing murder.

After the landlord's exit, the drunkard's mania ensues. A manuscript "side" written in Smith's hand, comprising Middleton's lines bookended by abbreviated cues, survives in a collection of Smith's scripts; he may have used it while performing at the Boston Museum in 1844. In the side, the DTs sequence features more fragmentation and confusion than the version that appears in the 1847 published edition.

[MIDDLETON:] (*delirium*) Here friend—take it off. Will you?—there—that serpent coiling round my leg—there—pull—pull—ah! How strong they are—there—don't kill it—give it liquor—poison it slowly with rum—it shall be punish'd justly—Toads and Serpents—drown'd with brandy—excellent punishment—justice! justice!

[WILLIAM: He does] not know me.

[MIDDLETON:] Hush! Gently—gently—while she's asleep I'll kiss—she would reject me did she know it—there—hush! God bless my Mary, Bless her and my child—hush—if the Globe turns round once more, we shall slide from its surface into infinite nothingness—or eternity—ha! Ha! Great idea that—a boiling sea of wine—fired by the torch of fiends. ha! ha![33]

William slips off to get help, and Middleton's hallucination ends. After regaining his senses, he recognizes that he has descended into utter depravity and produces a vial of poison. Before he can consume it, Rencelaw—an upstanding member of the community who is a reformed drunkard himself—arrives, seizes the poison, and cajoles, "Nay, friend, take not your life, but mend it" (40). Middleton accepts Rencelaw's help, and the pieces are in place for the hero's eventual recovery and redemption.

The prospect of institutionalization—whether in a prison, a poorhouse, or an insane asylum—haunts the drama from the outset. In the first act, Cribbs remarks that Mrs. Wilson "has a claim upon the Alms House" if she cannot remain in the cottage on the Middleton estate, which has been her home for many years. Mary finds the idea of her mother being warehoused with paupers to be so horrible that it elicits a corporeal reaction: she "shudders" upon hearing Cribbs's statement (10). Cribbs invokes the insane asylum specifically during an exchange with Mrs. Spindle, a somewhat befuddled old maid. Mrs. Spindle admits, "I buy all the affecting novels, and all the terrible romances, and read them till my heart has become soft as maiden wax" (13); during the early nineteenth century, novel reading was sometimes cited as a cause of mental illness in women.[34] When Cribbs has a frustrating exchange with Spindle in Act II, he declares, "Get your friends to send you to the Insane Hospital, and place you among the incurables, as the most fusty, idiotic old maid that ever knit stockings" (22).[35]

But more than any other character, insanity is embodied by William's sister, Agnes, a young woman driven mad by the premature death of her fiancé.[36] Her most important purpose is to represent the omnipresent prospect of madness, clearly indicated by her designation as "A Maniac" in the cast of characters. Called "my poor, little, half-witted sister" by William and "crazy" by Cribbs, in many ways Agnes invokes another theatrical madwoman, Ophelia in *Hamlet.*[37] When Agnes encounters Cribbs during her first appearance, she is unable to hold a coherent conversation with him; instead, she sings a song, later mimicking Ophelia by scattering flowers across the stage. He complains, "Who let you out? You distress the neighborhood with your muttering and singing. I'll have you taken care of" (17–18), and also grumbles, "Why don't the Alms House keep such brats at home?" (17). Interestingly, at the end of the scene Agnes departs from her Shakespearean predecessor and invokes instead the hallucinatory terror of the *delirium tremens.* After William rescues her from Cribbs, he instructs Agnes to stay put until he comes back. When he exits, she sings another verse then offers a short, stilted soliloquy that concludes with an episode of sheer panic.

> I will sit on this rock till I hear the bells that are far off, for then,—I think of his words, who says he did not love me. It was a good character he wanted of the parson. A girl out of place, is like an old man out of his grave. (*Bells chime piano.*) They won't ask me to their merry makings, now, though I washed my best calico in the brook. (*Sings.*)
>
> "Walk up young man, there's a lady here,
> With jewels in her hair."
>
> (*Suddenly clasps her hands and screams*) Water, water! hear him, oh, hear him

cry for water; quick, quick! he'll turn cold again! his lips are blue; water, water! *Exit frantically* (19)

Although it is not entirely clear what causes Agnes to scream, it seems possible she is reliving her fiancé's death from the DTs—the traumatic episode that originally drove her mad. By reenacting her part in the spectacle of his death, she offers a preview of Middleton's delusions in Act IV.

Agnes eventually experiences a miraculous recovery and effects the villain's comeuppance—thereby demonstrating that a deviant individual, whether a drunkard or a madwoman, can be restored to society. But more significantly, throughout the play she represents the archetypal person-out-of-place, a misfit whose excesses and lack of inhibition disrupt the community. As she herself states prior to her panic attack, "A girl out of place, is like an old man out of his grave." Her broken mind causes her to wander the countryside, well beyond the boundaries of her proper sphere (the home). Her presence inspires the people around her, especially Cribbs, to invoke the threat of institutionalization. Agnes's mutterings, screams, and confusion operate in close partnership with Middleton's DTs episode to render visible the spectacle of insanity that, by 1844, asylums had essentially hidden from view.

Interestingly, most scholars who have written about *The Drunkard* have omitted Agnes in their discussions, aside from brief mentions in plot synopses, as if she were a minor character unworthy of attention. But it seems that Agnes lingered in the minds of spectators. For example, John Bouvé Clapp singles her out in a 1903 *Boston Evening Transcript* article about the drama's premiere at the Boston Museum: "Agnes Dowton, the poor insane girl, has a mad scene that never fails, in the hands of a capable actress, to arouse the sympathy and pity of the spectators."[38] In addition, cast lists kept by the Boston Museum's stage managers indicate that the second-ranked actress in the company usually portrayed Agnes. In the 1849 revival of *The Drunkard* at the Boston Museum, Mrs. J. W. Thoman (née Elizabeth Anderson, a descendant of the first Joseph Jefferson) played the role. Thoman's repertoire included Nerissa, Regan, Lady Anne, and the Nurse in *Romeo & Juliet*.[39] According to one newspaper account, Thoman, a soubrette, could "adapt herself to parts of a more serious kind without the least display of extravagance"; and William Winter reports that she "became a favorite in Boston." Audiences appreciated her fine singing voice, which may be another reason why she was cast in the part.[40]

Agnes's importance is evident in the concluding tableau of *The Drunkard*, which displays the Middleton family in domestic tranquility. The final stage direction reads,

> *EDWARD plays on a flute symphony to "Home, sweet home." . . . The burthen is then taken up by chorus of villagers behind . . . The melody is repeated quicker, and all retire with the exception of EDWARD, MARY, JULIA, WILLIAM, & AGNES, singing, and becoming gradually dimuendo. Air repeated slowly. JULIA kneels to EDWARD, who is at table, R. H. seated in prayer. EDWARD'S hand on bible, and pointing up. MARY standing leaning upon his chair. WILLIAM and AGNES, L. centre. Music till curtain falls. Picture.* (50)

Although McConachie, Mason, and Frick have all discussed this scene, they focus on Middleton, Mary, and Julia; they do not note that Agnes and William are also present. In other words, Agnes is hidden in plain sight. This omission signals, I think, a noteworthy gap in our understanding of *The Drunkard* and its historical moment. Her presence in the tableau is significant because her recovery, like Middleton's, reassures spectators that redemption is possible. As Bastide argues, every illness works in partnership with its cure: "The dynamics of mental disorder operate within a system where both the deviant and society are in collaboration. . . . it is not only the appearance of the illness which is part of the system, but also its disappearance." Agnes's inclusion in the final tableau suggests that every American, despite personal failings and lapses in respectability, could rehabilitate and join the ranks of ordinary citizens once more.[41]

Acting the *Delirium Tremens*

The *delirium tremens* scene was powerful and popular, in part, because the spectacle of insanity was swiftly hidden whenever it occurred in the real world. Enactments of the DTs provided audiences with the opportunity to see a sensation that was usually secreted away.[42] Intensely physical and strikingly visual, it also exemplified the body *as* spectacle, relying exclusively on the actor's expertise. Several performers became well known for their portrayal of Middleton in *The Drunkard*. None attained the legendary status of Edwin Forrest for Metamora, Joseph Jefferson for Rip Van Winkle, or James O'Neill for Edmond Dantès; but they leveraged their talent for enacting the DTs as a way to advance significantly in their profession.

The American actor Harry Watkins (1825–94) is a case in point. He became so well known for his rendition of Middleton's delirium that he often chose the play (and sometimes just the scene) for benefit performances. Watkins wrote nearly every day in his diary during the first fifteen years of his career and frequently credited the role of Middleton—and particularly the DTs scene—for his early professional success. Most historians know Watkins's diary by way of Maud and Otis Skinner's biography of the actor, *One Man in His Time;* but Watkins's original manuscript, which is housed in the Harvard Theatre Collection, offers more insight into his performances of *The Drunkard.*[43] During his debut in the role, Watkins reports that by the end of the second act, "*I had the audience with me.*"

> I was discovered lying in the streets, a ragged drunken miserable wretch—with the *delirium tremens*—the scene progressed—*the audience still with me*—applauded every speech—until, through my ravings I fell upon the stage in convulsions—*then*—they *shouted*—at the fall of the curtain I was called out—received *nine cheers*—made a speech—and went off. Congratulations poured in upon me from every side—*friends* and *enemies*—it was pronounced a great piece of acting.

In November 1849, Watkins landed an engagement at the Arch Street Theatre in Philadelphia, where manager William Burton allowed the actor to play Middleton for several nights. Writing of his first night at the Arch Street, Watkins states, "My success equalled all I could have wished for, as at the end of the piece I was loudly called for, and upon my appearance before the curtain was greeted with three cheers. I made a short speech, and upon retiring, three more cheers were given me. I must labor hard to keep up the impression I made." The actor enjoyed continued success as Middleton and played the part during his New York debut in 1850 at the National Theatre, writing afterward, "I brought them down in the 'delirium tremens,' and everyone said that I made a hit." Watkins relays an interesting story describing two spectators' experiences of his performance. In the anecdote, he seems to express a hope (perhaps even an expectation) that his rendition of the DTs might have a lasting impact on certain audience members.

> During my delirium tremens scene in the "Drunkard," a lady in the boxes fell from her seat, fainting, and had to be conveyed home—her husband came

> to me afterwards to tell me that I ought not play that part again. I have since understood that he was not the most sober of men—may the incidents of this night prove a warning.

Here, Watkins suggests that his performance of the DTs sometimes sparked an equally sensational scene in the audience: in this case, a woman making a spectacle of herself in the house, followed by her husband's confronting the actor, followed potentially (in Watkins's imagination) by the man's recognition of his errant ways.[44]

The success of the DTs sequence hinged on a performer's ability to enact it convincingly. The day after his very first performance as Middleton, Watkins wrote in his journal, "My body is very sore from the effect of the delirium tremens scene of 'The Drunkard.'" Similarly, after his fifth night in *The Drunkard* at the Arch Street Theatre, he lamented, "I wish they would discontinue it[,] my body is sore enough."[45] Because actors like Watkins went to great lengths to make the scene believable, it sometimes took a physical toll—an overlap between the virtual and the real.[46]

Some producers recognized the audience's interest in this fine line between character and actor, and attempted to capitalize on it. As Michael L. Quinn asserts, "The personal, individual qualities of the performer always resist, to some degree, the transformation of the actor into the stage figure," and spectators at temperance melodramas may have been attracted to this phenomenological tension.[47] In some productions, real-life sobriety was an essential prerequisite; McConachie notes that P. T. Barnum advertised his 1848 production of *The Drunkard* in Philadelphia as featuring an entire company of pledged teetotalers.[48] But when the actor in the role was not a pillar of sobriety, and his drinking problem (whether past or present) was a matter of public knowledge, the dynamic was different. Whenever a reformed alcoholic played Middleton, spectators likely read the DTs scene as "dramatized biography," as Geoffrey S. Proehl observes.[49]

In these instances, the actor's real self ghosted his staged self, increasing and deepening the audience's sense of his body *as* spectacle. Rumors and stories about the drinking habits of actors were ubiquitous; this is evident, for example, in Joseph Daly's biography of his brother, theater manager and playwright Augustin Daly. Daly describes the theater industry of his youth—before managers like Kimball, Barnum, and his brother instituted changes intended to attract respectable, middle-class audiences—as "the day of the 'talented drunkard.'" In his recollection, "The player too often was more convivial than ambitious. After the performance he resorted to taverns and coffee-houses (all well known and respectable enough) and entertained the patrons of the theatre (all well known and respected too), and there until the early hours he discussed the glories of the stage . . . [over] many tobies of strong ale." Daly makes this observation as a way to emphasize his brother's achievements in the late nineteenth-century theater industry, so his comment veers toward hyperbole. Nevertheless, his description of the "talented drunkard" reflects a widespread cultural assumption regarding actors' appetite for drink.[50]

A "talented drunkard" penned *The Drunkard,* in fact. Smith was addicted to alcohol and struggled to maintain his sobriety while working as Kimball's stage manager. One of his journals reveals that he experienced several relapses during the early 1850s. On his forty-fourth birthday in 1852, Smith wrote, "At 11PM, with trembling fingers, but a most sincere profound repentance, I, with *God's help! Most sincere* and *firm Resolve,* from this day, I will *never taste anything that can intoxicate.* If after my death these lines should meet the Eye of any true hearted man inclined to drink, may he ponder on them and *profit.*" Despite this fervent pledge, he continued to wrestle with his addiction. During a particularly bad episode in the spring of 1853, Kimball took the intoxicated Smith to the Cambridge Street Jail—apparently because he believed such an action to be "the safest and best plan" for his stage manager's recovery.[51]

Smith's drinking problem seems to have been widely known. Watkins writes in his diary,

> Mr. W. H. Smith, an old actor, and who at that time was a hard drinking man—signed the pledge of total abstinence—this play [*The Drunkard*] was written for him—in fact he wrote the greater portion of his own part, himself—he made a great hit in the performance of it—the people looked upon it as a faithful portraiture of himself—it was but playing his own life. He was *the part*—under these circumstances, when I was cast for the part, I felt inadequate to the task assigned me.[52]

Here, Watkins reveals his belief that, in some respects, Smith *was* Middleton, and that the actor's personal struggle with alcohol informed the role he wrote. Perhaps this is why Watkins, who generally abstained from drinking, claimed to feel "inadequate to the task" of portraying Middleton. In contrast, whenever Smith played the part, he spectacularized both a sordid past and an unstable present. He also revealed to his audience a deeply personal horror: the spectacle he made of himself whenever (if ever) he suffered from the DTs. Undoubtedly, this was one reason why spectators came to see him.

Opportunities to witness reenactments of dipsomania occurred in other contexts, too. Renditions of the DTs appeared not only in theaters but also in lecture halls, where activists and reformed drunkards relayed sensational stories about the effects of drink. During the antebellum period and beyond, the stories they told, as well as stories told *about* them, contributed greatly to perceptions of inebriates within the American imagination. Temperance speakers mythologized and materialized the drunkard—as character, as cultural fetish, as social problem—and spectators reveled in the slippage between past and present while hearing their affect-mobilizing stories of distress and redemption. The relationship between these two performance genres warrants consideration.

The Spectacle(s) of John B. Gough

Both Frick and Mason assert that "experience speeches," a type of oratory popularized by the community of working-class temperance advocates that came to be known as the Washingtonians, probably fostered an appetite for temperance melodrama.[53] Instead of relating facts and figures about the prevalence of drunkenness, its impact on society, and the ways in which drinking compromised one's health—topics that constituted the bread and butter of texts penned by clerics and physicians—experience speakers told dramatic personal stories at public meetings that, in many ways, imitated both the structure and the emotionalism of melodrama. Indeed, *The Drunkard* owes a significant debt to the experience speech not only in terms of dramaturgy (as Frick and Mason contend) but also in terms of performance. Take, for instance, John B. Gough, a reformed drunkard inspired and supported by the Washingtonians whose career as a temperance speaker began and flourished in New England during the early 1840s. In many respects, the orator constituted a spectacle in himself—especially when, in 1845, he allegedly suffered a relapse in New York City that generated a firestorm of commentary in the press. Many dimensions of the Gough phenomenon—the anecdotal and the actual, the public and the private—help to illuminate why the *delirium tremens* played a prominent role in antebellum entertainment culture.

Established by a small group of Maryland artisans in May 1840, the Washington Temperance Society of Baltimore quickly caught the imagination of the nation. Although most of their chapters disbanded or transformed into fraternal lodges within a decade, the Washingtonians had an indelible impact on the antebellum temperance movement.[54] During the early nineteenth century, most temperance orators were pillars of sobriety, hailing from the clergy or the New England elite; in contrast, the Washingtonians targeted and embraced working-class individuals and actual drunkards. According to Ian R. Tyrrell, "The older evangelicals had lacked personal experience of drink and sought converts chiefly among the already sober; the new group of reformers focused the attention of the temperance movement on the drinkers themselves." In addition, the Washingtonians popularized the notion of total abstinence to a greater degree than any other temperance society had been able or willing to do. Earlier organizations, such as the Massachusetts Society for the Suppression of Intemperance (founded in 1813) and the American Temperance Society (established in 1826), urged restraint rather than abstention. In the 1830s, a philosophical shift occurred within the movement when reformers shifted away from the notion of "temperance" (moderate drinking) toward "teetotalism" (absolute avoidance). Although at first not all reformers embraced this ethic, it gradually gained traction across the board.[55] By 1843, Washingtonian strategies of reclamation and mutual support had spread to such a degree that the society claimed more than a million converts. According to Thomas R. Pegram, its efficacy "owed much to its willingness to provide a popular culture of temperance for working-class people."[56] Because organizers recognized that drinking was a social practice, they sponsored a wide variety of alternatives to the tavern. Dances, picnics, minstrel shows, concerts, and other amusements numbered among their offerings.

Another signature accomplishment of the Washingtonians was their approach to temperance meetings, which harnessed the affective power of confession.[57] Juxtaposing his sordid past with his happy present, the speaker recounted the horrors, trials, and tribulations of his personal history, urging his fellow men and women to beware of drink and join the cause. The before/after dynamic of such experience speeches lent them the sense of the spectacular. As Tyrrell observes, "The contrast between past degradation and present respectable condition which the reformed man presented on the stage carried tremendous dramatic force. The stark alternatives—poverty then, respectability now—were embodied in the person of the reformed man." During the first

Figure 2.5: John B. Gough. Engraving by J. J. Cade from a painting by Sir Daniel Macnee (ca. 1855). Frontispiece, John B. Gough, *Platform Echoes: Or, Living Truths for Head and Heart* (Hartford, CT: A. D. Worthington, 1886). Courtesy of the American Antiquarian Society.

years of the Washingtonian movement, some speakers, such as John Hawkins, traveled all over the country recruiting converts to the temperance cause using this passionate mode of oratory.[58]

Gough was such a convert. After becoming sober in the wake of an encounter with a Washingtonian, he began telling his story publicly in 1842. He was a different sort of spectacle—odd, anomalous, freakish (fig. 2.5). Indeed, he seems to have had what Joseph Roach terms "It": the peculiar charisma we perceive in "abnormally interesting" performers. In myriad ways, Gough embodied the paradoxical qualities of "strength *and* vulnerability, innocence *and* experience, and singularity *and* typicality" that Roach describes.[59] Gough was only twenty-five years old when he started speaking, and many witnesses of his first performances described feeling shocked and surprised by his youth. Middle-class audiences viewed Gough as relatively innocent due to his lack of polish and education (he never finished school, coming from an impoverished family). And yet, he also had a wealth of "experience" as a former drunkard, which not only informed his lectures but also gave him authority. He had a powerful voice and an uncanny ability to imitate characters—strengths that contrasted with his youthful vulnerability. Finally, Gough was both singular and typical because even though he was yet another orator within a virtual army of temperance speakers, he was unusual, distinctive, unique—strikingly different from others who frequented the lecture circuit.

Such contradictions can be detected in the plethora of newspaper clippings that Gough collected in his personal scrapbooks.[60] Spectators genuinely struggled to pinpoint what made Gough so compelling. A writer in the *Flushing Journal* once lamented, "It needs a more competent hand than mine to give anything like a sketch of the speaker's fire and power. . . . One must be *present,* as in a battle or a ship-wreck, to be able to form a just idea and estimation of such things."[61] More than anything, the clippings reveal that his admirers considered his performances to be not only *e*ffective but also *a*ffective. Gough's appeal seemed to center on two talents: his power of imitation and his ability to generate breathless moments of emotional collectivity in his audiences. But another mystery attracted spectators, too. As Baz Kershaw asserts, one of the defining features of spectacle is the simultaneous "curiosity and contempt" that it tends to inspire among audiences.[62] In many ways, Gough trafficked in this paradoxical dynamic. Suspicions about whether or not he was truly reformed dogged him throughout his life; such questions plagued many Washingtonian speakers, who collectively constituted a new class of lecturer. Simultaneously attracted and repulsed, fans and foes wondered if the drunkard before them was genuinely rehabilitated. Gough's public testimonials gave inquisitive spectators an opportunity to read the truth upon his body.

Apparently, a unique ability to conjure images was one of Gough's special talents. He performed, in essence, one-man sensation scenes. Accounts of his orations frequently mention the pictorial vivacity of his stories. A reporter for the *New York Tribune* in December 1844 writes that Gough's scenes were "brought before the mind, as though they were Daguerreotyped upon the wall." The *Princeton Whig* attempts to describe the orator's gifts by comparing him to Charles Dickens.

> Mr. Gough certainly possesses a rich fund of humor, and has a great command of details, always at his service; but we are disposed to think that his chief power lies in his *graphic delineations of thrilling scenes.* In this respect he resembles Dickens. His description of the poor shivering child in the streets—of the sister supporting the head of her degraded brother and weeping over him—and of the heartbroken girl who confronted the inhuman monster who persisted in selling rum to her father—and many, very many other scenes which we could recall, and which all his hearers will long remember—were worthy of the pen which described the trial of "Fagin" and the murder of "Nancy."

These descriptions of Gough's spectacular performances account for another trope that emerges in press coverage: one had to be in Gough's presence to understand fully his power. "No report, however able, could impart a just and vivid idea of the real thing," the *Daily Mail* of Boston declares. "You must have the man himself before you; you must hear the peculiarly winning, animating, soul-moving, mirth-provoking tones of his voice."[63]

Perhaps more than any other topic, critics discuss Gough's ability to inspire a palpable collectivity among his spectators. Wherever he went, it was said that Gough stirred intense emotions in the auditorium. A writer for the *Columbia Washingtonian* observed, "He possesses in an eminent degree, that electric, or magnetic power, by which he instantly fixes, and holds fast the undivided attention of his auditors. . . . It seems to be no part of his design to move the feelings of his audience, yet he evidently sways them at his will." The *Crystal Fount* describes a meeting at which "a thrill of intense admiration seemed to pass through the audience. . . . seldom have we seen an audience so completely carried away. At one time there would scarcely be a dry eye in the house, and the very next moment, with tears on every cheek, a roar of laughter would come from every lip." The *White Mountain Torrent,* detailing Gough's visit to the New Hampshire State Prison in February 1844, reports that at the conclusion of his lecture, every prisoner rose his hand to take the temperance pledge, "instantly and together, as if moved by one will, the tears at the same time gushing from every eye." In addition to emphasizing the affective dynamism of Gough's lectures, these accounts describe the experience as having a distinctly *corporeal* dimension: the audience breathes, sighs, laughs, and cries as one.[64]

His pleasing voice, his elaborate gestures and postures, and, above all, his mutability of character may be why critics frequently compared him to famous actors. A *Gloucester Telegraph* reporter asserts, "The stage actor's varied accomplishments were never nearer the pulpit: and never were their evident comedial [*sic,* comedic] attractions exhibited or exerted in a better cause." A writer for the *Commercial Advertiser* went even further in likening Gough's oratory to theatrical performance: "I have listened to [some] of the greatest tragic actors of the time when theatres were in fashion; but none of them in the highest wrought scenes of Shakspeare could ever move my feelings as they were moved by that son of Nature in his simple lectures in favor of temperance."[65] Whether intentionally or not, such comparisons alluded to a somewhat embarrassing detail in the orator's past: before taking the pledge of sobriety, he worked for a time as a professional actor, including short stints at the Franklin Theatre in New York City and the Lion Theatre in Boston. Gough occasionally mentioned this in his writings or lectures in order to illustrate the depths to which he had sunk as a drunkard.[66] Telling the story of how he (unsuccessfully) sought a position at Thomas S. Hamblin's Bowery Theatre, Gough exclaims in his autobiography, "so low had I fallen and so desperately had I backslidden, that at the very door of that same theatre, which I had, five years before, wished destroyed, as a temple of sin, I stood applying for a situation as an actor and comic singer!"[67] However, it is difficult to ascertain whether Gough's disavowals of the theater were genuine or strategic. In critiquing the theater, he may have been attempting to buttress his persona as a respectable and trustworthy man. In the unpublished manuscript of an oration he wrote late in life, Gough enthusiastically discusses his youthful love affair with the stage, admitting that as a playgoer, "I cried and *laughed,* I was thrilled by the tragedy, and *convulsed* by the farce. It was a new world."[68] It seems that he was ambivalent, even conflicted, about performing.

One of Gough's journals reveals just how much of a phenomenon he had become in the months leading up to the premiere of *The Drunkard* at the Boston

Museum. In one notation, Gough indicates that he gave a lecture for the "first time in Boston" on September 16, 1843. In his autobiography, Gough writes that this debut was a momentous event for him: "I felt rather apprehensive in view of speaking in Boston, for I had heard it spoken of as the modern Athens, and knew that as to intelligence it stood very high amongst the cities of the Union."[69] Subsequent entries in Gough's journal reveal that this was but the first of many appearances in Boston. In the time between September 1843 and the premiere of Smith's play in February 1844, Gough gave more than forty lectures in that city, including engagements at Faneuil Hall, the Boston Tabernacle, the Odeon, the Melodeon, and the Tremont Temple, among other venues. During the initial run of *The Drunkard,* Gough continued to lecture regularly there.[70]

Interestingly, the account book he kept during this period suggests that he made a special visit to the Boston Museum to see *The Drunkard* at the height of the production's popularity. An entry for Saturday, March 16, 1844, indicates that Gough purchased "Tickets to Museum 50¢ Candy 50¢ Omnibus Tickets 1.00." According to an advertisement in Boston's *Evening Transcript,* Kimball offered a special matinee of the play that day "for the convenience of families and strangers, commencing at 3 o'clock." Admission was twenty-five cents. This seems to have been the first of what would be many matinees at the museum catering to women, families, and other individuals for whom an evening performance was either inconvenient or morally problematic. According to McConachie, matinees of this type became a staple of not only Kimball's museum in Boston but also P. T. Barnum's in New York. If this entry in Gough's account book was, indeed, for two tickets to the Boston Museum, it suggests he was aware of Kimball's lauded show and wanted to see it for himself—especially when given the opportunity to attend a special matinee.[71]

Because Gough tended to speak extemporaneously, it is impossible to identify textual ties between the orator's version of the DTs and that of Smith.[72] However, newspaper accounts frequently mention that one of Gough's most effective bits was "his vivid portraiture of the horrors of the delirium tremens," which the *Princeton Whig* declared to be "the masterpiece of the whole performance. . . . the whole assembly stood aghast." Another testimony regarding Gough's rendition of the DTs similarly emphasizes the sensational, bodily nature of his spectators' response: "He made the flesh to creep with horror, as he described, with startling distinctness, the horrible terror, the dreadful, the terrible inflictions, of that intensely terrifying disease, the *delirium tremens*—the last stage of the drunkard's terrible career." Since Gough was admired for

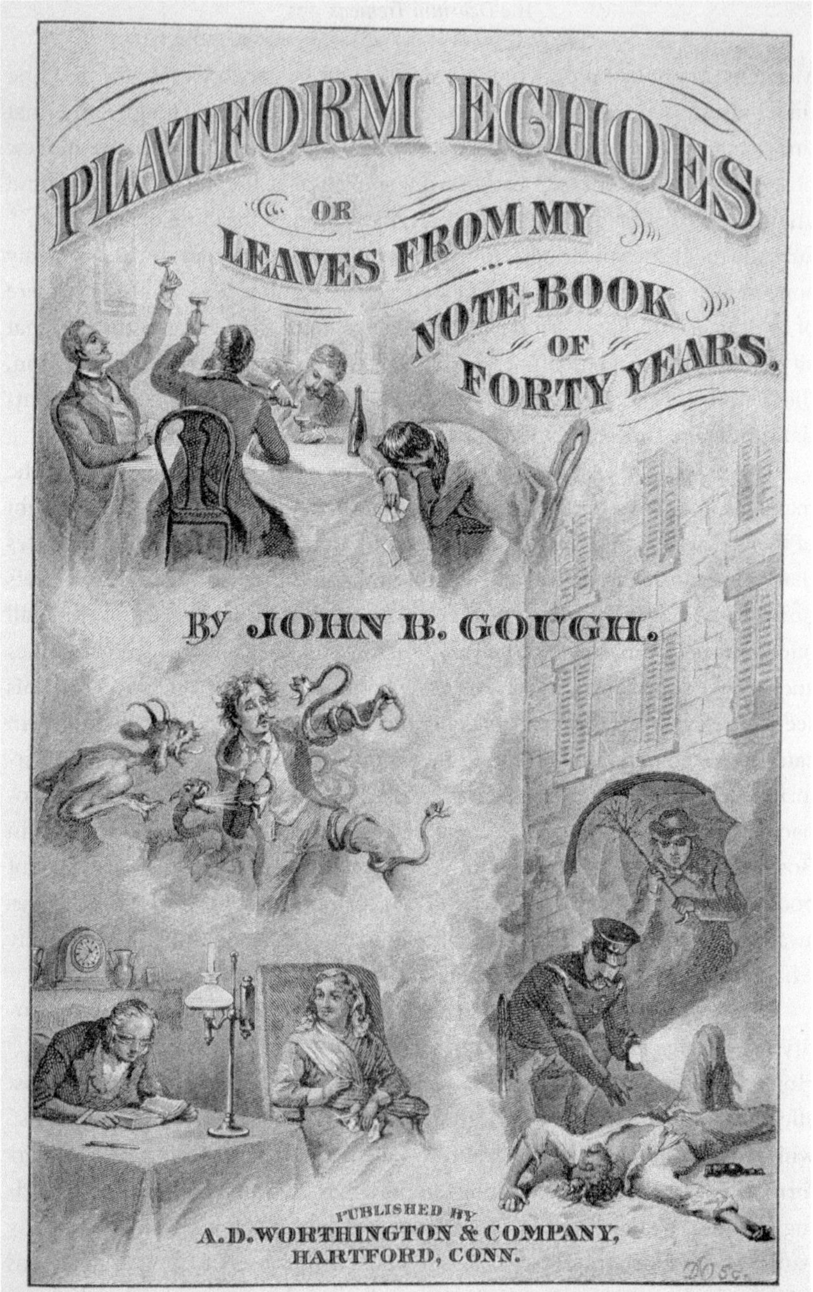

Figure 2.6: A man suffering from the DTs, depicted underneath the author's name, figures prominently on the title page for John B. Gough's *Platform Echoes* (Hartford, CT: A. D. Worthington, 1886). Courtesy of the American Antiquarian Society.

his gift of imitation—investing, according to the *Pilot* in Boston, "his whole soul into his representations of character, and [becoming], for the time being, a genuine actor"—it is probable that during these moments, the lecturer created a scene that had something in common with the *delirium tremens* sequence in *The Drunkard.*[73] Indeed, Gough's rendition of the DTs, which became one of his most popular routines, may have inspired Smith to include such a scene for himself in his temperance drama.

Platform Echoes; Or, Living Truths for the Head and Heart, a collection of Gough's oratorical texts first published in 1884, provides additional evidence that the *delirium tremens* played a prominent role in his lectures and legend. For example, the illustrated title page depicting "the beginning, middle, and end of a drunkard's career" features four images. Representing the "middle," located immediately beneath Gough's name on the title page, is a man battling snakes and demons during a bout of the DTs, suggesting that this spectacle was strongly associated with him (fig. 2.6). At one point in the book, Gough details drink's terrible toll on the body and declares, "Did you ever see a man in *delirium tremens,* biting his tongue until his mouth was filled with blood, the foam on his lips, the big drops upon his brow? . . . it is the *delirium tremens, mania a potu*—a trembling madness, the most terrible disease that can fasten its fangs on man. *Delirium tremens* is a species of insanity." Here, Gough casts the listener (or reader, or spectator) in the role of witness, conjuring the image of the drunkard before him and invoking the spectacle of derangement. Soon after this passage, Gough changes tactics slightly, casting the listener *as* the drunkard rather than mere onlooker.

> Suppose at night an animal frightful in expression and proportions was to enter your room with heavy tread, what would you do? If it were a reality, you would spring at it, you would fight with it, and gather fresh courage from every resounding blow. You are fighting a tangible thing. . . . Your weapon passes through the horrid thing . . . You grasp at it, and clutch nothing; still there is a mocking look on its frightful face. . . . You are not simply frightened, but transfixed with horror. The skin lifts from the scalp to the ankles; your hair stands on end, for you know there is nothing to fight. . . . That is the horror of *delirium tremens.*[74]

The use of second-person address suggests that in his lectures, Gough encouraged his spectators to imagine *embodying* the inebriate, which possibly explains why critics report sensing a palpable response in the audience when Gough described the horrors of the DTs. The orator first invited spectators to bear witness to the undisciplined drunkard's body; then, he conjured them *as* that body.

Making a Spectacle of Himself: Public Responses to Gough's 1845 Relapse

An inherent contradiction in the experience speech is that the speaker embodies both dissipation and redemption: the saved man portrays the fallen man. This disconcerting overlap between past and present is one reason why enactments of the DTs were so sensational. The Washingtonian project demanded an official declaration of sobriety that in many respects was a promise to embody American middle-class virtues. At temperance lectures, reformers urged audience members to come forward, sign the pledge, and vow never again to consume alcohol of any kind. The pledge placed enormous value on individual commitment, requiring the drunkard to participate actively in his own rehabilitation.[75] The speaker's present performance (his persuasive and affective speech) capitalized on his past vow (a performative utterance) to abstain from alcohol. Therefore, Gough's offstage life—especially his ability to model the temperance pledge's efficacy through his personal conduct—constituted a critical component of his persona. His reputation hinged on his daily adherence to middle-class norms despite his nightly conjuring of the old ghost. Therefore, when Gough relapsed into drunkenness on two occasions in the 1840s, the ghost materialized in a sensational way. Instead of creating spectacles in the lecture hall, he became one himself. The public debates surrounding these events help to illuminate why temperance performers' personal struggles fascinated spectators and, perhaps, added to their popularity and appeal.

His first relapse occurred in 1843, five months after he signed the pledge and began his career as a temperance lecturer. In his autobiography, Gough confirms this setback and states that it was a "fact notorious at the time," widely discussed within his home community of Worcester, Massachusetts. Fatigued by a rigorous speaking schedule, he explains that he traveled to Boston one evening, fell in with some old friends at the theater, and when one of them offered him a glass of alcohol, he did not refuse. This single glass roused his "powerful and now successful enemy"—his appetite for drink—and he resumed the habit for a short time. Gough eventually sought help from his temperance associates and began giving addresses again. "I was almost broken-hearted, and felt as if

I were insane," he writes, "but . . . cheered by the considerate kindness of my friends, I determined, God helping me, to be more than ever an uncompromising foe to alcohol." Because his admirers and acquaintances rallied around him, encouraging him to continue his good work, Gough was able to cast this unfortunate experience in a positive light. When he recommenced lecturing, sympathetic audiences embraced him. Incorporating his mistake into his life story, he moved on.[76]

However, the next time Gough fell from grace, he was not as fortunate. By 1845, Gough had obtained celebrity status, with newspapers in most major Eastern cities regularly reporting his activities and whereabouts. During an engagement in New York City in September, he disappeared for a week and was eventually discovered in a brothel on Walker Street, suffering from the effects of *delirium tremens*. The news sparked a veritable firestorm of criticism, with sensational publications like the *Police Gazette* and *New York Herald* leading the ruthless charge. Unlike his relapse in 1843, this time Gough did not accept responsibility or blame. He distributed a statement claiming that a stranger invited him to engage in conversation over a glass of soda water, and somehow drugged or poisoned him. Apparently, the proffered concoction whetted Gough's appetite for drink and caused an uncontrolled spiral that ended in a house of ill repute.[77]

The voluminous press coverage about the scandal in Gough's scrapbooks suggests that the public followed the story with intense interest. Several newspapers underscored its theatricality, describing it in terms of spectacle and sensation—calling attention to the importance of a temperance speaker's "performance" in life, offstage. One paper noted, "The singular disappearance, and as singular re-appearance, of this distinguished and eloquent Temperance Lecturer creates more and more of a sensation." Along these lines, the *Herald* declared, "It is, in fact, a singular spectacle—a moral phenomenon, worthy of exciting admiration, and of leading to enquiry." The *Christian World* faulted the "injudicious kindness of his later friends [who] kept him forever in the field. . . . They forgot that when but a boy he was of the *dramatis personae* of our 'Lion Theatre.' They unconsciously made life for him a *spectacle*, in which he was to bear the only, the single part. I do not wonder that he fell." Writers in the *Police Gazette* repeatedly argued that the incident was evidence of Gough's hypocrisy, which (they boasted) they had suspected all along: "Take one backward glance upon his whole career, and the mind reels back sickened and disgusted with the spectacle." The event gave the press an opportunity to resurrect accusations leveled against Gough during his fast and furious rise to fame, including the claim that he had personally enriched himself through the philanthropic machinery of the temperance cause.[78]

Supporters and detractors alike participated in the debunking of the popular mythology that had formed around Gough. The lecturer's alleged "humbugging" of the public—as the *Gazette* asserted on at least one occasion—was of particular concern. The *Herald* declared that temperance reformers (especially reformed drunkards) collectively comprised "a moral ulcer on the community" by trying "to prove that a rogue is not a rogue—that a deceiver is not a deceiver—that a drunkard is not a drunkard." The anonymous author of a pamphlet conceded that Gough should not be criticized for his desire to consume ardent spirits, since "The appetite for drink is one that, once thoroughly acquired, is rarely, if ever wholly conquered." Gough's denials and lies, the pamphlet asserted, constituted his real crime.[79] While cynics brutally attacked his character and motives, sympathizers urged the public to lend Gough their compassion. They insisted that the event posed an opportunity to pity the humiliated orator and, by association, drunkards everywhere. As the *Pittsfield Washingtonian* declared, "We trust that this melancholy event will be . . . a warning to all, to be ever on their guard against the temptations of the adversary." Others maintained that if Gough was a victim of deception he should not be blamed, because he had not consciously violated his pledge; rather, he was tricked into doing so. In the process, however, such writers tacitly questioned the veracity of Gough's explanation of events.[80]

The raucous public discourse about Gough's relapse confirms that the sensational drunkard, in both oratory and melodrama, derived its capital from the slippage between storied/past and actual/present failure. As Roach argues, an audience's attraction to celebrity relies in part on the performer's vulnerability, on "the empathic tension of waiting for the apparently inevitable fall, [which] makes for breathless spectatorship."[81] Temperance speakers fascinated audiences because each reformed drunkard might someday fall again, stumbling spectacularly from normalcy into disorder. For them, disaster perpetually loomed, one step—or one drink—away.

When Gough enacted his apparently inevitable fall, it only seemed to add to his fame. In his journal during this tumultuous period, Gough indicates feeling "sick" for several weeks after his scandalous discovery on Walker Street, during which time he rested and recovered at home. Despite the controversy, the questioning, and the ridicule he endured, he held out hope for not only a physical recovery but also a public one: "I am encouraged by my friends and do not fear what [my enemies] can do to me as long as I feel that I am right."[82] His friends' encouragement was warranted. In December of that year, Gough began speaking again. For the most part, his audiences welcomed him with open arms, and he enjoyed a celebrated career that spanned four decades.

Dénouement: The Paradox of Sensationalism and Reform

In contrast to sensation scenes featuring a character at her heroic best, the *delirium tremens* sequence displays a character at his deplorable worst. The disorderly excess of the DTs scene seems unseemly, out of place, in moral reform melodrama—a genre strongly associated with nineteenth-century museum theaters, which "hinged on [the proprietors'] personal reputations and their production of moral drama," according to McConachie.[83] In soliciting the audience's sympathy for the drunken protagonist, did reformers and theater producers encourage spectators to be more understanding or more critical of the fallen man? Furthermore, did the sensationalism of the scene distract or detract from the messages it conveyed?

Theater historians who have explored these questions provide disparate answers. McConachie, for example, argues that the exhibits and melodramas at museums "helped to fold thousands of status-anxious urbanites into the embrace of the emergent business-class culture."[84] He proposes that contract-making and vow-keeping are of central concern in moral reform plays because characters suffer dire consequences when they do not adhere to their social and familial obligations—suggesting that melodramas like *The Drunkard* served a disciplinary function by celebrating business-class values. Although Mason views the question through a slightly different lens, his conclusions are somewhat similar to McConachie's. In his theoretical analysis of melodrama as a genre, Mason maps some of the distinctions between myth and ideology and warns against conflating the two, arguing that melodrama's tendency toward *myth* (which he defines as "a form of symbolic narrative," representing "the voice not of individuals but of entire peoples") contrasts starkly with *polemic,* "or any other mode that eschews symbol, narrative, allegory, and overt fiction." By focusing on the public character of myths and their apparent ambition to "bring everyone together," Mason suggests that myths are conservative, collective, and static whereas polemic tends to be progressive, particular, and active. In his discussion of *The Drunkard,* he argues that temperance melodramas "fostered a myth that promoted the ideology of the rising middle class" and "appeared only when the mainstream temperance rhetoric and publications . . . had evolved to the point at which popular theatre was possible."[85] In short, he asserts that the play conveyed values that were widely accepted at the time of its premiere; therefore, it was mythic (conservative) rather than polemic (progressive).

In contrast, Frick suggests, "Temperance drama was born of the intersection of temperance motives and ideology with *progressive* trends in literature and the arts." He argues that "the more sensationalist reformers" embraced performative and theatrical activities because "they were directed principally at the senses; they appealed to the emotions rather than to reason; and, they were perceived by many as being potentially subversive."[86] Frick's reading has much in common with those of cultural historians who characterize antebellum temperance activists as antitraditionalist—refuting, in many respects, earlier studies by Richard Hofstadter (*The Age of Reform,* 1955) and Joseph Gusfield (*Symbolic Crusade,* 1963) that describe the movement as an attempt by conservative individuals to solidify their hegemony by promoting traditional values.[87] Still others assert that it is important to examine reformers' methods when exploring questions about the conservative or progressive nature of temperance activity. Tyrrell contends that Washingtonian tactics, such as the controversial use of amusements, reveal a "strong anti-traditional bias." Blocker claims that "temperance reformers have generally remained good liberals," and that the methodologies employed by different groups can serve as "a recurrent test of their attachment to the liberal dream." Mintz highlights some of the contradictory objectives of nineteenth-century activists but also criticizes historians who "cynically conclude that antebellum reform was in its essence an instrument of class hegemony or control," calling such a conclusion "a mistake of the highest magnitude."[88]

In many respects, these scholars have helped rehabilitate antebellum temperance reform as a serious subject of study. By drawing attention to the innovative means adopted by activists, Frick, Tyrrell, Blocker, and Mintz implicitly critique the contempt that seems to exist regarding Prohibition and its nineteenth-century precedents—a widespread perception that teetotalism was merely "a cranky fad," to employ Joel Bernard's apt phrase.[89] Jessica Warner and Janine Riviere blame this collective cynicism for the curious absence of scholarship on "abstinence," broadly defined.[90] But while fixating on the innovative character of the Washingtonians and their amusements, have scholars obscured their fundamental content?

I suggest that a focus on audiences rather than producers helps to address some of these concerns. Instead of studying the means of production, perhaps we should consider the mechanics of reception. The question of what a moral reform melodrama communicates hinges on how spectators make decisions regarding "morality": the collection of conventions, ethics, and behaviors that are considered right and correct. By accounting for the complexity of moral subjectivity, such a focus potentially offsets the conservative/progressive binary—a construct that, all too often, tends to dominate scholarly discourse about activism (moral, political, and otherwise). Psychologist Jonathan Haidt and his collaborators have developed a theory of "moral foundations" that helpfully destabilizes conservative/progressive binarism.[91] In brief, Haidt proposes that our ethical judgments are made by way of five innate and cross-cultural intuitions, each of which is a "preparedness to feel flashes of approval or disapproval toward certain patterns of events involving other human beings." According to Haidt, moral decisions are guided by one or more of these goals or "virtues": to protect and help unfortunate and/or suffering individuals (harm/care); to ensure the autonomy and equal treatment of individuals within a society (fairness/reciprocity); to support, sustain, and strengthen the communities to which one belongs (ingroup/loyalty); to acknowledge one's place within a social hierarchy and adhere to its conventions (authority/respect); and to avoid dirty or disgusting experiences, objects, and behaviors (purity/sanctity). These values constitute a complex matrix rather than a linear scale. Not all decisions (or deciders) take all five criteria into account when making a moral appraisal, but they might consider some or all in any given situation.

By analyzing how moral foundations manifest in public discourse, we can begin to perceive how individuals privilege certain intuitions over others, and also ascertain why they affiliate with particular political positions. Haidt's preliminary research indicates that liberal and progressive thinkers tend to discount concerns related to ingroup/loyalty, authority/respect, and purity/sanctity—privileging instead the harm/care and fairness/reciprocity criteria. In contrast, traditionalist and conservative thinkers keep in mind all five moral foundations when making ethical judgments. This essential, almost structural, difference helps to explain why liberals and conservatives strongly disagree on certain issues, and why both sides experience considerable bafflement when trying to understand the opposing point of view.[92]

Which moral virtues did audiences see and sense in performances of the *delirium tremens* during the 1840s? I contend that, despite its inherent sensationalism, the DTs scene appealed most strongly to the spectator's understanding of purity and sanctity—concerns that are closely tied to and expressed by the body. Haidt points out that this moral intuition tends to carry more weight in conservative cultures: "Those who seem ruled by carnal passions (lust, gluttony, greed, and anger) are seen as debased, impure, and less than human, while those who live so that the soul is in charge of the body (chaste, spiritually minded, pious) are seen as elevated and sanctified."[93] Antebellum temperance discourse and iconography tended to spectacularize normalcy and deviance, setting them side by side. The pure and sober man ensured economic, professional, and familial stability; whereas the impure drunkard, his mind pickled with liquor, lost all. Horrifying and grotesque, the DTs served as sensational evidence of a man's abjection, his deplorable failure to stay within the boundaries of middle-class normalcy. In light of these tropes, it is not altogether surprising that an absolutist notion of discipline—total abstinence—supplanted moderation within the temperance movement. Through the adoption of the teetotaler's pledge, working- and middle-class activists endorsed and reinforced the restrained, disciplined body as a universal common denominator for all Americans.

So, somewhat paradoxically, sensational depictions of dipsomania played an important role in the construction of the "normal" body during the early and mid-nineteenth century. In melodramas, lectures, and pictorial media, the DTs revealed the spectacular consequences of departing from this new norm. It promoted values that we generally associate with fundamentalist politics: corporeal self-regulation (the thrashing dipsomaniac is, essentially, *un*disciplined), the stable nuclear family (which the drunkard radically destabilizes), and social decorum (as modeled by the respectable middle class). Essentially, the mad man helped to define the rational man. In this way, the DTs scene was a conservative spectacle, albeit effected through excess. Reformers employed sensational tactics to advance their cause, but they nevertheless communicated a mandate of restraint.

Of course, renditions of the *delirium tremens* were temporary and fleeting, constituting just a few moments in a relatively long performance. DTs scenes fulfilled practical and capital needs as well, providing actors with opportunities to leverage their talent and offering spectators the pleasure of witnessing an actor's tour de force. But the sensationalism of the DTs sequence derived from the audience's belief that such scenes occurred in the real world. It increasingly appeared in lecture halls and theaters at a time when new concepts of normativity were emerging. Physicians and activists conceived the DTs as a kind of temporary insanity and, perhaps even more important, a manifestation of moral deviance. A spectator's perception of a performer's feigned madness was likely informed, in whole or part, by this understanding. Reformers employed many images to advance the temperance cause, especially pictures of the drunkard's ragged family; but it was through spectacles of insanity that dramatists, performers, and activists reinforced the orderly middle-class body in a powerful and visceral way. John B. Gough, whose personal struggle to become normal made him famous, succinctly endorsed the ideal of the orderly body in one of his orations: "Time would fail to enumerate the many habits that, acquired and indulged, mar the beauty and destroy the symmetry of the true man."[94] During the DTs scene, that beauty was marred and destroyed for a spectacular instant—and in subsiding, the absolute symmetry of the normal man materialized once more, a ready model for the masses.

3

The Fugitive Slave

Eliza's Flight in *Uncle Tom's Cabin*

Slavery has never been represented; Slavery never can be represented.

—WILLIAM WELLS BROWN (1847)[1]

The agency of the enslaved is only intelligible or recognizable as crime.

—SAIDIYA V. HARTMAN, *SCENES OF SUBJECTION*[2]

Despite William Wells Brown's declaration that "Slavery never can be represented," antebellum writers, artists, and performers sought to expose the spectacles of slavery. Harriet Beecher Stowe, author of *Uncle Tom's Cabin; or, Life among the Lowly* (1852), figures prominently within the community of reformers who, through literary and visual revelation, hoped to persuade US citizens to emancipate those in bondage. Producers and playwrights immediately recognized her novel's potential as a dramatic text. Their melodramas, working in tandem with public discourse on the slavery question, reflected and refracted various tropes in the American debate about abolition. A sensation scene in Stowe's story, Eliza's flight over the Ohio River, became one of the most recognizable images from *Uncle Tom's Cabin* due to its appearance on stage. Spectacle serves as both method and matter in Eliza's escapade, during which she scurries across the ice floes while clinging to her child. Leslie A. Fiedler suggests that it "transcend[s] somehow not just the ordinary criteria of taste, but of credibility itself"; and indeed, incredulity itself plays a role in the scene, as a bewildered onstage audience—a band of slave-catchers—watches from the riverbank.[3]

For all its drama and pathos, the sprawling cultural history of this image reminds us that politically progressive texts often become ambiguous once they begin circulating in the collective imagination. Many scholars have pointed out these ambiguities. Lauren Berlant has called attention to the multiple (and moderately incompatible) suppositions driving the scene: it celebrates the human potential to achieve sublimity, but also conveys naturalized, conventional notions of motherhood. Others, such as Sarah Meer and Saidiya V. Hartman, have argued that characters in the novel that are clearly derived from the minstrelsy tradition, like Topsy, cause sympathetic figures like Eliza to recede into the background.[4]

But *Uncle Tom's Cabin* emerged at a time when stories of escaped slaves were of great public interest, and the spectacle of Eliza's flight evoked many of the moral dilemmas at the heart of the Compromise of 1850. Stowe wrote her novel in response to this legislation, which strengthened the Fugitive Slave Act (FSA) by facilitating the return of runaways to their owners.[5] The slavery question gained momentum in its wake, and Stowe and other writers began deploying actual and fictional fugitives as affective lightning rods. As a result, representations of runaway slaves played an increasingly important role in abolitionist propaganda. In order to understand this shift, I pursue the fugitive as both archetype and subject, hunting for iconographic forebears of Eliza and figurations of slaves crossing the river to freedom. Building on the work of scholars like Meer, Robin Bernstein, Jo-Ann Morgan, and Patricia A. Turner, who have tracked vestiges of Stowe's novel in popular culture, I examine visual and discursive portrayals of Eliza in a wide range of sources, including almanacs, newspaper advertisements, illustrated sheet music, and typographers' specimen catalogs.[6] The tribulations that Eliza and her husband George endure underscore the absolute injustice of the law; and the white characters in the story who aid the absconders are portrayed as answering to a higher, Christian law. These cultural reverberations of the Compromise in Stowe's story reveal that producers and audiences championed the figure of the hotly pursued runaway.

The enhanced FSA immediately criminalized slaves who had successfully entered Northern states as well as whites who assisted them on the quest for freedom. It also reinforced the idea that *any* act of free agency by the slave was a violation of law. To understand what the scene articulates about the immanent subjectivity of the fugitive slave, I examine how the outlaws in *Uncle Tom's Cabin* foreground these ethical quandaries. Escape constitutes a desperate seizure of subjectivity: the slave "steals" himself from the master, realizing and declaring agency through criminality. The Ohio River scene derived its power, in part, from its celebration of this reclamation of self, even though it also conveyed relatively conservative notions of gender, motherhood, and universal humanity. Audiences seeing the sensation of Eliza's flight may have perceived a radical protest of the erasure of personhood demanded by the slavery system. This reading, I argue, possibly preceded or even exceeded spectators' appraisal of the heroine's ethnicity.

Eliza's Flight on Stage

Although it ultimately became one of the most enduring images associated with *Uncle Tom's Cabin,* the Ohio River incident was not illustrated in the original two-volume edition of Stowe's novel issued by John P. Jewett in early 1852, which features six plates by Hammatt Billings. A lavish, single-volume edition published by Jewett at the end of the year—timed to take advantage of the Christmas season—includes more than 150 illustrations; Eliza's escape is depicted for the first time in this version[7] (fig. 3.1). In the interim, a number of theaters in the eastern United States prominently featured the scene in plays based on the novel. Its frequent appearance on stage and spectators' enthusiastic response to it suggest that the theater helped popularize what eventually came to be known as "Eliza's Flight."[8]

Dramatizations of the novel were numerous and widespread; I focus primarily on three versions produced in Boston and New York during the years 1852 to 1854. For close textual readings, I rely principally on George L. Aiken's *Uncle Tom's Cabin,* first presented in 1852 by George C. Howard in Troy, New York, and then at A. H. Purdy's National Theatre in New York City.[9] I also examine materials related to a rendition by C. W. Taylor (no longer extant) mounted at a small number of theaters in 1852. Because H. J. Conway's adaptation, produced at Moses Kimball's Boston Museum in 1852 and at P. T. Barnum's American Museum the following year, omits Eliza's flight, it provides an intriguing contrast to the other plays as well as the panoply of American pictures and objects that depict the scene.[10]

Taylor's *Uncle Tom's Cabin* premiered at Purdy's National Theatre in August 1852, nearly a year before Aiken's version ran there. Taylor gave George and Eliza Harris new names—Edward and Morna Wilmot. According to the *New York Herald,* the play followed "the general plot" of Stowe's novel, but in true melodramatic style, it ended happily: "Instead of allowing Tom to die under the cruel treatment of his new master in Louisiana, he is brought back to a reunion with Wilmot and his wife—returned runaways—all of whom, with Uncle Tom and Aunt Chloe, are set free, with the privilege of remaining upon the old plan-

CHAPTER VII.

THE MOTHER'S STRUGGLE.

T is impossible to conceive of a human creature more wholly desolate and forlorn than Eliza, when she turned her footsteps from Uncle Tom's cabin.

Her husband's suffering and dangers, and the danger of her child, all blended in her mind, with a confused and stunning sense of the risk she was running, in leaving the only home she had ever known, and cutting loose from the protection of a friend whom she loved and revered. Then there was the parting from every familiar object,—the place where she had grown up, the trees under which she had played, the groves where she had walked many an evening, in happier days, by the side of her young husband,—every thing, as it lay in the clear, frosty starlight.

10

Figure 3.1: Eliza crossing the Ohio River. Engraving by Hammatt Billings in Harriet Beecher Stowe, *Uncle Tom's Cabin; or, Life among the Lowly,* illustrated ed. (Boston: John P. Jewett, 1853), 73. Courtesy of the American Antiquarian Society.

tation." Playbills indicate that the adapter recognized the dramatic potential of the Ohio River sequence. Although he gave the heroine a different name, Taylor retained her crossing of the ice floes. A scene list from August 30, 1852, reads, "Ohio River Frozen over; Snow Storm; Flight of Morna and her child; Pursuit of the Traders, Desperate Resolve and Escape of Morna on Floating Ice." An advertisement in the *Herald* lists only two names—the actors playing Morna and Edward—suggesting that the runaway slaves served as the play's focal point. Subsequently, Uncle Tom, Little Eva, and Topsy would eclipse George and Eliza in popularity; but in 1852, it seems Purdy believed that the fugitives (or, at least, the actors in those roles) would be the biggest draw. The run comprised fewer than a dozen performances, even though the *Herald* reported that the audience was "pleased with the novelty, without being troubled about the moral of the story."[11] In October, Taylor's drama was presented at W. Cowell's Eagle Theatre in Boston; a playbill for the production lists Morna/Eliza's escape and promises, "No expense has been spared in placing this immense production on the Stage in the most effective manner."[12]

Around the same time, the first part of Aiken's version premiered in Troy, New York—a hotbed of antislavery activity in the state, particularly for free African Americans. One of Troy's most notable residents was Henry Highland Garnet, an escaped slave, minister, and radical abolitionist who had urged slaves to rebel against their masters in a controversial speech at the National Convention of Colored Citizens held in Buffalo in 1843. According to Harry Birdoff, newspaper reports in Troy's *Budget* and *Daily Times* indicate that over a ten-week period, the play attracted an impressive array of spectators, in part because of "the thrilling scenes." Soon, Aiken adapted the second half of Stowe's novel under the title *The Death of Uncle Tom; or, The Religion of the Lowly.* Howard eventually offered both plays together in a single evening, thereby initiating what Birdoff terms "a radical change to the American stage": presenting one melodrama instead of an eclectic bill of assorted entertainments.[13]

After a successful run exceeding one hundred performances, Howard presented the production in Albany, the site of the first national convention held by the Liberty Party (a political organization calling for immediate emancipation) in 1840. Then, the company traveled to New York City, where it began its famous engagement at the National Theatre in July 1853. The Ohio River sequence, which was the first of eight tableaux, turned out to be a crowd-pleaser, with spectators responding vocally in typical nineteenth-century fashion. The *Times* describes the audience's reaction to the scene as follows: "The boys are now wrought up to the highest pitch—and when, finally, *Eliza* is seen with her child, sailing across a blue river on a piece of paste-board ice, and the slave-hunters are shivering and shaking their whips on the shore; one grand cheer goes up from pit and galleries."[14] Later in the run, Purdy freshened up the production by commissioning new scenery by S. Culbert and J. Whytal, adding four tableaux. A playbill from this time indicates that the Ohio River scene now consisted of three components: "A Winter Scene near the Ohio River," "Perspective Ice Scene on the Ohio," and "New Ice Scene, Banks of the Ohio." Meanwhile, a competing version by H. E. Stevens at the Bowery Theatre, featuring T. D. Rice as Uncle Tom, made a similar investment in the spectacle of Eliza's flight. A playbill boasts, "Loud applause is given to the FROZEN OHIO, exhibiting a splendidly located Panorama of the same," and "Eliza's Peril on the Ice" is listed as the second of nine tableaux.[15]

Cast lists confirm that in these early productions, Eliza was portrayed as a conventional melodramatic heroine intended to attract the audience's sympathy; actresses in the leading-lady line almost always performed the role. In Troy, Mrs. G. C. Germon (née Jane Anderson, a third-generation descendant of the first Joseph Jefferson) played Eliza. A review in the *Northern Budget* singled her out as someone who acted "admirably" in the production. At the National Theatre the following year, Mrs. W. G. Jones (née Julia A. Wagstaff) originated the part. Interestingly, in Taylor's *Uncle Tom's Cabin* in 1852, a different actress, Mrs. H. F. Nichols, played Eliza at the National, while Jones performed two comic parts: Crazy Meg in Taylor's melodrama and Desdemona (opposite T. D. Rice) in a blackface burlesque, *Otello,* which shared the bill.[16] It seems Jones had a wide range and played an impressive variety of parts throughout her career; T. Allston Brown asserts, "Her great natural talents have been perfected by diligent study, and she not only knows but comprehends all the parts she undertakes. A more versatile actress has never been seen on the stage." Jones became a regular member of the National's acting troupe around this time, "having previously only played on special occasions." As such, she may have performed in different lines as she settled into the company. At any rate, the *Times* review of Aiken's *Uncle Tom* described her as "obviously the favorite actress and the heroine of the play." In October 1853, Mrs. J. J. Prior took over the role of Eliza at the National. Fifty years later, Henry F. Stone dubbed her the best actress ever to perform the part and "one of the best leading women of former years . . . a Shakespearean actress of repute." Similarly, leading lady Mrs. Wulf Fries (née Louisa Gann)—whose repertory included Portia, Cordelia, and Ophelia as well as Mary in W. H. Smith's *The Drunkard*—originated Eliza in Conway's *Uncle Tom's Cabin* at the Boston Museum in 1852.[17]

Casting is important to take into account because, as Marvin Carlson has argued, a spectator's overall impression of an actress and her previous roles inevitably ghost subsequent performances.[18] The *Times* writer who saw Jones in Aiken's play describes her as "a very pretty white girl"—suggesting that the production endeavored to elicit the audience's sympathy for Eliza by "whitening" her.[19] The writer also observes that the opening scene, during which Eliza and George bid each other farewell, was "not especially different from most plays, where lover and mistress part" (a statement that highlights, perhaps inadvertently, the couple's inability to marry legally under the slavery system). By following a familiar form and structure, the scene instructed spectators who were unfamiliar with the novel that George and Eliza were the hero and heroine. Turner notes that the positioning of this conversational exchange "shift[s] the emphasis from the 'Tom sold to the South plot' and privil[eges] the 'Harris taking the Underground Railroad' one." Mason seems to suggest that the Harris plot distracts from larger concerns in the drama; in his view, the issue of slavery serves "as mere background to the Harrises' domestic situation." However, because spectators had previously seen the same actress in other leading roles, they were primed to sympathize with Eliza and her plight—and perhaps, by association, the plight of all fugitive slave mothers.[20]

Eliza's sensational escape has its own scene in Aiken's version (Act I, scene vi) and consists of a single stage direction: "*The entire depth of stage, representing the Ohio River, filled with Floating Ice.—Set bank on R. H. and in front. ELIZA appears, with HARRY, R. H., on a cake of ice, and floats slowly across to L. H.—HALEY, LOKER and MARKS, on bank, R. H., observing.—PHINEAS on opposite shore*" (12). Two scenes earlier, Phineas—a rugged Kentuckian who assists both Harrises in their attempts to escape—describes the river as follows.

> Chaw me up into tobaccy ends! how in the name of all that's onpossible am I to get across that yer pesky river? It's a reg'lar blockade of ice! . . . (*Goes to window.*) That's a conglomerated prospect for a loveyer! What in creation's to be done? That thar river looks like a permiscuous ice-cream shop come to an awful state of friz. If I war on the adjacent bank, I wouldn't care a teetotal atom. Rile up, you old varmit, and shake the ice off your back!

At this point, Eliza enters with her son Harry, telling him, "Courage, my boy—

we have reached the river. Let it but roll between us and our pursuers, and we are safe!" (9). She later exclaims, "That dark stream lies between me and liberty! Surely the ice will bear my trifling weight. It is my only chance of escape." As she begins to cross, the fugitive mother declares, "The river is my only hope!" (12).

She successfully dashes across the ice floes, creating a memorable spectacle that is recalled in future scenes. When they are reunited in Act III, Eliza and George discuss the incident in considerable detail, as if to underscore the danger and peril she risked.

GEO. It seems almost incredible that you could have crossed the river on the ice.

ELIZA. Yes, I did. Heaven helping me, I crossed on the ice, for they were behind me—right behind—and there was no other way.

GEO. But the ice was all in broken-up blocks, swinging and heaving up and down in the water.

ELIZA. I know it was—I know it; I did not think I should get over, but I did not care—I could but die if I did not! I leaped on the ice, but how I got across I don't know; the first I remember, a man was helping me up the bank—that man was Phineas.

GEO. My brave girl! you deserve your freedom—you have richly earned it! (28)

Here, George explicitly connects Eliza's river-crossing with liberty—a liberty realized through courage, fortitude, and faith, and therefore "richly earned."

Newspaper reports about Aiken's *Uncle Tom's Cabin* at the National indicate that the audience's reactions intrigued journalists as much as, if not more than, the drama itself. Champions celebrated and critics feared the energetic collectivity that the play allegedly inspired. Birdoff suggests that the exchange between Uncle Tom and Aunt Chloe in the third scene (which generally lacked the minstrel comedy associated with black characters at that time) had a disciplining effect on the National's notoriously rowdy audience: "The coldest listeners in the gallery had shown the closest attention to the plot, and there was a multiplicity of 'Hi! hi's!' They called out, 'It isn't right!' and gone were the offending boots over the railing."[21] Although Birdoff may be exaggerating (as did, probably, puffers and reporters), this and other narratives underscore how questions of political import and impact played a role in the public mythology forming around *Uncle Tom's Cabin* at the time. For example, in a lecture she gave in New York City in 1854, abolitionist and suffragist Lucy Stone cited the Ohio River scene as a particularly effective moment in the novel, claiming that parents who read the story to their children could help transform the next generation into staunch antislavery citizens.[22]

In stark contrast to Aiken's play, H. J. Conway's version of *Uncle Tom's Cabin* omits Eliza's escape. Conway transforms the incident into a joint getaway by the Harrises, essentially combining two sensation scenes, "Eliza's Flight" and "The Freeman's Defense" (during which George exchanges gunfire with slave catchers who are pursuing him).[23] A letter written by Conway to Kimball several months before the play's premiere at the Boston Museum indicates that the question of the fugitives' escape may have been settled early in the writing process. "I find much difficulty in handling it [the novel] dramatically," Conway admits, describing dramaturgical challenges like the combination of characters, the portrayal of the passage of time, and other issues related to the "unity" of the work. Although he briefly alludes to "the escape of George and Eliza at the end Act 1st," Conway does not explicitly propose combining the Ohio River and Freeman's Defense scenes in the letter, suggesting that the issue may have been previously considered and decided.[24]

Admittedly, Conway's decision may have had little to do with the scene's politics. The playwright explains to Kimball that "Eliza must not be a mother" because it would necessitate Cassy's being a grandmother, which "would destroy her not only with the audience but the personator." He also states he will merge the parts of Eliza and Emmeline because "it will never do to divide the sympathies of the audience." In his analysis of the correspondence, Bruce A. McConachie suggests, "Conway sacrificed the Eliza-clutching-her-baby-while-crossing-the-Ohio-on-the-ice-floes scene . . . to allow for a melodramatic recognition scene between mother and daughter nearer the dramatic climax of the show—a decision that probably reflected astute play-carpentry."[25] In other words, the playwright might have omitted Eliza's flight for pragmatic or dramaturgical reasons.

But regardless of why the choice was made, it nevertheless had a serious impact on the characterization of Eliza. In Conway's revision, the men take control of the situation. Instead of escaping separately, as in the novel, the Harrises flee together, with George masquerading as a white man and Eliza as his slave. From the moment the fugitives enter the tavern by the Ohio River, it is clear that George is in charge and that Eliza relies on him for guidance. She role-plays the servant, at one point saying, "Yes, Massa," to her disguised husband, then exits to "see to the trunks" at his direction. George, in an exchange with Mr. Wilson (a former employer whom George serendipitously encounters in the tavern), claims that he ran away because of his wife: "Now, Sir, I have found a wife, you've seen her, you know how beautiful she is. When I found she loved me, when I married, I scarcely could believe I was alive. But now what. I am to be dragged, forced to live with another, and this your laws give him the power to do." At this point, Eliza rushes back in and cries, "Oh, George! The dogs, the dogs! They come this way. We are lost. They will tear me to pieces." Paralyzed with fear, she looks to George to save her.[26]

But in the end, it is a white man who takes charge and saves both George and Eliza. Drover John—who pontificates at one point about the proper way to manage human property—helps the couple escape not because he finds slavery to be objectionable, but because he disagrees with the way they have been treated. Upon hearing the barking dogs, he picks up his rifle and swears, "No dogs shall pull down a gal while I can pull a trigger." John decides to aid the Harrises because he objects to physical violence and cruelty, especially when the fugitive to be "pulled down" is a woman. In the process, John offsets George's role as protector. When Eliza tells her husband that the dogs are after her, George declares, "They shall tear my heart out first." But before he can fully enact the hero's part, John reenters, smashes the window, tells George to go through, and "assists out Eliza."[27]

It is intriguing (and telling) that Barnum advertised this particular *Uncle Tom's Cabin* as "deal[ing] with FACTS, INSTEAD OF FICTION" and as "the only truly sensible version of Mrs. Stowe's great work."[28] Conway's reconceived heroine probably contributes to this alleged realism, because in many respects the playwright transformed her into a damsel in distress. Other early adapters—Aiken, Taylor, Stevens—retained the Ohio River sequence as it was written in the novel, and so the young mother's autonomy remains intact. In contrast, Conway changed the incident into a traditional, gender-appropriate chase scene in which two men rescue the anxious (and childless) Eliza, who is debilitated by her fear of bloodhounds. It is a marked departure from Stowe's original conception of the heroine who saves herself and her son.

Fugitive on the Move: Eliza's Flight in Visual and Material Culture

Uncle Tom's Cabin jumped quickly from page to stage, but it did not stay there; cultural producers brought it into other settings and spaces—sometimes on principle, sometimes for profit, sometimes for both. Bernstein, drawing on

Diana Taylor, argues that Stowe's novel is best understood as a "repertoire": a rich cache of cultural material that is "neither a sprawling-yet-coherent phenomenon nor a multiply-authored 'inadvertent epic,' but instead . . . a formation of influence and cross-influence that is internally contentious and surprisingly tightly woven without ever becoming unified; that constantly transposes among theatrical, visual, literary, and crucially, material genres; and that is not always authored."[29] Bernstein focuses on how figurations of Little Eva and Topsy infiltrated (and continue to permeate) American visual and material culture, but Eliza, too, circulated in homes by way of objects such as sheet music, children's books, figurines, toys, and games. The prevalence of artifacts depicting the Ohio River scene demonstrates that women who acquired domestic objects found the quadroon mother's heroics to be both respectable and appealing. On a daily basis, the consumer, upon seeing or engaging these objects, could experience a sensation of sympathy for the slave.

What made the scene so appealing, affective, and memorable? One possible explanation is the river itself. Rivers have always figured prominently in the spiritual and cultural imagination. From the River Styx to the River Jordan to the Mississippi River in Mark Twain's *The Adventures of Huckleberry Finn,* water serves as a radical test of faith, a border between enslavement and liberty, or a transition between earthly and heavenly life. River crossings are invoked in a variety of African American folk songs and spirituals, such as "Deep River," "Michael, Row the Boat Ashore," and "Swing Low, Sweet Chariot." Howard Thurman observes that for slaves who sang these songs, "the river may have been for many the last and most formidable barrier to freedom. To slip over the river from one of the border states would mean a chance for freedom in the North—or, to cross the river into Canada would mean freedom in a new country, a foreign land."[30] The fording of a river occurs in many escape stories, including the fugitive-slave narratives of Harriet Tubman and William Wells Brown, among others.

In *Uncle Tom's Cabin,* the river symbolizes hope and danger, the potential for freedom as well as the dark possibility of death. Like spectacle itself, the river derives its power from paradox and contradiction: it liberates and eradicates, sometimes in the same moment. Rivers and other watery boundaries test the courage and mettle of many characters in Stowe's novel, as Jane Tompkins observes.

> Bodies of water mediate between worlds: the Ohio runs between the slave states

> and the free; Lake Erie divides the United States from Canada, where runaway slaves cannot be returned to their masters; the Atlantic Ocean divides the North American continent from Africa, where Negroes will have a nation of their own; Lake Pontchartrain shows Eva the heavenly home to which she is going soon; the Mississippi River carries slaves from the relative ease of the middle states to the grinding toil of the southern plantations; the Red River carries Tom to the infernal regions ruled over by Simon Legree.[31]

In Aiken's adaptation of the novel, water also represents the menacing threat of being sent "down river." In the opening scene, George announces that he will flee his master rather than be sold and sent away from his family, telling Eliza, "I will never go down the river alive" (5). In the tavern scene, Mr. Wilson reiterates this sentiment. He warns the fugitive, "If you're taken it will be worse with you than ever; they'll only abuse you, and half kill you, and sell you down river" (21).

Eliza's escape on the ice floes reflected iconographic strategies already percolating in mid-nineteenth-century American abolitionism. Rivers appear in many pictorial renditions of fugitive slaves produced around this time. The cover illustration of the sheet music for "The Fugitive's Song," published in the mid-1840s in honor of Frederick Douglass (discussed in detail in the next section), features a river that divides Douglass from the white men who pursue him (fig. 3.8). *Effects of the Fugitive-Slave-Law,* an 1850 lithograph by Theodor Kaufman published by Hoff and Bloede, is another case in point (fig. 3.2). It depicts four male slaves on the run, just beyond a cornfield; several men carrying farm tools and rifles are in the background. Similar to images of Eliza's flight, the absconders are close to the viewer, separated from their pursuers by a topographic obstacle—in this case, a river-shaped cornfield, which the slave-catchers must ford in order to capture their prey.

Prior to its inclusion in the illustrated edition of the novel, the Ohio River scene served as the subject of at least one song: "Eliza's Flight, A Scene from Uncle Tom's Cabin," written by M. A. Collier with music by E. J. Loder, and published by Oliver Ditson in Boston during the same year that Taylor's *Uncle Tom's Cabin* played at the Eagle Theatre in that city (fig. 3.3). Conspicuously displayed on the parlor's pianoforte, this illustrated artifact gave Stowe's story a material presence in the domestic sphere. Given the timing of the song's publication as well as the inclusion of "scene" in the title, it is tempting to wonder whether the cover illustration reflects, in whole or part, the Ohio River

Figure 3.2: Theodor Kaufman, *Effects of the Fugitive-Slave-Law.* The cornfield divides the pursuers and the pursued, not unlike the river in depictions of Eliza's flight in *Uncle Tom's Cabin.* Lithograph, Hoff and Bloede, 1850. Courtesy of the American Antiquarian Society.

sequence in Taylor's adaptation as it was presented at the Eagle Theatre. In the drawing, a dark-complexioned Eliza ("Morna" in Taylor's version) holds her child tightly, a dazzled and fearful expression on her face. She is mid-dash, one foot nearly submerged in water as she balances on a thin plate of broken ice. Her three pursuers—faces gashed with rough indications of eyes and mouths—watch incredulously from the shore behind her (what would be upstage left). Their bodies, rather than their faces, indicate surprise and anger: one holds a long whip pointing toward the river; the other lifts his arms high in the air, shocked by what he sees. Inside, the lyrics emphasize the mother's bravery as well as her faith.

> Hope lights with her undying gleam
> The wand'rer and her child.
> She clasps him closely to her heart,

Figure 3.3: Cover illustration for “Eliza's Flight, A Scene from Uncle Tom's Cabin,” a song by Miss M. A. Collier and E. J. Loder (Boston: Oliver Ditson, 1852). Courtesy of the American Antiquarian Society.

Her only one—her joy;
For nought but death the two shall part,
The mother and her boy![32]

The song invokes Eliza's declaration "the river is my only hope!" as well as her insistence that she would rather die than be captured and separated from her child.

Images of Eliza also circulated in domestic spaces by way of juvenile literature, which allowed parents to inculcate the values embedded in Stowe's story in the next generation. In late 1852 or early 1853, John P. Jewett published *Pictures and Stories from Uncle Tom's Cabin,* a children's book featuring illustrations and songs. According to Stephen Railton, it was originally printed in England by T. Nelson & Sons and then offered to the US market by way of Jewett. The title page announces that the book intends to adapt "Mrs. Stowe's Touching Narrative to the understanding of the youngest readers and to foster in their hearts a generous sympathy for the wronged negro race of America," instructing boys and girls how to "feel right" about the slavery question. Eliza plays a prominent role in this project, in that the cover displays a vivid rendition of her crossing the ice floes; the image is reproduced inside as well (fig. 3.4). The book also includes a song titled "Eliza Crossing the River."[33]

A copy of *Pictures and Stories* in the American Antiquarian Society (AAS)'s collection, inscribed "Agnes M. Burleigh 1854," offers an intriguing portrait of the type of consumer who acquired it. The Oxford South Congregational Church Cemetery in Worcester County, Massachusetts, includes a gravestone for an Agnes M. Burleigh, who died May 18, 1861, at fifteen years of age. Assuming that this is the same Agnes, the date of the inscription suggests that she obtained the book when seven or eight years old. The AAS acquired it through a bequest by Charles Lemoyne Burleigh (1877–1938), the grandson of John O. and Evelina Burleigh, Agnes's parents. (Had Agnes survived her teens, she would have been Charles's aunt.) Other materials in the bequest offer clues about the Burleigh family and its interests. For instance, *Abolitionrieties,* a pamphlet of short poems about prominent abolitionists, is inscribed with Evelina's name—suggesting that the matriarch of the family had an interest in antislavery literature. Perhaps the Burleighs wanted their daughter to share in their practice of reading abolitionist texts. Agnes's parents might have considered *Pictures and Stories* to be appropriate reading for another reason: Eliza's flight over the Ohio River conveys potent assumptions about a woman's role and natural pro-

Figure 3.4: Eliza's flight was chosen for the cover of this children's book, issued by Stowe's publisher. Cover illustration, *Pictures and Stories from Uncle Tom's Cabin* (Boston: John P. Jewett, 1853). Courtesy of the American Antiquarian Society.

clivities. This spectacular instant, both in the novel and on stage, suggests that a mother—no matter her race—endeavors to protect her children at any cost.[34]

Figurines, dolls, and other souvenirs associated with *Uncle Tom's Cabin* encouraged reflection, and possibly compelled the viewer to feel (or perform) compassion for the slave. Jill Weitzman Fenichell asserts that three-quarters of ceramics inspired by the novel depicted one of two scenes: Eliza's flight across the ice floes or Little Eva decorating Uncle Tom with a flowered garland. She describes the latter as "representing the highest 'moral moment'" in the novel, due to the presence of the Bible on Tom's lap and the Christian affection evident in Eva's gesture. In contrast, Fenichell says, Eliza's escape is "the lowest moral and greatest melodramatic moment"—a statement that somewhat contradicts her later acknowledgment that the scene "reminded contemporary viewers that slave owners separated family members from one another for commercial reasons and sent bounty hunters across state lines to find escaped slaves and return them, as chattel, to their owners."[35]

Hartman warns that empathetic identification, a practice that many antislavery advocates espoused, may have resulted in "the dissimulation of suffering through spectacle" because it invited the white individual to put herself in the slave's place, thereby erasing the personhood of the black subject.[36] However, because women lacked access to electoral means of change during this period and were frequently criticized when they expressed themselves in public spaces, I contend that the consumption of abolitionist texts and objects constituted a means by which women could assert themselves politically. In other words, for disenfranchised Americans, the accumulation of *Uncle Tom* images and objects might have been a political act—one that could be reenacted and reprised through the everyday rituals of domesticity.

The Escape as Transformation from Property to Person

In his critique of Taylor's *Uncle Tom's Cabin* at the National Theatre in September 1852, James Gordon Bennett of the *New York Herald* refers directly to the Compromise of 1850 and its stipulations regarding fugitive slaves. Complaining that entrepreneurial "catchpenny imitators" of Stowe were "imperil[ing] the peace and safety of the Union," he declares,

> The Fugitive Slave Law only carries out one of the plain provisions of the con-

> stitution. When a Southern slave escapes to us, we are in honor bound to return him to his master. And yet, here in this city . . . we have nightly represented, at a popular theatre, the most exaggerated enormities of Southern slavery, playing directly into the hands of the abolitionists and abolition kidnappers of slaves, and doing their work for them. . . . We would, from all these considerations, advise all concerned to drop the play of *Uncle Tom's Cabin,* at once and forever. The thing is in bad taste—it is . . . calculated, if persisted in, to become a firebrand of the most dangerous character to the peace of the whole country.[37]

Bennett's diatribe is deeply informed by the tumultuous political context in which early stage adaptations of Stowe's novel were produced and consumed. Allusions to the FSA and its moral dilemmas surface repeatedly in the plays themselves as well as in accounts of spectators' responses to them. For the slave, running away was both a desperate act of agency and a crime. In liberating herself, she filched her master's property. I assert that audiences appreciated the Ohio River scene, both in performance and in print and material culture, because it celebrated and endorsed the radical subjectivity seized by slaves who chose to flee. Stories of escape played a vital role in fugitive slave narratives, not only due to their sensational character but also because they represented the moment of transition from thing to human; as Leonard Cassuto points out, "it made rhetorical sense for many fugitive slave narrators to spotlight the escape as the central symbol of their rebellion against objectification." Escape catalyzes the slave's conversion from object to subject; the struggle to become free is, at its core, a struggle to become a person. It seems likely that audiences' perception of Eliza's flight was influenced by a plethora of precedents, including personal stories told by fugitives and various textual and pictorial ephemera. This sensation scene was shaped and inspired by emergent, complicated ideas regarding the transformation of property to person through escape.[38]

In the mid-nineteenth century, the question of how to handle fugitive slaves was not new; on the contrary, it was as old as the nation itself.[39] To ensure the widespread adoption of the US Constitution, the founders addressed slave states' concerns regarding runaway chattel in the following provision: "No Person held to Service or Labour in one State, under the Laws thereof, escaping into another, shall, in Consequence of any Law or Regulation therein, be discharged from such Service or Labour, but shall be delivered up on Claim of the Party to whom such service may be due."[40] In 1793, Congress reiterated this gesture by passing the Fugitive Slave Act, but the new law did not address the problem of enforcement. As a result, it was generally ineffective, especially since several Northern states responded by establishing "personal liberty laws" placing significant obstacles in the way of the FSA's implementation. As sectional tensions mounted during subsequent decades, a desire to preserve the Union led to the Compromise of 1850: a series of bills that made California a free state and eradicated the slave trade in Washington, DC, but also mandated federal involvement in the capture of runaways and punishments for citizens who helped them.

The legislation inspired reactions ranging from complacency to outrage. Stanley W. Campbell argues that the majority of Northerners complied with the law, viewing it as a necessary evil: "Public opinion in the Northern states . . . was ambiguous, but on the whole it was acquiescent." In contrast, Jane H. Pease and William H. Pease contend that the strengthened FSA served as fuel for the abolitionists' fire, causing frustrated activists to lose faith in the strategy of "moral suasion" (the use of rhetoric and petitioning to effect change). Sometimes, entire communities would harness the power of spectacle in elaborate protests against the FSA. The arrest of fugitive slave Anthony Burns in Boston in May 1854 is a case in point. Residents rioted and stormed the courthouse in an attempt to rescue Burns, but local and federal officers successfully resisted these efforts and eventually remanded him to his owner. Such acts of protest, which the press widely publicized, infuriated Southerners who had always suspected the FSA would not be fully enforced.[41]

All the while, cultural and legislative constructions of human chattel as "things" structured and maintained the slavery system. As Frederick Douglass argued in 1850, "The first work of slavery is to mar and deface those characteristics of its victims which distinguish *men* from *things.*" Stowe herself seems to have shared this belief, because the initial subtitle for *Uncle Tom's Cabin* was "The Man That Was a Thing."[42] Cassuto observes that in many respects US law characterized slaves as nearly but not quite human—bizarre monstrosities somewhat akin to freaks.

> Whether portrayed as a child who never grows up, an inferior race of human being, or simply as a piece of property to be used, the slave stands out as an anomaly of human existence: at once outwardly normal yet inwardly abnormal, a living thing that has human form, but without the full complement of qualities that make someone into a person.[43]

An essay in the 1846 *Anti-Slavery Almanac,* "American Slavery Founded on a Lie," recognized and critiqued these principles by declaring the slave to be "an *I myself.*" Subject and object collapse in this rhetorical phrase, suggesting that self-possession is a definitional aspect of being: "The natural results of an activity, springing from *I myself,* must of course belong to *I myself.* But all this slavery denies. It seizes on *I myself* and reduces *personality* to *property.* Thus the *I myself* vanishes, and leaves behind nothing but a chattel." In essence, slavery transforms personalities into property; slavery turns men into things.[44] Within this discursive context, Eliza's escape may be interpreted as a slave's spectacular seizure of personal subjectivity.

The transformation from property to person involves self-actualization, resistance, and, ultimately, movement: the slave literally "steals away," and in doing so, steals a body that lawfully belongs to her master. When a slave's desire for self-possession conflicts with his master's wishes, an intense negotiation begins. One of the most well-known portrayals of this negotiation, one in which education plays a pivotal role, is in Douglass's biographical narrative.[45] For slaves, learning to read was a violation of law, and it is this act, this "crime," that allows Douglass to comprehend the illegitimacy of keeping human property. In his narrative, he relays that his master, Hugh Auld, was alarmed to discover that his wife had taught the young Douglass the alphabet, telling her, "If you learn him now how to read, he'll want to know how to write; and, this accomplished, he'll be running away with himself." Mrs. Auld's tutelage enables Douglass to teach himself to read, and he secretly steals time and opportunities to practice his newfound skill. Eventually, Douglass's relationship with his mistress, which originally resembled something akin to mother and son, turns to gall. "Nature had made us *friends;* slavery made us *enemies.* My interests were in a direction opposite to hers, and we both had our private thoughts and plans." When a schoolbook titled *The Columbian Orator* comes into his possession, he becomes acquainted with some of the abolitionist arguments against slavery. He finds a theatrical dialogue between a slave and slaveholder, during which the former persuades the latter that slavery is immoral, to be particularly provocative. Douglass reports, "The dialogue and the speeches were all redolent of the principles of liberty, and poured floods of light on the nature and character of slavery. . . . The more I read, the more I was led to abhor and detest slavery, and my enslavers." The small but significant gift of the alphabet, offered unwittingly by Mrs. Auld, paves the way for Douglass's engagement with anti-slavery literature; and his education—his enlightenment—kindles his desire to escape.[46]

Eliza, too, enacts a fretful negotiation between master and slave. She enjoys habits of living and laboring on the Shelby estate that are rarely afforded to chattel like her. Ambiguously positioned on the scale of subjectivity, she is introduced in the first scene of Aiken's play as a mulatto woman who has been carefully nurtured and educated by the Shelbys. George observes, "They have brought you up like a child—fed you, clothed you and taught you, so that you have a good education" (4). But Eliza's privileged place in the household is threatened when Shelby feels forced by his financial circumstances to sell her and her son. The Harrises' impending separation necessitates an aggressive act of resistance. They fly, severing themselves from the structures, routines, and behavioral norms of enslavement. They break the cycle by breaking the law.[47]

For George and Eliza, mere survival is not enough: liberty alone makes life worth living. They state this radical philosophy at multiple points in Aiken's drama. The first declaration of this type occurs in the opening scene, when George insists, "I'll be free, or I'll die" (5). George reiterates this belief when he is reunited with his family: "I'll fight to the last breath before they shall take from me my wife and son!" (26). Eliza makes similar statements, especially during the Ohio River scene. She announces that it would be "better to sink beneath the cold waters, with my child locked in my arms, than have him torn from me and sold into bondage"; and as she nears the river, she exclaims, "we will be free—or perish!" (12). These words invoke real-life slave mothers who murdered their children rather than give them up to slavery—desperate acts that were widely publicized. In Stowe's *A Key to Uncle Tom's Cabin* (1853), a compilation of texts and commentary intended to substantiate the situations in her novel, the author defends her daredevil characterization of Eliza by pointing out, "Instances have occurred where mothers, whose children were about to be sold from them, have, in their desperation, murdered their own offspring, to save them from this worst kind of orphanage."[48] In such stories, the distraught mother seizes agency through violence: she steals her offspring from the master by taking their lives. Indeed, Stowe's broken and disconsolate character Cassy, who mourns the newborn son she murdered in order to protect him from a life in bondage, embodies a fate that Eliza refuses to accept.

Abolitionists often recognized the law's role in shaping, controlling, and hindering slaves' subjectivity. Stowe's frustration with the law helps to explain why so many characters in *Uncle Tom's Cabin* are celebrated for breaking it.

George and Eliza defy the Shelbys' legal "right" to divide their family, and the white characters who assist the Harrises violate man's law and adhere instead to God's. Moreover, in her *Key*—which explores the legal architecture of slavery at some length—Stowe quotes, cites, and summarizes a variety of codes and court decisions, offering personal commentary and analysis in the process. At one point, Stowe declares, "The slave-code is designed *only for the security of the master, and not with regard to the welfare of the slave*," arguing that laws intended to protect slaves nevertheless reduce human beings to things: "Even such provisions as seem to be for the benefit of the slave we often find carefully interpreted so as to show that it is only on account of his property value to his master that he is thus protected, and not from any consideration of humanity towards himself." Stowe seems to find so-called protective statutes, which offered provisions for the bodily preservation of human chattel, to be particularly egregious because they invariably included exceptions triggered by a slave's breach of discipline.[49]

Stowe also discusses statutes related to "outlawry," the legal process by which a master could disown a runaway and sanction his or her assassination. By officially outlawing a runaway, the owner authorized the slave's transformation into hunted game. Sometimes, fugitives took refuge in topographically challenging areas, such as swamps, where small communities of outlawed slaves formed. A North Carolina statute quoted by Stowe reads, "Many times slaves run away and lie out, hid and lurking in swamps, woods, and other obscure places, killing cattle and hogs, and committing other injuries to the inhabitants of this state." This description invokes visions of skulking monsters and swamp creatures, half-man and half-animal, freakish "What Is It?" exhibits set loose from Barnum's museum. In this fashion, the law aggressively dehumanized runaways. Presumed dangerous because they were free agents, outlaws caused enormous social anxiety. It was absolutely impermissible for a slave to become a freeman, even in the dark recesses of a swamp.[50]

Fugitive slave advertisements also played an important role in the abolitionists' attempts to reveal how slavery reduced men to things. For one, such ads offered evidence of the horrific tortures suffered by human chattel. Jennifer Putzi observes that, by quoting and reproducing such ads, reformers used "the marked black body to prove to readers the cruelty of white slave owners and their willingness to publicize the evidence of such treatment to reclaim their runaway slaves."[51] Stowe uses this tactic frequently in the *Key*.[52] Advertisements seem to work well for Stowe, not only because they substantiate her claims but also because they avoid sensationalism: ruthlessly expository, dry, and clinical, they reveal the truth while skirting grotesquerie. Stowe applies a rigorous hermeneutic to them, carefully tracking the punishments inflicted on slaves. Tacitly, Stowe suggests that despite their matter-of-fact rhetoric, the advertisements are miniature discourses in which *the body tells.* The body is at once evidence and archive, revealing its history through wounds and scars. As Theodore Dwight Weld had done in *American Slavery as It Is: Testimony of a Thousand Witnesses* (1839), she italicizes text describing identifiable marks: "middle finger on the right hand off at the second joint," "a scar over the left eye," "the left arm and right leg somewhat scarred," "two or three marks on his back, a small scar on his left hip," "lost a part of the finger next to his little finger on the right hand; also the great toe on his left foot." In addition, she italicizes phrases like "no scars," "no scars recollected," and "no marks, save one, and that caused by the bite of a dog," as if to emphasize that even unscathed slave bodies are routinely read and ruthlessly objectified.[53]

But fugitive slave advertisements usually comprised more than text. Many included a small type ornament to draw the reader's attention and to communicate instantly what the ad was about (fig. 3.5). I argue that within American visual culture, the thrilling, inspiring image of Eliza's flight served as a powerful contrast to this flat and lackluster ornament. Depicting a slave on the run carrying a walking stick or bindle (a cloth-wrapped bundle of belongings tied to the end of a pole), the symbol became widely recognizable because of its constant iteration in print. During the mid-nineteenth century, many type foundries, even those with bases of operation in free states, sold these tiny icons through "specimen" books distributed to potential buyers. The ubiquity of the ornament in type specimens indicates that there was a significant market for them. In some catalogs, it appears alongside other depictions of property, such as horses or cattle—underscoring, whether intentionally or not, the etymological and capital relationship between "cattle" and "chattel"[54] (fig. 3.6).

Typographically generic and ruthlessly repeated, the icon—literally, the stereotype—erased the runaway's individuality through duplication. Like the famous abolitionist emblem "Am I Not a Man [Woman] and a Brother [Sister]?" it came in gendered versions and featured other minor variations (the absence or presence of footwear, for example). But in general, it disavowed the singularity of the individual through its consistency. Because fugitive-slave ornaments circulated widely and were frequently appropriated, I contend that, collectively, they served as a Baudrillardian "scenario of deterrence," in which

1838] *Anti-Slavery Almanac.* 35

ger would suppose there was NO African blood in him. He is so very artful, that in his language it is likely he will deceive those who might suspect him. He was with my boy Dick a short time since in Norfolk, and offered him for sale, and was apprehended, but escaped under the PRETENCE of being a WHITE MAN.

ANDERSON BOWLES,

Jan. 6, 1837. Dentonville P. O.

$100 REWARD.

RANAWAY from James Hughart, Paris, Ky., the Mulatto Boy NORBON, aged about 15 years; a *very bright* mulatto, and would be taken for a WHITE BOY if not *closely* examined; his hair is black and STRAIGHT. Aug. 4, 1836.

ABSCONDED from the subscriber, HER negro man JOHN. He has a VERY LIGHT complexion, *prominent nose*, &c.

Charleston Mercury, 1837. W. J. SANGLOIS.

$100 REWARD.

RANAWAY from the Subscriber, living in Sumter Co. Ala., a *bright mulatto* man slave named SAM, calls himself SAM PETTIGREW*... LIGHT SANDY HAIR and *blue eyes*, RUDDY complexion, very stout built, and will weigh about 180 pounds; he is SO WHITE as *very easily* to pass for a free white man.... He carries a small memorandum book in his pocket, and will pass *very easily* for a *white man* unless *closely* examined—is a first-rate blacksmith and barber. EDWIN PECK.

Mobile, April 22, 1837.

V. The fifth point to be proved is that FREE men are often sold into slavery to *pay the expense* of THEIR OWN UNJUST IMPRISONMENT.

SHERIFF'S SALE.

COMMITTED to the Jail of Warren County, by WM. EVERETT, one of the JUSTICES of said county, a Negro MAN who calls himself JOHN J. ROBINSON; says that he is FREE. The OWNER of the said BOY is requested to come forward, prove PROPERTY, pay charges and take him away, or he will be dealt with as the law directs. WM. EVERETT, Jailer.

And how does the law direct? Read the following:

NOTICE is hereby given, that the above described BOY, who calls himself John J. Robinson, having been confined in the Jail of Warren county as a Runaway for SIX MONTHS—and having been *regularly advertised* during this period,—I shall proceed to SELL said Negro boy at public auction, to the highest bidder for cash, at the door of the Court-house in Vicksburg, on Monday, 1st day of August, 1836, between the hours of 11 o'clock A. M. and 4 o'clock P. M. of said day, in pursuance of the *STATUTE* in such cases made and provided. E. W. MORRIS, Sheriff.

Vicksburg, July 2, 1836.

* So we might, perhaps, see, "ARCHY, calls himself ARCHY MOORE," advertised by Col. Carter.

Figure 3.5: Fugitive slave advertisements reproduced in N. Southard, ed., *Anti-Slavery Almanac for 1838* (Boston: D. K. Hitchcock, 1837), 35. Southard featured these particular ads to show that mixed-race children were usually enslaved by their fathers; some were nearly indistinguishable from free white Americans. Courtesy of the American Antiquarian Society.

Figure 3.6: Type ornaments for sale. Alexander Robb, *Specimen of Printing Types and Ornaments* (Philadelphia: A. Robb, 1844), n.p. Courtesy of the Library Company of Philadelphia.

"a moribund principle [is reiterated] through simulated scandal, phantasm, and murder—a sort of hormonal treatment through negativity and crisis."[55] Designed to inure rather than intrigue, the symbol denied the fugitive's personhood even though the text of the ad explicated what made the runaway unique (visible scars, nuances in complexion, distinguishing behaviors). It rejected the outlaw's subjectivity by reiterating her status as property. And, through its relentless recurrence, it attempted to erase the human, the *I myself.* In stark contrast, activist representations of fugitives on the run, such as Eliza crossing the ice floes, celebrated the slave's seizure of subjectivity. By boldly challenging the stock-quality of the ornament and other depersonalized depictions of human chattel, images like Eliza's flight counteracted attempts to reduce subjects to objects. Eliza participated in the recovery of the slave subject by offering a spectacular counterpoint to the cookie-cutter icon.

The ethical dubiousness of the type ornament was widely recognized, so it was frequently copied, cited, and manipulated. The first fully reproduced advertisement in *A Key to Uncle Tom's Cabin* appears where Stowe describes the inspiration behind her fugitive hero, George Harris. Unlike many other ads in the book, this one includes the imprint of the runaway. Its placement at this precise point in her text is jarring, as if Stowe is underscoring the mark's significance as a cultural signifier. In the novel, Stowe personalizes the reductive icon through her characterization of the Harrises. She fleshes out and transforms the stereotype into the valiant George: intelligent laborer, faithful husband, loving father, self-declared "freeman."

The ornament also became fodder for artists and illustrators, who adopted and adapted it in a variety of products. It appears on at least two Civil War envelopes, for instance (fig. 3.7). A form of printed ephemera, war stationery infiltrated the daily lives of Americans, moving from merchant to consumer to mail carrier to recipient. By turns, participants in the chain of communication were exposed to pictures of Union patriotism as they wrote, handled, opened, and perhaps saved decorated correspondence. The envelopes in figure 3.7 employ the fugitive-slave ornament as a kind of iconographic shorthand; both depict and celebrate runaways fleeing the plantation to become human "contraband" in North. "The Fugitive's Song," a piece of illustrated sheet music printed around 1845 in honor of America's most famous fugitive, Frederick Douglass, constitutes another intriguing example of how the symbol was adapted in visual art (fig. 3.8). On the cover, a young Douglass looks squarely at the viewer, body in motion and one finger pointed toward his destination, New England. A river is behind him, and on the opposite bank, his furious and confused pursuers can be seen, riding their horses and accompanied by a pack of bloodhounds. Douglass's posture, bare feet, and bindle echo and enact the fugitive-slave ornament. This suggests that the icon was fully incorporated into the American pictorial vernacular by the 1840s.

Interestingly, all of the playwrights that I discuss in this chapter knew about and capitalized on the public's fascination with runaway slave advertisements. A bill for Taylor's play at the National Theatre in 1852 alludes to an "Advertisement Extraordinary" in the third-act tavern scene; apparently, Taylor retained the conversation in Stowe's novel when the notice seeking George is discussed. The review in the *Herald* confirms that the ad figured prominently in the production, describing it as one of several "extravagant exhibitions of the imaginary horrors of Southern slavery"—suggesting that such advertisements did indeed serve as ideological lightning rods during this time.[56] In Aiken's version, the ad for George plays a central role in the third scene of Act II. The opening stage direction indicates that "a printed placard" detailing George's physical characteristics and announcing a $400 reward for his return is visible on one of the tavern's walls. Phineas spits, signaling his disgust at the document, and announces he would also spit on "the writer of that ar paper, if he was here." He

Figure 3.7: Illustrated Civil War envelopes inspired by type ornaments depicting fugitive slaves. Courtesy of the American Antiquarian Society.

takes issue especially with the ad's description of a brand on the fugitive's hand, saying that a man who would do such a thing to his slave "*deserves* to lose him. Such papers as this ar' a shame to old Kaintuck!" (19; emphasis in original).

The equivalent scene in Conway's *Uncle Tom's Cabin* poses an intriguing contrast. In Stowe's novel, the conversation in the tavern about the handbill involves Drover John. Unlike Aiken, who replaces the slaveholding John with the slaveless Phineas, Conway keeps the episode from the novel relatively intact. In his play, Drover John spits after reading the advertisement, complains about abusive masters, then pontificates at length about the proper way to manage human property.

> I've got a gang o' boys, and I just tells em, run row—cut—dig—[illegible; paint?]—just when you wants to. I shall never come to look arter you. That's the way I keeps mine. Let 'em know they're free to run any time, and it just breaks up their wantin' to. More'n all, I've got free papers for 'em all recorded in case I gets keeled any o' these times, and they knows it—and I tell you, stranger, no man in our parts gets more out of his niggers than I do. Why my boys have been to Cincinnati with five hundred dollars worth of cotes and brought me back the money all stret [*sic*] time and again. It stands to reason they should. Treat 'em like dogs, and you'll have dogs' work and dogs' actions. Treat 'em like men, and you'll have men's works. Ha! (*spits and hawks*)[57]

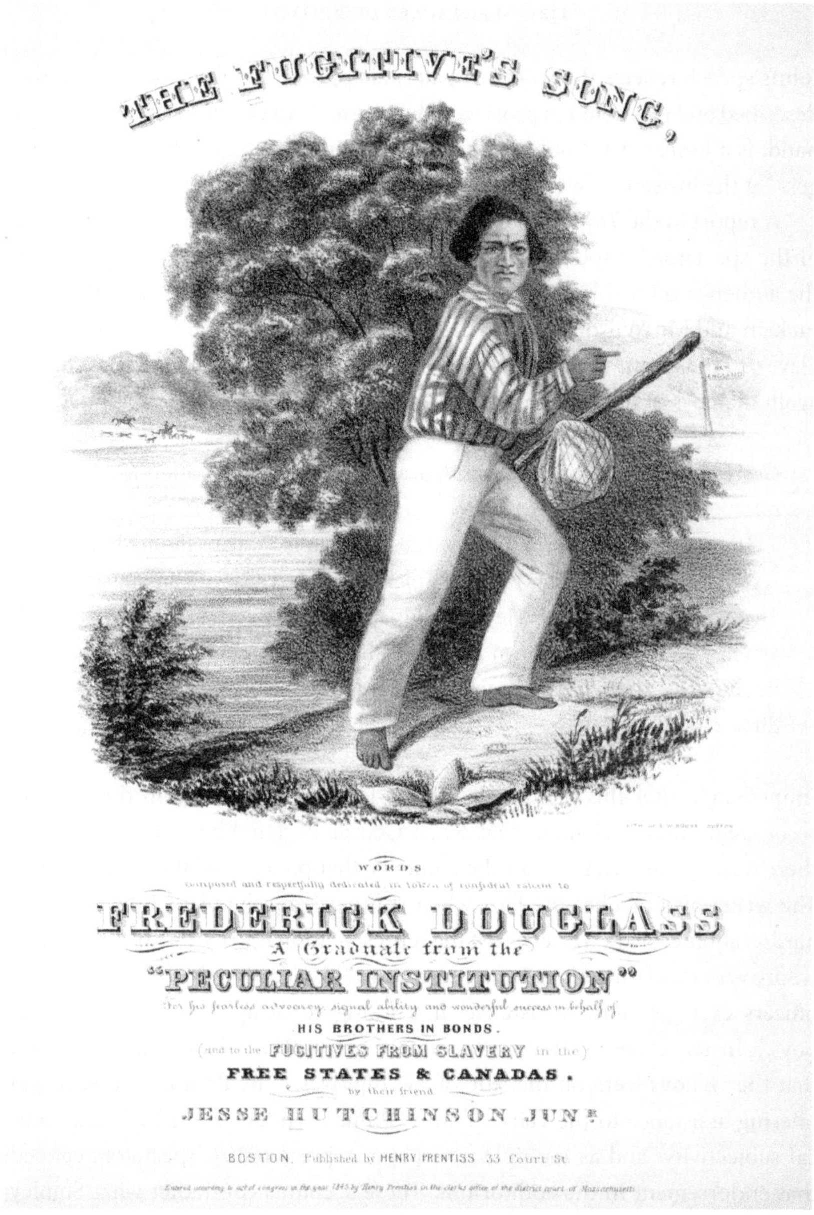

Figure 3.8: Cover illustration (E. W. Bouve, lithographer) for "The Fugitive's Song" by Jesse Hutchinson Jr. and J. M. White (Boston: Henry Prentiss, ca. 1845). Douglass's physical stance and bindle echo the type ornament that accompanied newspaper advertisements for runaways. Courtesy of the American Antiquarian Society.

John's speech reflects the so-called paternal approach to slaveholding that was described and promoted in proslavery literature.[58] Aiken's Phineas, on the other hand, is a *former* slaveholder: he tells Marks that he let go of his "grist of niggers" at the insistence of the Quaker woman he wishes to marry.

A report in the *Times* about Aiken's version at the National offers a glimpse of the spectators' response to the advertisement seeking George. Apparently, the audience echoed Phineas's disgust. The writer reports that when the Kentuckian and Mr. Wilson "spy, at length, the notice on the walls, of 'A Runaway Slave' . . . the Kentuckian spits on it, with 'That's what I think of that!' Whereat again the boys of the pit are convulsed with delight." The report continues,

> *George Harris* now appears disguised, and holds his conversation with *Mr. Wilson.*
>
> The audience are by this time well absorbed in it. Perhaps the actor knows he is uttering real sentiments of these times—for he speaks with an unusual spirit. The caps wave, and the "Hey" sounds with almost every sentence, at words which would be hissed down in most public meetings, and be coldly received in churches—but which, somehow, seem to strike some strange chord in the dirty, ragged audience.

Immediately after this paragraph, several lines of dialogue from the play are recounted. The writer notes that when George declared himself a "*freeman,*" there were "great cheers" from the audience that punctuated the actor's words. The writer also invokes the FSA when summarizing the play's impact on the hardscrabble crowd: "The effect of the representation is to elevate the black; and we are very much mistaken, from the tone on this occasion, if the United States' officers ever get much assistance, in chasing runaways, from the 'Bowery-boys.'" In its review of the production, the *New York Tribune* also affirmed that the "B'hoys were on the side of the fugitives."[59] By flouting the FSA and offering assistance to the Harris family, Phineas endorsed the fugitives' radical subjectivity; and as multiple newspaper reports testify, spectators echoed that endorsement in the auditorium. These accounts contradict what Stanley Campbell perceives as a general acceptance of the FSA during the 1850s.[60] Indeed, the audience's response suggests anything but complacency. Spectators who attended the first run of Aiken's play at the National signaled their support of George and Eliza's defiance of the law through their cheers.

Dénouement: The Ambiguity of an Enduring Image

"Slavery never can be represented," Brown declared before the Female Anti-Slavery Society of Salem in 1847. But is it the subject matter that makes representation problematic, or something else? The answer may be in one of Brown's subsequent statements, when he acknowledges both the necessity and the impossibility of representation: "Your fastidiousness would not allow me to do it. . . . Were I about to tell you the evils of Slavery, to represent to you the Slave in his lowest degradation, *I should wish to take you, one at a time, and whisper it to you.*"[61] The tension between desire and ability in his statement does not seem to derive from a belief that slavery cannot be represented, but rather from the conviction that it would be in bad taste—especially in the presence of respectable women. In talking about *talking about* slavery, he offers a private, intimate exchange in lieu of a spectacular exposé. In other words, "incendiary pictures" of anguish and misery—men cruelly whipped, women immodestly stripped, husbands and wives divided, parents and children separated—are too sensational, *too much,* to be seen.

This leads to a crucial question: Was the vision of the stubborn, daring, semisuicidal, lawbreaking Eliza in good taste? One testament to the image's palatability was its circulation in domestic spaces. Berlant observes that *Uncle Tom* objects and toys brought "politics into the home as much as the novel form did, but this time the consciousness it produce[d] must be shared and noncontroversial, requiring a group consensus conventional to melodrama about what winning would mean, where evil resides, and how to read the moral meaning of different deaths."[62] Women who wanted to assert their views about slavery, at a time when the law inhibited them from doing so electorally, could acquire sheet music and objects depicting the fugitive slave mother, free and fleeing. Because this sensational scene contrasted markedly with other abolitionist images in circulation—such as slaves suffering or supplicating—women could feel confident that no matter who visited their homes, the song on the pianoforte or the figurine on the hearth would be viewed favorably by visitors.

Moreover, I contend that the scene's dramaturgy, in and of itself, addresses Brown's concerns about representation. Not content with mere survival, Eliza rejects the distasteful scenes of misery that await her, running from the Shelbys and the auction block. Refusing to serve at the center of a spectacle, Eliza *becomes* the spectacle through escape. She appeals to spectators' innermost interests while keeping the more gruesome sensations of slavery (heartbreak, pain, death) from view. Perhaps this is why so many types of audiences appreciated and applauded her.

Admittedly, the complexities of the slavery question inspired an extraordinary range of political opinions, making a one-size-fits-all reading of Eliza's flight impossible. It communicates multiple, sometimes contradictory, ideas: the "natural" tenacity of mothers; the innate potentialities of women, regardless of color; the relative value of preserving one's life, when doing so means living in bondage; the insistence on subjectivity despite the suffocating limits of law. Perhaps these contradictions are also the image's attractions. As Michel de Certeau contends, readers are always "poachers," actively mining a text for different meanings.[63] Eliza even seems to haunt a political cartoon that circulated soon after the publication of Stowe's novel. In it, Daniel Webster—who played a central role in the passage of the Compromise of 1850—chases a slave mother fleeing with her two children.[64] Still, scenes derived from *Uncle Tom's Cabin* probably continued to convey abolitionist sentiment, which of course is what inspired Stowe to write in the first place. Changes made by conservative playwrights and producers could not fully eradicate the novel's political orientation. For example, Meer suspects that Conway's version "retained something of Stowe's antislavery tone" despite efforts to soften it. Perhaps this was inevitable, given the subject matter and the historical context in which the play took shape.

An anecdote relayed by Birdoff regarding the production at Barnum's museum offers evidence of this. At one point during the run, "Barnum dug deep into his pocket" and commissioned a banner to be displayed in his lecture hall. According to Birdoff, "High along the cornice, some fifty feet, the title of the play was blazoned forth in ornamental letters. Below floated some five hundred yards of cotton muslin, representing on one side a Negro dance, and on the other the anti-fugitive slave law fight between runaways and pursuers."[65] Materially and figuratively, Barnum's banner invoked the contradictions at the heart of *Uncle Tom's Cabin,* which have plagued it for more than a century and a half. One image conjured minstrelsy's "Old Folks at Home" vision of the happy plantation, while the other invoked the polemical FSA, exhibiting slaves turned into subjects.

The curiosity and contempt with which scholars continue to regard Eliza's flight attest to not only the scene's cultural significance but also the uneasiness it inspires. Much of the disquiet seems to stem from the heroine's ambiguous racial status. Because Eliza mimics the color, speech, and behavior of the Shelbys, some argue that she has been whitewashed beyond recognition. Meer asserts, "In the process of dramatizing *Uncle Tom's Cabin* many of the more powerful female characters were watered down or even dropped." Along these lines, Hartman argues, "In antislavery dramas, beleaguered slave heroes and heroines supplemented rather than replaced darky fanfare."[66] Certainly, Topsy and other blackface characters function as counterparts—perhaps even as antidotes—to the amalgamated fugitives, potentially offsetting the story's progressive politics. And when viewed through a feminist lens, Eliza does not strike a wholly radical pose, because she personifies essentialized notions of gender and motherhood that endure to this day. But it is important to acknowledge that she embodied both the best intentions and the worst assumptions of the abolitionist project. Plus, if paradox and contradiction are essential to spectacle, as Kershaw argues, then the blackface characters may have amplified Eliza's heroics on the river.

At any rate, the proliferation of this sensation scene in multiple media attests to both its playability and its palatability. Tompkins observes, "The text that becomes exceptional in the sense of reaching an exceptionally large audience does so not because of its departure from the ordinary and conventional, but through its embrace of what is most widely shared."[67] Apparently, the quadroon heroine represented values, ideals, and hopes that could be admired by many. Even after the Civil War, Eliza's crossing of the ice floes continued to be adopted and adapted for myriad uses. A set of twelve magic lantern slides produced around 1881 offers evidence of the image's endurance. Produced by C. W. Briggs Company and painted by Joseph Boggs Beale, the slides reproduce Billings's pictures in the illustrated edition of *Uncle Tom's Cabin.*[68] The illustrated edition includes more than 150 pictures, yet "Eliza's Flight" made the cut. Clearly, the scene became obligatory in the telling of Stowe's story, as its inclusion in a postbellum lantern show attests.

Discussing the danger and the potential of sentimental texts such as *Uncle Tom's Cabin,* Berlant asserts, "The possibility that through the identification with alterity you will never be the same remains the radical threat and the great promise of this affective aesthetic."[69] Perhaps the radical threat and great promise of Eliza was that everyone could find something to appreciate in her, even after the question of slavery had been settled and the harrowing process of Reconstruction had begun.

4

The Railroad Rescue

Suffrage and Citizenship in *Under the Gaslight*

Some tell us that this is not the time for woman to make the demand; that this is the negro's hour. No, my friends, we have a broader question than either on hand to-day. This is the Nation's hour.

—ELIZABETH CADY STANTON (1867)[1]

And these are the women who ain't to have the vote!

—SNORKEY IN AUGUSTIN DALY'S *UNDER THE GASLIGHT* (1867)[2]

When Augustin Daly's sensation drama *Under the Gaslight* premiered at the Worrell Sisters' New York Theatre on August 12, 1867, it was an instant success, playing first for six weeks then another eight when it was remounted a month later. Since this was a time when, in the words of Marvin Felheim, "a month's run meant a real hit," the sheer number of performances reveals that *Gaslight* was extremely popular.[3] Audiences found the "wondrous Railroad Sensation" especially affecting. Early advertisements list all of the sensation scenes in the drama; later ones focus exclusively on the railroad sequence. One ad in the *New York Times* boasts, "*Under the Gas-Light,* Witnessed by 100,000 people, and pronounced the most interesting, truthful and exciting picture of Life and Love at the present day. The wondrous Railroad Sensation, the universal topic of conversation." Even after accounting for puffery and hyperbole, this suggests that the play was on the public mind—a sought-after event to see and experience.[4]

Widely considered "one of the most famous spectacles on the American stage," and the first train scene to capture the attention of US audiences, the railroad rescue eventually appeared in other melodramas (most notably, Dion

Boucicault's 1868 play *After Dark,* which led Daly to file a copyright lawsuit) and later, after the turn of the century, in films.[5] In Daly's version, the female protagonist, Laura, breaks out of a locked shed with an axe and saves a one-armed Civil War veteran named Snorkey from the tracks. The gender of both the victim and the rescuer was part of the point: Snorkey proclaims at the end, "And these are the women who ain't to have the vote!"—referring to the debate, in full swing by 1867, regarding which Americans would receive electoral rights in the wake of the Civil War. The placement of Snorkey's prosuffrage statement, at the height of the play's most spectacular instant, constitutes a notable intersection of sensationalism and reform culture.

Gaslight premiered at a time of tremendous political ferment: one year after Elizabeth Cady Stanton and Susan B. Anthony founded the American Equal Rights Association, which advocated voting rights for women; and a year before the full ratification of the Fourteenth Amendment, which laid the foundation for the enfranchisement of African American men but in the process excluded all women. In addition to Snorkey's climactic line, Daly refers to the suffrage question in the cast of characters, where he describes a minor role, Sam, as "a colored citizen, ready for suffrage when it is ready for *him.*" How did spectators read and interpret these statements about suffrage and citizenship in 1867? Bruce A. McConachie asserts that spectators probably dismissed Snorkey's declaration at the end of the railroad sequence, going so far as to characterize it as "a throwaway remark."[6] I offer an alternative reading that situates the scene in its historical context and also sheds light on its astonishing longevity in US entertainment culture. In contrast to the sensation scenes examined in previous chapters, this one exemplifies spectacle's potential to communicate subtly yet profoundly to audiences.

Since many of the cultural resonances in Daly's railroad rescue have been lost to us over time, its politics are harder to detect than those of the temperance play or abolitionist drama. Nevertheless, *Gaslight* addressed an incendiary political issue that until that point had received little attention in the American theater. As Emma Dassori has observed, the majority of mid-nineteenth-century plays addressing voting rights were "anti-suffrage comedies, satirizing the New Woman and her plight for equality" performed in amateur settings.[7] The marked absence of references to this reform movement on the commercial stage, and the delicacy and deftness with which it is handled in *Gaslight,* suggest that women's suffrage was indeed a radical idea in 1867—one that audiences could only swallow, perhaps, with a spoonful (or several) of spectacle.

Like Robert Darnton, I seek to "get the joke" by considering each component of the railroad rescue as a kernel of culture—a fragment evoking historically specific customs, controversies, and ideas.[8] For example, competing conceptions of "true womanhood" articulated by proponents and opponents of women's suffrage reveal how Laura exceeds the limits of conventional gender roles throughout Daly's play. Similarly, discursive and pictorial depictions of Civil War "citizen-soldiers" and disabled war veterans illuminate Snorkey's significance in the story, both as type and as victim. Laura's use of an axe during the train scene is also noteworthy, because the American version of this tool (literally, the "American axe") came to be associated with a host of gendered, nativist values during the late eighteenth and early nineteenth centuries.

Strangest of all is the enduring presence of the railroad rescue, in modified form, in the public imagination. How and why did this melodramatic scenario transform over time into a more "gender-correct" image—a woman tied to the tracks saved by a man (fig. 0.1), which Peggy Phelan has called "the epitome of cross-cutting, neck-wrenching melodrama"? Like Rebecca Schneider, I am interested in "the curious inadequacies of the copy, and what inadequacy gets right about our faulty steps backward, and forward, and to the side." The stamina and stickiness of this Baudrillardian simulacrum, which has somehow eluded the material confines of the archive, attest to its unrelenting influence on notions of heroism and victimhood in US culture.[9]

From Moral Suasion to Electoral Politics: Transitions in Equal-Rights Feminism

In the early nineteenth century, it was generally believed that public, political, and economic activities fell within the purview of men. Women, on the other hand, served as homebound ethicists, responsible for inculcating standards of decency and morality in husbands and children. This assumption helped to rationalize "separate spheres" for each gender, with men engaging in the sordid, messy worlds of business and government while women advised boys and men in the home.[10] However, for some women, the idea that females were morally superior seemed to warrant—even demand—some manner of participation in social reform. According to Keith E. Melder, "Because of her purity, woman occupied a moral pedestal that permitted her to judge the behavior of others. This same virtue gave woman new responsibilities: within the home she should be the moral head of the household; and outside the home she would be vigilant against all evil and destructive influences." As a result, by the 1830s female reformers were "band[ing] together in fledgling organizations to struggle to abolish slavery, aid prostitutes, fight the debilitating effects of the unregulated sale of alcoholic beverages, and claim their rights as persons and citizens," as Karlyn Kohrs Campbell notes. Gay Gibson Cima asserts that women skirted and stretched the boundaries between public and private by adopting abstract "host bodies," both in print and in person, that facilitated their participation in reform activities. Female reformers argued that because intemperance and slavery tended to victimize mothers and children, women's participation in campaigns to eradicate these ills was justified. Petitioning and similar activities provided these activists with socially acceptable opportunities to agitate, since such tactics involved one-on-one persuasion rather than public protest or exhibitionism.[11]

The abolition movement particularly benefited from and encouraged the involvement of women, who played an instrumental role in the promulgation of antislavery ideology. William Lloyd Garrison, the radical leader of the abolitionist project, enlisted women nearly from the start. As they became more and more emboldened, female reformers flouted social prohibitions more and more, speaking in public and attending meetings with "promiscuous" (mixed-gender) audiences. They explained these unorthodox behaviors by citing the moral degradation of slavery and the pressing urgency of its eradication. Garrison did not, in Suzanne M. Marilley's estimation, "envision women's participation in his abolitionist movement as a first step toward their winning equality"; but as social tensions about slavery increased, female abolitionists (most of whom were "native-born, white, educated, middle-class, and from religious denominations such as the Quakers that called for equality at home as well as in public") began conceiving a more-universal notion of freedom and liberty. They envisioned a nation in which women, as well as slaves, could be politically enfranchised.[12]

By the 1840s, the Garrisonian philosophy regarding natural rights—which held that slaves were human beings and therefore were entitled to the basic privileges enjoyed by all humans—eventually stimulated discussions about the natural rights of women as well. Many of Garrison's male colleagues strongly opposed such talk, which led to strife within the American Anti-Slavery Society. In 1840, a substantial number of members defected and formed another body, the American and Foreign Anti-Slavery Society. By the time the first women's rights convention took place in Seneca Falls, New York, in 1848, the "woman question" was inextricably bound up with that of abolition. A woman's ability to keep property, file for divorce, time her own pregnancies, and access educational and vocational opportunities were among the topics discussed. A woman's right to vote was, perhaps, the most controversial subject of all, and was not wholly embraced. At the Seneca Falls convention, Elizabeth Cady Stanton proposed a resolution related to women's suffrage; Frederick Douglass spoke in favor of it, aligning himself with Stanton and other proponents of universal suffrage. Nevertheless, it was not unanimously supported.[13]

As Lori D. Ginzberg notes, women reformers became more overtly political during the 1850s, increasing their demands for legislative recourse. Ginzberg contends that this shift occurred due to a dawning realization: moral suasion—the strategy that had dominated most early nineteenth-century antislavery activity—"had, quite simply, failed." In 1856, a writer in Amelia Bloomer's temperance publication *Lily* complained, "Why shall [women] be left only the poor resource of petition? . . . For even petitions, when they are from women, without the elective franchise to give them backbone, are of but little consequence." Ginzberg suggests that this prompted some women to believe they needed electoral privileges to effect real change: "Voteless, women discovered that benevolent work's growing dependence on electoral means had by the 1850s rendered 'female' means for change less effective and thus less popular."[14]

Although the onset of the Civil War in 1861 shifted everyone's attention to the battlefield, it did not silence women suffragists completely. In May 1863, Stanton, Susan B. Anthony, Lucy Stone, Angelina Weld Grimké, and other female activists formed the Woman's National Loyal League, an organization dedicated to supporting Union war efforts.[15] Members coordinated petitions, wrote letters to soldiers on the warfront, promoted household economy, and provided medical assistance in order to bolster the Union cause. The question of women's suffrage persisted in the league's discussions. A resolution proposed at the first meeting stated, "There can never be a true peace in this Republic until the civil and political rights of all citizens of African descent and all women are practically established." Stone, who presided at the meeting, defended the resolution during a vigorous debate by asserting, "If justice to the negro and to woman is right, it can not hurt our loyalty to the country and the Union. If it is not right, let it go out of the way; but if it is right, there is no occasion that we should reject it or ignore it."[16] As had happened in Seneca Falls in 1848, it was the only resolution that was not adopted unanimously; yet the proposal reveals that the fight for women's rights was not fully in abeyance during the Civil War.[17]

When the war ended in 1865, the process of reconstruction commenced. The Thirteenth Amendment was ratified that year, making involuntary servitude illegal throughout the United States. Next, through the Fourteenth Amendment, Congress began to establish rights for former slaves, including due process and equal protection. This landmark legislation had a dark side for women suffragists: it attached the word *male* to its definition of US *inhabitants* and *citizens*. In that way, it constituted the first time a gendered adjective was used to designate who would have the right to vote. Before this time, electoral participation was unmarked, requiring no adjectival descriptors; it was, unequivocally, a male privilege. The deliberate association of suffrage with sex in the Fourteenth Amendment suggests that members of Congress felt obliged to be explicit: women activists had generated enough heat that the masculine qualifier was suddenly necessary. The amendment was proposed in June 1866 and began the process of ratification that year.

The legislation propelled women suffragists to step up their efforts to obtain the vote along with black men. Flouting Wendell Phillips's assertion that it was "the Negro's Hour"—in other words, that women should wait patiently for their turn—members of the Women's Rights Society (formerly a subdivision of Garrison's Anti-Slavery Society) dedicated their organization to the fight for universal suffrage in May 1866. They renamed themselves the American Equal Rights Association (AERA), and Anthony and Stanton became its leaders.[18] In December of that year, the AERA held a convention in New York City and passed several resolutions, including one that declared,

> Resolved, That the ballot, alike to the woman and the negro, means bread, education, intelligence, self-protection, self-reliance and self-respect. To the daughter it means industrial freedom and diversified employment; to the wife it means the control of her own person, property and earnings; to the mother it means the equal legal right to her children; to all it means social equality, colleges and professions open, profitable business, skilled labor, and intellectual development.

Another resolution at the convention suggests that the AERA's activities in New York received wide and favorable press coverage: "We are rejoiced to see so friendly a spirit towards our new enterprise by the newspaper press of the country generally, as well as of this State; and we are still more happy to know that this acknowledgement is due alike to the religious and literary as well as the political journals, irrespective of party."[19]

Nevertheless, differences in opinion continued to plague the organization. After investing their talent and energy in the antislavery cause, for some female suffragists the passage of the Fourteenth Amendment represented a huge blow. Others considered it a temporary setback that would help their cause in the long term. Stone maintained that both populations deserved the vote, which led her eventually to break with the AERA. Douglass, who had advocated for universal suffrage before the war, now insisted that men of color needed the vote more urgently than women did. Abby Kelley Foster agreed that securing suffrage for African American men was a step in the right direction, even if it meant women would have to wait. Growing frustrated with these colleagues, Anthony and Stanton adopted racist rhetoric, asserting that native-born, educated white women were more deserving of the vote than black men.[20]

Defining the True Woman: Nature, Gender, and the Suffrage Debate

Laura Courtland, the heroine of *Under the Gaslight,* tumbles from her comfortable bourgeois life and is forced to navigate New York City's underworld for a time, but she ultimately regains her place among the elite. Many people in the play discuss Laura's character and actions in light of what it means, to them, to be a *true woman.* And yet, in the 1850s and 1860s the definition of womanhood was itself a source of debate. A woman's "nature" often played a prominent role in these discussions. Progressives like Anthony and Grimké argued that a woman's innate sense of morality made her an excellent decision maker, domestically and politically. But opponents of female suffrage, such as Sarah Josepha Hale and Horace Bushnell, also invoked nature to advance conservative notions of femininity. For the most part, members from both factions hailed from the middle and upper classes; and like other midcentury reformers, they sought to establish a moral telemetry that would apply to all Americans, regardless of social and economic station. Any woman could be a true one, they argued, because every woman had the same inherent proclivities.

The *true woman* as conceived by suffragists derived, in part, from what Linda A. Kerber calls "Republican motherhood," a formulation of femininity that emerged in the United States around the time of the Revolution.

The concept of the "republican mother" had developed in the era of the Ameri-

> can Revolution as a way of deflecting male criticism that the woman who "meddled" in political ideas necessarily desexed herself; it also develops, as Elizabeth Blackmar has argued, as a language that permitted the wives of upwardly mobile, entrepreneurial men to account for their household responsibilities as productive, even civic, duties requiring them to supervise working-class women as domestic workers.[21]

Rather than looking to fathers and husbands for direction, the Republican mother took an active role in her family as nurturer and counselor. In the mid-nineteenth century, prosuffragists adapted and updated this idea when asserting that women's natural ability to provide ethical guidance made them indispensable in the political arena. In this manner, they emphasized the utility of their irrepressible and indispensible moral authority.

Antisuffrage activists capitalized on the concept of Republican motherhood, too. As Luce Irigaray notes, a common tactic employed by opponents of women's liberation is the appropriation and manipulation of arguments originally advanced by progressives. She observes that this is one of "the difficulties women encounter when they try to make their voices heard in places already fixed within and by a society that has simultaneously used and excluded them, and that continues in particular to ignore the specificity of their 'demands' even as it recuperates some of their themes, their very slogans." Opponents of suffrage argued that a woman's natural virtue actually *exempted* her from the corrupt world of politics. Feminine morality was most effective when exercised within the home. On those rare occasions when a true woman desired political influence, she should work behind the scenes and above the fray.[22]

In making such arguments, antisuffragists often focused on the "natural" differences between men and women. For example, the writers of *Godey's Lady's Book*, a popular magazine catering to "respectable" women, routinely articulated biologized notions of womanhood.[23] An issue published around the time of *Gaslight*'s premiere includes an editorial exploring the question, "Ought American Women to Have the Right of Suffrage?" It cites biblical evidence regarding the distinguishing characteristics of men and women and the responsibilities associated with them: "The Word of God settles the question of differences between the sexes in perfect accordance with the natural laws that indicate the best way of human happiness and progressive improvement. . . . Man is the *protector, provider,* and *lawgiver.* Woman is the *preserver, the teacher,* or *inspirer,* and *the exemplar.*" Here, men's and women's roles—dictated by "the

Word of God" and "natural laws"—are defined in terms of labor. Whereas a man's work is active (protector, provider) and public (lawgiver), a woman's is passive (inspirer, exemplar) and domestic (teacher). By 1869, when Bushnell published his treatise *Women's Suffrage: The Reform against Nature,* opponents of women's suffrage habitually cited biological reasons for limiting voting rights to men.[24]

Conservatives often declared that female reformers were abnormal—even freakish. *Godey's* routinely characterized suffragists as eccentric and aberrant. A pamphlet written by an anonymous "Member of the Press," titled *An Appeal against Anarchy of Sex* and published during the same year that *Gaslight* premiered, reveals the category crisis that female suffragists inspired.

> The assurance with which these few so-called "strong-minded" women and their few followers claim to represent the sex which disowns them with virtual unanimity, is extraordinary, and is really worthy of a stronger term. It would be truly deplorable if the general sense of the citizenship should be so misled as to foist upon women a position which they do not desire, and which is out of their legitimate sphere, because of the outcry of a few persons, who seem to constitute substantially a kind of *third sex,* so to speak, *of somewhat monstrous aspect.*[25]

In this manner, antisuffragists portrayed women activists as radical exceptions to the rule: their opinions and activities did not reflect the vast majority of normal, genuine, bona fide women. A *true* woman would never subject herself to the distasteful dominion of civic activity.

Progressives rigorously challenged these restrictive definitions of womanhood. Grimké, defending a suffrage resolution at a Woman's National Loyal League convention in May 1863, portrayed the domestic sphere as frivolous and restrictive, neither pleasant nor pleasurable.

> True, we have not felt the slave-holder's lash; true, we have not had our hands manacled; but our *hearts* have been crushed. . . . A teacher said to a young lady, who had been studying for several years, on the day she finished her course of instruction, "I thought you would be very glad that you were so soon to go home, so soon to leave your studies." She looked up, and said, "What was I made for? When I go home I shall live in a circle of fashion and folly. I was not

made for embroidery and dancing; I was made a woman; but I can not be a true woman, a full-grown woman, in America."[26]

In other words, a woman cannot be *true* unless she is able to follow a variety of pursuits. Hence, Grimké offers an alternative to the submissive, subjugated womanhood espoused by *Godey's Lady's Book* and other opponents of women's rights.

The True Woman in *Under the Gaslight*

Prior to the premiere of *Under the Gaslight,* Anthony declared during a speech in Brooklyn, "After these false customs are all swept away, woman will rise up in her native strength and dignity, and be woman still."[27] Daly's heroine Laura seems to embody a "native strength and dignity" that is realized most vividly when she rises up out of her place—out of her home, out of her element—and, in effect, becomes a "true woman," as Snorkey repeatedly calls her. In many respects, she reflects a progressive conception of femininity that subtly contests the conservatism of *Godey's,* Bushnell, and other antisuffragist commentators.[28]

Despite a drastic change in her fortunes in the first act, Laura maintains an air of dignity and poise. When her fiancé Ray discovers she is an adopted rather than a natural daughter of the Courtlands, he grows cold, announcing his intent to break their engagement. Laura barely bats an eyelash, pretending lofty unconcern; a stage direction specifies, "*Laura looks at him a moment, smiles and then crosses without further noticing him*" (10). Surprised by her reaction, Ray eventually rethinks his rejection of Laura and pledges his devotion once more; but Laura does not greet his pronouncement with effusive joy. Rather, she laughs, expressing her dismay that feminine charms blind men's eyes to the true woman within: "How happy must those women be, who are poor, and friendless, and plain, when some true heart comes and says: I wish to marry you." Ray, baffled, replies, "Laura, you act very strangely to-night" (10). And indeed, she does. Unlike heroines whose race or class status undermines their matrimonial aspirations (such as Zoë in Dion Boucicault's *The Octoroon*), Laura does not revel in self-loathing or woe, but instead reacts to the situation calmly and matter-of-factly.[29] Even when the Courtlands' well-to-do friends reject her at the end of the first act, she does not falter, but "proudly waves [Ray] away" (14).

Laura's severance from the Courtland clan not only forces her to leave the confines of her comfortable home but also necessitates her becoming a laborer. She disappears into the city's underworld, never asking for help from her friends and family, and moves into a humble apartment. Laura retouches photographs for a meager income while searching for a position as a tutor. Although she expresses concern about the people she left behind, she remains lighthearted despite her circumstances. Getting ready to make a meal for herself in Act II, her sense of humor is evident: "Now to be cook. (*Laughing*) The 'Tuesday Sociable' ought to see me now. Artist in the morning, cook at noon, artist in the afternoon" (18). As she is preparing the repast, Snorkey leads the pining Ray to her apartment. Rather than expressing relief and joy at his arrival, she deflects his dismay and reasserts her independence.

RAY: Alone, without means, exposed to every rudeness, unprotected, is this not misery for you?

LAURA: (*Laughing*) Oh, it's not so bad as that.

. . .

RAY: Laura, by the tie that once bound us—

LAURA: (*Going up.*) Yes, *once.* It *is* a long time ago.

RAY: What have I said?—the tie which still—

LAURA: (*Sharply turning.*) Mr. Trafford must I remind you of that night, when all arrayed themselves so pitilessly against me? When a gesture from you might have saved me! . . . No, you made your choice then—the world without me. I make my choice now—the wide, wide, world without you. (20–21)

Laura's willingness to forgo the comforts of marriage for the "wide, wide, world" directly challenges conventional expectations regarding what women desire most, as well as the notion of separate, gendered spheres. By embracing and celebrating her self-reliance, she implicitly criticizes Ray's passivity and lack of faith.

Claiming that *Gaslight* belongs to an emergent mid-nineteenth-century American dramatic genre focusing on business-class concerns, McConachie suggests that Laura's composure derives from her bourgeois blood and breeding. In his estimation, *Gaslight* and other sensation dramas "shift[ed] the definition of respectability from inner qualities of character and morality to 'natural' attributes resulting from birth and upbringing." He points out that when Byke (the villain in *Gaslight*) and his wife Old Judas capture Laura, Old Judas remarks, "How her blood tells—she wouldn't shed a tear" (30).[30] While acknowledging the value of McConachie's observation regarding the naturalization of class in *Gaslight,* I suggest that his reading does not take into account the political context in which the play premiered, when the nation was struggling with monumental questions regarding the racial and gender qualifications of US citizenship. *Gaslight* spectacularizes Laura's womanhood at least as much as her breeding. For instance, Byke's reply to Old Judas's line "How her blood tells" underscores how Laura defies his expectations of her *as a woman:* he says, "Bah! If she'd been more of a woman and set up a screaming, we shouldn't have been able to get her at all. Success to all girls of spirit, say I." In other words, Laura *exceeds* Byke's expectations, impressing him with her unusual (for a woman) response to adversity.

Laura's courage is displayed most dramatically in the railroad rescue itself: the spectacular instant that thrilled audiences, inspired imitations, and generated "universal conversation" (42–43).[31] When she escapes the clutches of Byke, Laura tries to catch a train back to New York City from the Shrewsbury Bend train station. When told by the signalman that no trains will stop there until the following day, she asks him to lock her in a storage shed overnight (40). Snorkey, eager to protect Laura and her family from the murderous Byke, also arrives at the station in hopes of boarding a train to New York. But Byke has followed him. He quickly overcomes Snorkey, ties his legs with rope, and fastens him to the rails, leaving him there to be crushed by an oncoming locomotive. Snorkey calls out for help, and when Laura hears him, she finds an axe inside and uses it to bash her way out. Emerging with axe in hand, she reaches him just in time to move him off the tracks before the train rushes by.[32]

The railroad sequence begins when Laura glimpses Snorkey through a window in the station shed and cries out, "O Heavens! He will be murdered before my eyes! How can I aid him?" On the brink of death, Snorkey seems to mistake the flesh-and-blood female for a heavenly figure of salvation; he expresses surprise when he realizes that it is in fact Laura, exclaiming, "I almost thought I was dead, and [the voice] was an angel's." Snorkey is disabled in two senses: tied up and incapacitated by Byke, and one-armed due to his service in the Civil War. Laura is his only hope.

SNORKEY: Never mind me, Miss. I might as well die now, and here, as at any other time. I'm not afraid. I've seen death in almost every shape, and none of them scare me; but, for the sake of those you love, I would live. Do you hear me?

LAURA: Yes! Yes!

SNORKEY: They are on the way to your cottage—Byke and Judas—to rob and murder.

LAURA: (*In agony.*) O, I must get out! (*Shakes window bars.*) What shall I do?

The shuddering door, the clanking metal, and Laura's cries foreshadow the cacophonous train that will soon appear. These sounds signal Laura's willingness to dive into the fray and become the guardian angel Snorkey hopes to see.

SNORKEY: Can't you burst the door?

LAURA: It is locked fast.

SNORKEY: Is there nothing in there?—no hammer?—no crowbar?

LAURA: Nothing! (*Faint steam whistle is heard in the distance.*) O, heavens! The train! (*Paralysed for an instant.*) The axe!!!

As the tension builds, it seems that Laura—crying out helplessly to the heavens—will lose her signature composure and spiral into panic. But after a mere "instant" of paralysis, her senses return and she is struck with an epiphany: she can use one of the axes in the shed to break down the door.

The axe, in contrast to the hammer or crowbar, is a striking symbol of destructive power. It is a man's tool, employed in tasks ranging from the mundane (splitting firewood) to the heroic (breaking into a burning building). The stage directions indicate that Laura's axe makes a spectacular noise.

SNORKEY: Cut the woodwork! Don't mind the lock—cut around it! How my neck tingles! (*A blow at the door is heard.*) Courage! (*Another.*) Courage! (*The steam whistle heard again—nearer, and rumble of train on track. Another blow.*) That's a true woman! Courage! (*Noise of locomotive heard—with whistle. A last blow; the door swings open, mutilated—the lock hanging—and Laura appears, axe in hand.*)

Soon, however, the blows of Laura's axe are punctuated by the train whistle—louder this time—as well as a new sound, a "rumble" of the train on the tracks, which adds to the dramatic tension. Determined and seemingly unconcerned for her own safety, Laura ultimately gains her freedom by "mutilating" the door.

It is important to acknowledge that Laura departs dramatically from what we generally expect from a melodramatic heroine, whose "vulnerability" and "passivity" characterized "her perfect goodness," as David Grimsted notes. In many respects, this fictive figure is the melodramatic counterpart of the "true woman" espoused by conservative antisuffragists. Grimsted further observes, "the heroine's weakness was such that she had to be carefully sheltered."[33] But clearly, Laura is not this kind of heroine. Snorkey's declaration "That's a true woman!" is an exultant expression of faith in her strength of character. Prior to this climactic point in the play, he has witnessed Laura display courage, steadiness, and independence in myriad ways. Plucky and unconventional, she responds to adversity with laughter; she rejects the hero's apologetic pleas for reconciliation; she violently chops her way out of a shed with an axe. In these ways, she represents a progressive construction of true womanhood.[34]

What we know about Rose Eytinge, the actress who played Laura during the initial run of *Gaslight,* supports this contention. According to the *New York Times,* Eytinge as Laura "presented an exceedingly good picture of a young girl with *genuine American pride and sense,* and was the pet of the spectators from the first scene to the conclusion." Upon her death in 1911, the *Evening Transcript* in Boston described Eytinge as "a strong and persistent advocate for the advance of woman and the extension of her rights," reporting that she once declared, "I want my rights afforded me, even if I do not use them." Prior to playing Laura, Eytinge had enjoyed accolades for her portrayal of Nancy Sykes (a role Lewis C. Strang describes as the epitome of "melodramatic horror") in *Oliver Twist* at Wallack's Theatre. In her autobiography, she reports that the managers originally rejected her request to play Nancy because "in every particular—physically, mentally, and temperamentally—I was wholly unequipped for it." She continued to press for the opportunity, and they eventually agreed, under the condition that she conclude the evening in "some light one-act piece . . . in order that the audience should not take away with them the ghastly picture of Nancy in her death throes."[35]

Snorkey's final line in the railroad sequence reveals his feelings about the type of "true woman" that Laura represents. As the train appears, the sensation scene concludes with a direct allusion to women's suffrage.

SNORKEY: Here—quick! (*She runs and unfastens him. The locomotive lights glare on the scene.*) Victory! Saved! Hooray! (*Laura leans exhausted against the switch.*) And these are the women who ain't to have the vote!

McConachie asserts that spectators probably dismissed Snorkey's line, stating that it is "clearly intended as a throwaway remark to spark a laugh" and that "because it is said by the comic and not by the hero or heroine, it carries less dramatic weight."[36] Surely, audiences found aspects of the scene humorous; reports about the earliest performances indicate that this was especially true when the scene's machinery went awry. Joseph Daly admits that on opening night, "The intensely wrought feelings of the spectators found vent in almost hysterical laughter when the 'railroad train' parted in the middle and disclosed the flying legs of the human motor who was propelling the first half of the express." But he also says that "the suspense and emotion created by the whole situation . . . was beyond chance of accident," pointing out that despite such mishaps, it was a hit with spectators.[37] Even though the scene's comic qualities may have blunted its edge, it seems doubtful that they fully extinguished its affective impact.

The notion that Snorkey's social position lessened his "dramatic weight" is also questionable. Similar to the Yankee character that appears in many American melodramas, Snorkey not only offers comic relief but also articulates the basic moral codes at the heart of the play. Felheim notes that Snorkey "serves as the playwright's method of keeping the strands of the story together," in part because of his role as a professional messenger. He also functions as what McConachie describes as a "proto-detective," a label he uses to describe resourceful secondary characters like Badger and Myles-na-Coppaleen in Dion Boucicault's *The Poor of New York* (1857) and *The Colleen Bawn* (1860), respectively. The protodetective is more assertive than the melodramatic hero—which, I would argue, gives him *more* dramatic weight. McConachie observes that Ray, the hero of *Gaslight,* is typical of "bourgeois heroes" in midcentury sensation melodramas who "float passively through their plays." Ray's ineffectualness contrasts starkly with Snorkey's pluck and dedication—leaving one to wonder who the real hero is. Snorkey is a "heroic protagonist" who fills a dramaturgical vacuum left by Ray, who is "too self-divided and too ignorant to push to resolution the plots which entangle [him]."[38]

Moreover, casting may have impacted how spectators perceived Snorkey. During the two initial runs of *Gaslight* at the Worrell Sisters' Theatre, J. K. Mortimer played the role. T. Allston Brown describes Mortimer as an eccentric but popular performer, "one of the finest of American light comedians," who was well known for his portrayal of another protodetective, Boucicault's Badger.[39] The *Times* described Mortimer in the role as "a light-hearted, free, spirited soldier lad" and "a thing to be remembered."[40] Snorkey's body also made him "a thing to be remembered": as a wounded Civil War veteran, he evoked many of the central questions that lay at the heart of the suffrage issue in 1867 (described in the next section). For these reasons, Snorkey's line about the vote cannot be dismissed as the comic utterance of a minor figure.

Spectacles of True Women and Citizen-Soldiers

Military action has always been integral to the myth of America, a nation born of violence and revolt. Metaphors of war surface repeatedly in discussions about civil rights and social order as well. Since the country's founding, people who have deviated in some way from the normative model citizen (white, heterosexual, male) usually have to "fight" for power and privileges. Activists in minority groups "struggle" for equality; women "battle" sexism and harassment in the workplace. These oft-used phrases, some verging on cliché, reveal that—by necessity or design—efforts to broaden citizenship are often couched in the rhetoric of aggression. Such rhetoric is inevitably and inexorably gendered.

During the mid-nineteenth century, it took (masculine) force, rather than (feminine) persuasion, to eradicate slavery. As the bloodiest, most devastating conflict in US history, the Civil War affected a considerable number of American families because of the sheer number of men involved and the incredible losses suffered by both sides.[41] On the battlefield, soldiers engaged in violence—"the unique province of males," according to Jim Cullen—so that women would not have to do the same.[42] Yet *Under the Gaslight*'s famous sensation scene features a disenfranchised woman saving a disabled war veteran from certain death; it is the woman, not the soldier, who fights and protects. How did spectators interpret these reversals of role and occupation, of gender and job?

The radicalism of Daly's railroad rescue becomes evident when examined in light of the "citizen-soldier," an idealized figure that unrelentingly haunted the postwar suffrage debate.[43] Willing to lose his life to protect the Union, the citizen-soldier became a powerful myth in the North, circulating in pictorial media and political discourse. During the war, consumers could purchase a wide range of lithographs and stationery depicting soldiers laboring on the field, marching with their regiments, or exhibiting themselves in pride and glory. A variety of iconographic allegories, such as a troop's departure for the warfront or portraits of soldiers holding American flags, celebrated the spirit and bravery of Northern militiamen—and, by extension, the patriotism of the person who purchased them.[44] Supporters proudly displayed these images in their homes or wrote correspondence on decorated paper and envelopes that passed through multiple hands (printer, merchant, letter-writer, mail-carrier, recipient, collector). In some respects, these objects not only reflected but also shaped how Americans viewed each other and themselves. As such, they offer useful information about how spectators may have perceived a character like Snorkey.

As I discuss in the first chapter, strategies of juxtaposition and comparison/contrast—which capitalized on the scale, excess, and intensity of spectacle—were frequently employed in theatrical advertisements, children's literature, and temperance and abolitionist propaganda in order to foster a methodology of seeing that foregrounded the body. Such strategies are also evident in depictions of Union soldiers. *The American Patriot's Dream* (1861) by Currier & Ives sentimentalized the citizen-soldier's sacrifice by juxtaposing men on the field with their families at home (fig. 4.1). A soldier lies asleep in the foreground while his comrades mill around chatting, eating, drinking, or engaging in mundane tasks. Smoke from a campfire collects above the sleeping soldier and reveals his dream: a vision of homecoming in which his beautiful wife, strapping young son, and parents run to meet him. The scene communicates that the Union's troops are fighting not only for the nation's preservation but also for the families they left behind. Apparently, this tableau was popular, because it reappears in subsequent prints by Currier & Ives and other lithographers.[45]

The domestic utopias enacted in these soldiers' dreams also manifested in memorial placards, envelopes, and stationery. Such products, which circulated in domestic and community spaces, served as material archives of patriotic feeling. A case in point is an 1863 lithograph honoring volunteers in "Company C, 8th Regiment, of Connecticut."[46] It lists soldiers who had died or been injured sometime between September 1861 and August 1863. Allegorical imagery, miniature icons, and four larger scenes embellish the memorial. Two pictures exhibit soldiers on the battlefield, whereas two others illustrate scenes similar to the "soldier's dream," with men taking leave of wives and children. The print honors the soldiers' sacrifices by freezing on the last moment of domestic harmony they enjoyed: saying goodbye to their loved ones. Stationery produced

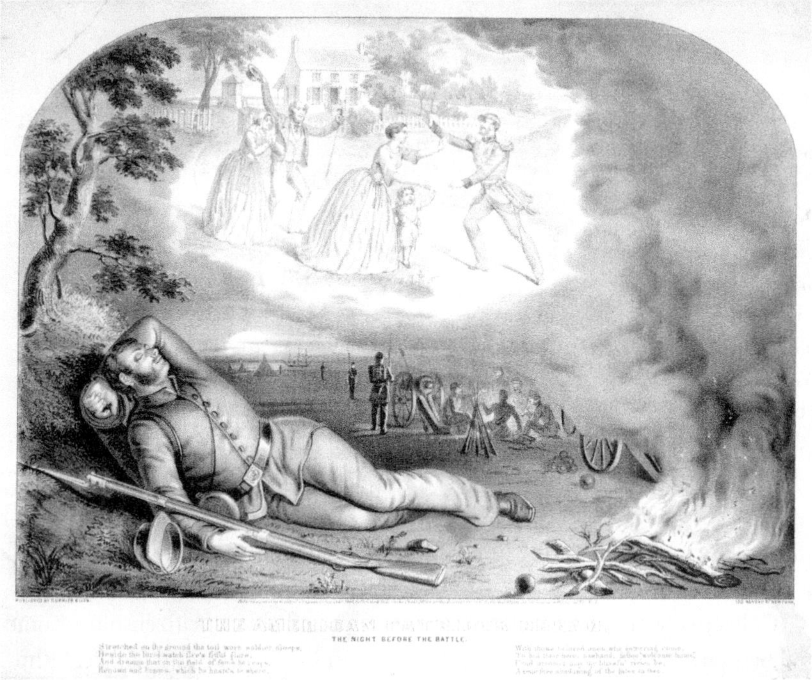

Figure 4.1: *The American Patriot's Dream.* Currier & Ives, 1861. Courtesy of the American Antiquarian Society.

during the war, featuring similar imagery, conveys similar sentiments. Some envelopes depict the soldier's dream, nearly identical in form and composition to the lithographs described above; others show scenes of farewell between wives and uniformed husbands setting out for the front.[47]

Illustrations of wives, sisters, and mothers performing household tasks provide a stark contrast to those of soldiers laboring on the battlefield—confirming William F. Thompson's assertion that "women were expected to help the Union only in ways that did not compromise their femininity."[48] In one example, the female subject works a needle and thread alongside the caption "Our hearts are with our brothers in the field" or simply "Our hearts are with them." In another, she washes clothes while wondering about her "boys gone to the war" and whether "they [her boys? the army?] would take me." In yet another, a woman hard at work in her kitchen declares, "If I cannot fight, I can feed those who do" (fig. 4.2). The scene celebrates women's desire to contribute to the war effort,

If I cannot fight, I can
feed those who do.

Figure 4.2: *If I Cannot Fight, I Can Feed Those Who Do.* Illustrated Civil War envelope, n.d. Courtesy of the American Antiquarian Society.

but it also circumscribes the limits of those contributions along conventional gender lines.

Collectively, these artifacts juxtapose types and sites of citizenship—home and battlefield, family and military, husband and wife, male and female. Lithographs and stationery depicting "the soldier's dream" preserve the separation of spheres by representing simultaneous narratives: the bold and brave husband on the warfront, the dainty and devoted wife on the homefront.[49] Their romanticized depictions of women—passive, pretty, and laboring at feminine tasks—evoke a fantasy of domesticity that disavows the rigorous, public, often belligerent actions of women involved in the temperance and abolition movements during the antebellum period. In other words, they represent what Simone de Beauvoir terms the patriarchal "myth of woman," which "claims woman for hearth and home [and] defines her as sentiment, inwardness, immanence."[50] The soldier's dream, in particular, employs this strategy. A dream, as a dramaturgical device (in literature and visual art as well as drama), communicates something to or about the subject; it serves as an idealizing space, at once virtual and visionary. Sometimes, dreams reveal keenly felt yet unattainable desires. Instead of a fragment or ferment of imagination, on some level the soldier's dream represents his hope for a peaceful and proper abode.

In a way, these tidy depictions of men and women in their correct roles, spaces, and places seem to be part of a cultural cover-up. For one, they deny the existence of any conflict over what, precisely, a *true woman* might be. The ideal of true womanhood was not a universal or unilateral concept; it was a site of theoretical struggle. These images of tough men and faithful women obscure—even erase—the controversial activities of female reformers prior to the Civil War, which had fostered fears and anxieties about "monstrous women." Perhaps the soldier's dream was, in part, a dream of postwar normalcy: average men living normal lives with normal wives.

Furthermore, these glorified representations resemble what Robert Bogdan calls the "aggrandized mode" in nineteenth-century freak shows. The notion of a *true woman,* in itself, is a kind of aggrandizement: different constituencies constructed her through the same tactics used by platform-show producers when they put extraordinary individuals on display. According to Bogdan, in aggrandized presentations of unusual people, "One, some, or all of the following attributes were fabricated, elevated or exaggerated, and then flaunted: social position, achievements, talents, family, and physiology."[51] I am not suggesting that artists and printers of patriotic iconography drew direct inspiration from freak shows, but there are intriguing parallels in technique. As de Beauvoir famously argues in *The Second Sex,* "one is not born, but rather becomes, a woman." Women are not born, but rather made—not unlike freaks.[52]

The Citizen-Soldier Is the One Who Gets the Vote

The strict division of spheres in these images may be further contextualized by examining postwar discourse conjoining electoral privileges and military service. As Kerber observes, in the United States "the association between soldiering and entitlement runs very deep."[53] And indeed, the sacrifices made by citizen-soldiers not only inspired an unprecedented pension program for veterans and widows after the Civil War but also buttressed efforts to give the vote to African American men.[54] In her study *Protecting Soldiers and Mothers: The Political Origins of Social Policy in the United States,* Theda Skocpol point outs that in contrast to today's entitlement programs, which are usually designated for the profoundly poor or needy, postwar pensions singled out "a group that ought to be generously and constantly repaid by the nation for their sacrifices" who "by their own choices and efforts as young men had *earned aid.*"[55] In other words, public assistance served as a form of compensation for citizen-soldiers who had contributed labor to the Union cause. Therefore, it is not altogether surprising that, during Reconstruction, opponents of universal suffrage often cited women's lack of military service as a reason to withhold the vote from them—especially as the nation inched toward giving the vote to African American men.[56] This tactic was deployed in debates about suffrage long before the war; for instance, a writer in the *New York Herald* reporting on the 1848 Seneca Falls women's rights convention sarcastically quipped that women should also be granted the "right" to fight.[57] After the war, comments like this appeared even more frequently in newspapers, pamphlets, orations, and other texts.

Keenly aware that such associations excluded women from enfranchisement, Parker Pillsbury sternly criticized the tendency to tie the vote to military service in his speech before the AERA in New York on May 9, 1867 (later published as a pamphlet, *The Mortality of Nations*). Pillsbury insisted, "The right of the black man to a voice in the government was not earned at Olustee or Port Hudson. It was his when life began, not when life was paid for it under the battle-axe of war." He implores,

> Must a brave soldier fight and bleed for the government, and, pruned of limbs, plucked of eyes, and scarred all over with the lead and iron hail of war—must he now hobble on his crutches up to a Republican, Democratic, yea, and a Christian throne, and beg the boon of the ballot in that government, in defense of which he periled all, and lost all but bare life and breath, only because an African instead of a more indulgent man looked upon him or his ancestors in their allotment of life?[58]

In this manner, Pillsbury underscored the laudable military service of men of color, while also insisting that women were entitled to the vote as well, despite their absence on the field. Further questioning this thread in the suffrage conversation, he insisted that active participation in government was a god-given right, as opposed to a "gift" doled out by privileged white men. Similarly, George William Curtis, in his remarks supporting women's suffrage at the Constitutional Convention of New York on July 19, 1867 (published later by the AERA under the title *Equal Rights for Women*), invoked popular wartime images of both the soldier's farewell and his dream of home: "Those homes were both the inspiration and the consolation of the field. They nerved the arm that struck for them. When the son and the husband fell in the wild storm of battle, the brave woman-heart broke in silence, but their busy fingers did not falter. . . . There are thousands and thousands of these women who ask for a voice in the government they have so defended. Shall we refuse them?"[59] Curtis invokes these sentimental visions to assert that women's war-work was no less worthy than men's.

More evidence of the pressure exerted by the citizen-soldier ideal can be found in *History of Woman Suffrage* (1882) edited by Stanton, Anthony, and Gage. Published more than a decade after the Reconstruction amendments, the *History* reveals that many of the rhetorical tropes circulating in the late 1860s continued to resonate years later. For example, the opening chapter of the second volume (covering 1861 to 1876) is titled "Woman's Patriotism in the War." It chronicles the burdens endured by women during the conflict—burdens that were, the authors assert, just as heavy as those borne by men. The vision of the American soldier haunts the narrative from the outset.

> While he buckled on his knapsack and marched forth to conquer the enemy, she planned the campaigns which brought the nation victory; fought in the ranks when she could do so without detection; inspired the sanitary commission; gathered needed supplies for the grand army; provided nurses for the hospitals; comforted the sick; smoothed the pillows of the dying; inscribed the last messages of love to those far away; and marked the resting-places where brave men fell.

The writers go on to discuss women who provided service during the war, including those who ventured, in disguise, onto the battlefield. In one lengthy footnote, no fewer than fifteen women soldiers are mentioned and briefly described, especially the physical injuries they suffered—as if to suggest that wounds are the best test of a soldier's mettle. Alluding to the question of whether African American men earned the vote by serving in the military, the authors assert, "When in the enfranchisement of the black man [women] saw another ignorant class of voters placed above their heads, . . . and demanded for the protection of themselves and children, that woman's . . . opinions in public affairs be expressed by the ballot, they were coolly told that the black man had earned the right to vote, that he had fought and bled for his country!"[60]

The notion that citizen-soldiers deserved respect and support helped to justify the enfranchisement of African American men despite rampant racist prejudice both during and after the war. This work commenced with the Emancipation Proclamation of 1863, when Abraham Lincoln tied military service to liberty in his announcement that slaves would be "received into the armed service of the United States to garrison forts, positions, stations, and other places, and to man vessels of all sorts in said service."[61] As Kerber notes,

> The Emancipation Proclamation itself merged emancipation and arms bearing, welcoming into the armed service of the United States the people whom Lincoln declared free. For enslaved blacks, arms-bearing for the Union was an experience that came before citizenship and helped to set the terms for it. Black men risked their lives for the Union long before the Thirteenth Amendment, and the claim that they had bought their rights with their blood suffused constitutional debate and also the discourse of Reconstruction.[62]

Although the Union desperately needed to increase and expand its military regiments during the war, Northerners were nevertheless ambivalent about black men's participation in combat; newspapers and patriotic stationery from the war period exhibit caricatures of slaves on the battlefield that often border on the grotesque[63] (fig. 4.3).

However, as the conflict continued, sympathetic depictions of African Americans appeared with more frequency. They make up a relatively small subset of popular iconography, but such images offered a striking contrast to the comic illustrations of slaves that generally dominated US visual and theatrical culture, especially in minstrelsy and in cultural products capitalizing on minstrelsy's tropes and stereotypes. Some illustrations showed slaves assisting the Union military, gathering intelligence, conducting reconnaissance, or caring for injured soldiers.[64] Others depicted dignified black soldiers in uniform and bearing arms. A lithograph portrait of Martin R. Delany, the first African American awarded the rank of major, is a case in point. The image has been cited as an example of how, in Cullen's words, "the Civil War did indeed mark a watershed for black manhood."[65] In it, Delany adopts the pose and posture of famous white officers who appeared in popular prints, such as George B. McClellan and Ephraim Elmer Ellsworth. Another intriguing portrayal of a black citizen-soldier appeared in *Harper's Weekly* on April 22, 1865, less than two weeks after General Robert E. Lee surrendered to Union forces in Appomattox, Virginia. In this illustration, a white veteran and a black veteran face each other as equals, shaking hands. Both of them have lost a leg in combat, so they stand with the aid of crutches (fig. 4.4). Titled "A Man Knows a Man," the picture suggests that by becoming a soldier, the slave—or, the "man that was

368
FRANK LESLIE'S ILLUSTRATED NEWSPAPER.
[OCT. 26, 1861.
DARK ARTILLERY; OR, HOW TO MAKE THE CONTRABANDS USEFUL.

Figure 4.3: "Dark Artillery; or, How to Make the Contrabands Useful." *Frank Leslie's Illustrated,* October 26, 1861, 368. Courtesy of the American Antiquarian Society.

a thing," to invoke both Douglass and Stowe—has been transformed, at last, into a man. The caption reads, "Give me your hand, Comrade! We have each lost a Leg for the good cause; but, thank God, we never lost Heart." It is unclear who is addressing whom—who is the speaker, and who is the comrade?—yet this ambiguity in the text, a marked departure from the legibility of the image, may be part of the point. Representations like these reflect a subtle shift (if not a total transformation) of white perceptions and constructions of black men, even though racial relations remained deeply troubled.

Of course, the two men in this image have something in common with Snorkey as well: amputated limbs. During the war and for decades afterward, depictions of veterans' maimed bodies circulated widely in pictures and print. Images of citizen-soldiers whose bodies had been transformed within the crucible of war inspired considerable public interest. An absent body part rendered a fighting man's war experiences visible, serving as a prominent and potent reminder of his sacrifices. When viewed within this context, Snorkey's missing arm may be understood as what Jennifer Putzi terms an "identifying mark": a physical scar that serves as a dense, complicated site of cultural meaning.[66]

A MAN KNOWS A MAN
"Give me your hand, Comrade! We have each lost a LEG for the good cause; but, thank GOD, we never lost HEART."

Figure 4.4: "A Man Knows a Man." *Harper's Weekly,* April 22, 1865. The caption reads, "Give me your hand, Comrade! We have each lost a Leg for the good cause; but, thank God, we never lost Heart." Courtesy of the American Antiquarian Society.

At first glance, the Civil War amputee might seem "unmanned"—someone in need of assistance, help, even (in Snorkey's case) rescue. But as Megan Kate Nelson observes, diverse interpretations of veterans' identifying marks circulated in popular culture by way of texts and images. The "Empty Sleeve" narrative, which celebrated soldiers' bravery in battle, became prevalent in both Northern and Southern states, "fram[ing] war wounds as proof of manly bravery, patriotism, and noble suffering." Simultaneously, the narrative of the "Incomplete Man" articulated "concerns about the masculinity of veterans, the role of women in shoring up that masculinity, and the return to 'normalcy' at home." Both during and after the Civil War, these contrasting ideas competed for attention in the public imagination, deeply informing the ways that Americans viewed disabled veterans.[67]

Many amputees, as well as the artists and writers who depicted and discussed them, described their war wounds as proof of their masculinity. As Frances Clarke has shown, veterans who wrote about their experiences in postbellum penmanship competitions characterized their injuries as badges of honor and "firm proof of their manhood." Their missing limbs evidenced not only their loyalty to the Union but also their hardiness, tenacity, and will to survive. ("A Man Knows a Man," the title of the aforementioned *Harper's* illustration, conveys this sentiment.) Henry C. Allen, a mechanic who served in the Civil War, described his amputation as an "honorable scar" and explained, "I wanted to bring a mark home with me to show that I had been w[h]ere danger came near me. I have that mark, and so conspicuous, that all can see it. I am proud of it. No man can say, that Allen was a coward and hid from danger."[68] Putzi, in her analysis of the depiction of disabled soldiers in mid-nineteenth-century American fiction, arrives at a similar conclusion regarding the cultural meaning of war injuries.

> The marked body of the white soldier has the potential to be reconfigured as a testimony to both the experience of fighting in battle and the personal characteristics that are said to develop as a result of such experience—strength, honor, bravery. Perhaps the more drastically "marked" the soldier's body, the better—hence the positive depictions of amputees. Above all, the wounded is not a victim.[69]

In other words, war amputees saw themselves, and were seen by others, as fighters rather than victims. This suggests that in the eyes of some audience members, especially those attuned to the "Empty Sleeve" narrative, Snorkey was not necessarily an emasculated figure. Rather than dismantling his masculinity, his missing arm underscored it.

However, other spectators—steeped in the idea that the disabled veteran was an "Incomplete Man"—may have viewed Snorkey in a different light. Ironically, the narrative of the incomplete man was partly constituted through portrayals of American women who had taken on new responsibilities at home and in their communities while men labored on the battlefield. Nelson's discussion of an 1863 cartoon published in a Northern newspaper highlights how women were elevated, perhaps even liberated, within this narrative of the emasculated hero. In the cartoon, a woman strolls with a man dressed in soldierly garb; her arm is draped around the waist of her suitor. He cannot reciprocate the affectionate gesture because both of his arms are missing—a double casualty of war. The caption reads, "This may seem very bold, and all that sort of thing, on Julia's part; but he cannot put his arm around HER waist—and something has to be done, you know." In her analysis of this illustration, Nelson writes, "Such scenes of successful courtship, as much as they affirmed amputees' masculinity, also betray an anxiety about the more powerful role of women within the family as a result of the wartime destruction of male bodies."[70] The tenderness, compassion, and subtle humor of the image paradoxically underscore and underplay the dilemma at its heart: disabled men returning from the war now had to rely on women—emboldened by circumstances and necessity (like Laura in *Under the Gaslight*)—to perform the male's part.

In sum, it seems likely that different audience members saw different degrees of manhood in Snorkey. But in many respects, his relative manliness is beside the point. In Daly's railroad rescue, spectators saw a citizen-soldier—the iconic American figure who had just saved the Union—being saved by a woman. If spectators believed that Snorkey was an "Incomplete Man," then they probably viewed Laura as one of the many American women who had become independent and brave when disabled men came into their lives. If, on the other hand, the audience regarded Snorkey as a courageous veteran with an "Empty Sleeve," a man who deserved deep admiration and respect, then Laura became an even greater hero upon saving him. The line "And these are the women who ain't to have the vote" seems all the more significant in light of postwar assertions that the sacrifices made by soldiers, both black and white, entitled them to electoral privileges. Snorkey's missing arm (likely rendered with some awkwardness by the actor, who had to camouflage his intact body part while portraying the character) is a constant reminder of that sacrifice. Even though he protected women and children while fighting in the war, it is a woman who rescues him now. Laura returns the favor and repays the debt by rising to the occasion in the face of crisis.

Laura and "The Axe! The Axe!"

In the prelude to Daly's railroad sequence, the signalman informs Laura that the last train of the day has already come and gone. He then agrees to lock her in the station shed overnight, apologizing that he must crowd her in with several packages dropped off by the train she missed. Loading the goods into the shed, he inventories them as follows: "hoes, shovels, mowing machines, and what is this—axes. Yes, a bundle of axes. If the Superintendent finds me out, I'll ask him if he was afraid you'd run off with these. (*Laughs.*)" (41). The signalman's joke suggests that Americans considered the idea of a woman wielding an axe to be ridiculous. Therefore, Laura's use of an axe to break out of the shed may have been as spectacular, in its way, as the rushing locomotive. Ronald Jager asserts that nineteenth-century America was "a culture aware and fond of its love affair with the felling axe as a noble national weapon."[71] For many, the single-bit balanced axe that eventually came to be called the "American axe" represented the ingenuity, creativity, and fortitude of those populating the continent. Although the political and cultural nuances of the American axe have been lost to us over time, reports about the initial run of *Under the Gaslight* suggest that spectators were well attuned to them. The mythology coalescing around this tool—which incorporated ideas of nationalism and imperialism as well as gender—added both comedy and clout to Laura's sensational exertions.

It is unknown precisely when, where, and how the American axe first emerged, but the earliest archaeological specimen dates to the Revolutionary era. During the colonial period, the most commonly used implement for felling trees was the British axe, which featured a short, straight handle positioned toward the blunt end of a thick blade. At some point, American colonists enhanced this model by adding a longer, curved handle, which increased its momentum and therefore its efficiency. The handle also shifted toward the center of the blade, giving it more balance and improving the accuracy of the logger's swing. Finally, the thickness of the iron wedge was reduced, allowing for a deeper cut. Because the continent's thickly forested land had to be cleared for farming, the new axe became both a necessity and a source of pride. Its designation as the "American" axe was the first step toward claiming it as a native treasure. This sentiment also manifested in the practice of naming axe patterns after specific regions (the Connecticut, the Wisconsin, and so forth).[72]

During the mid-nineteenth century, the American axe appeared repeatedly in print and pictorial media as a nationalist symbol. In 1851, a writer in *The Cultivator* of Albany proclaimed, "It is a maxim that 'necessity is the parent of invention;' and the great use required of the ax in this country, may have been the chief cause of its improvement; at any rate we believe it may be said that the 'American ax' has reached a perfection unknown in the old world." Ten years later, a writer in *Vanity Fair* cited the differences between British and American axes as a way to compare the efficiency of the two nations. Responding to a claim in the London *Times* that the British axe was better, he sardonically wrote,

> Many of our readers, probably, have never seen a British axe. . . . It takes two men so long to cut down a tree with one of these tools, that the birds are quite sarcastic about it. A crow has been known to build her nest in a tree after the first blow of the hatchet had fallen upon it; do up her incubation, hatch and educate her family, and soar jubilant away with them just as the tree began to fall . . . We defy the *Times* to have a Crow over the American axe. If the *Times* tries that little game, we shall only say that It, like the British axe, is a clumsy tool in the hands of a heavy party, unaccustomed to making clear tracks through a wood.

In 1862, the *New England Farmer* in Boston similarly portrayed the American axe as a sign of Western progress: "To the American *axe* there is nothing superior, and we may regard it as the emblem of the civilization of the western hemisphere."[73]

At the same time, American painters creating artworks for elite consumers depicted the tool ambivalently. Barbara Novak asserts that the axe is a paradoxical symbol in their work: "National identity is constructed and threatened by the double-edged symbol of progress, the axe that destroys and builds, builds and destroys."[74] Early paintings, such as the over-mantel painting of the Lazarus Hathaway House in Paris Hill, Maine (ca. 1805), depict deforestation positively. It shows several men felling trees and turning forest into usable land; their tools exhibit the signature characteristics of the American axe. According to Gary Kulik, "there is no ambivalence [in the painting]. This is a forceful and prideful image, representing an act played out daily as forests gave way in the new nation."[75] But later works, most notably the landscapes of Thomas Cole, seem more troubled by what a man can do with his axe. In Cole's *River in the Catskills* (1843), the axe and the railroad train combine in an unsettling image that Alan Wallach describes as "antipastoral." A man holding an axe stands in the foreground of the painting, surrounded by severed tree branches. His back is to the viewer as he watches a train in the distance, as if he is looking toward an industrialized future that his axe is helping to make possible. Cole seems to suggest that the logger must, in the words of Tony Tanner, "deface and then destroy" the land. Nevertheless, the artist's critique of such activity is subtle, at best; it is unlikely that buyers of paintings at this time would have welcomed a critical reading of railroads and other symbols of American progress, as Wallach points out.[76]

Despite variations in the ways that writers and artists deployed the American axe, its gender associations remained consistent. From a strictly material standpoint, the shape of the blade made it heavier than its European counterpart, and demanded quite a lot of strength to use. In contrast to the practice of girdling, felling trees with an axe required significant effort and toil. The emergence of the professional logger during the mid-nineteenth century further served to masculinize the American axe. As the country's borders stretched across the continent, professional axemen made careers out of forest-clearing. The grueling logger was eventually mythologized in the figure of Paul Bunyan, an icon of rugged manhood. As Kulik writes, "If later folklore surrounding Paul Bunyan tells us anything, American farmers, and later lumbermen, came to revel in that toil and especially in their strength and skill with an axe as they cleared prodigious, even mythic, amounts of land." Indeed, Bunyan is the American axe personified: a virile, efficient, and pioneering man who penetrates and disciplines the virgin forests of an uncharted continent.[77]

At the dawn of the Civil War, the axe became strongly associated with a man who became the nation's leader and a public icon: Abraham Lincoln. During his 1860 presidential campaign, Lincoln was often called "The Rail-Splitter"—a nickname referring to his early experiences splitting wood, particularly fence rails, with his axe. Born to an agrarian family in Kentucky, Lincoln "had an axe put into his hands at once, and from that time within his twenty-third year, he was almost constantly handling that most useful instrument," according to his campaign autobiography.[78] Gary L. Bunker notes that the "Rail-Splitter" appellation invoked several nativist themes, including the toughness and determination required to tame the frontier, as well as the rigorous work ethic of the self-made man.[79] Illustrations and cartoons featuring Lincoln with axes and fence rails strengthened the connection between America's axe and America's top executive. A color lithograph titled *Trial by Battle*, published by E. B. & E. C. Kellogg in Connecticut around 1861, is one example (fig. 4.5). In this image, President Lincoln faces off with Jefferson Davis, the president of the Confederacy. An American axe—easily identifiable due to its curved poll—is in Lincoln's left hand, while he holds a sword in the other. Davis holds a sword and a handful of cotton. According to Harold Holzer, who briefly discusses *Trial by Battle* in his study of Lincoln and American visual culture, in this image the artist deliberately depicts Lincoln "with one of the symbolic props that had been employed in earlier campaign prints to help introduce him to the public: the tools of the railsplitter who had risen inspiringly from frontier obscurity to national fame."[80] Given the tool's nationalist associations, its appearance in *Trial by Battle* asserts Lincoln's position as the nation's leader: he who holds the axe is the true president.

Admirers and supporters celebrated the "The Rail-Splitter" by way of material culture as well. Axes he held and rails he split were treated reverently during his life and fetishized after his assassination. D. W. Bartlett, in his 1860 biography *Life and Public Services of Hon. Abraham Lincoln,* relates a story from a Chicago journal in which fence rails hewn by Lincoln were transformed into spectacle. At the 1860 Illinois State Republican Convention, a man from Macon County (where the young Lincoln once spent a season splitting rails) paraded through the hall carrying two fence rails adorned with patriotic decoration and a placard proclaiming, "Abraham Lincoln, The Rail Candidate for President in 1860. Two rails from a lot of 3,000 made in 1830, by Thos. Hanks and Abe Lincoln—whose father was the first pioneer of Macon County." Apparently, "The effect was electrical. . . . The cheers upon cheers which rent the air could have been heard all over the adjacent country."[81] Furthermore, the last axe Lincoln ever wielded in public was saved for future generations. A week before his assassination, the president spent the day shaking hands with 5,000 Civil War veterans who were recovering from injuries at a field hospital in City Point, Virginia. Responding to a suggestion by a member of the crowd, he demonstrated his stamina by picking up an axe and chopping wood for several minutes. He also used it during a spectacle of strength: holding it by the handle, he raised the axe slowly until it reached a right angle to his body. Through his performance, Lincoln transformed this workaday object into a celebrated relic. In early 2008, when archivists at the Lincoln Presidential Library and Museum uncovered this particular axe in its collection, Illinois State Historian Thomas Schwartz compared it to Lincoln's top hat—another iconic object housed at the library.[82]

In sum, by the time *Under the Gaslight* premiered in 1867, the axe was not merely a utilitarian tool but a potent symbol of masculinity and nationalism.

Figure 4.5: *Trial by Battle*. E. B. & E. C. Kellogg, ca. 1861 or 1862. Courtesy of the American Antiquarian Society.

These connotations—embodied most spectacularly by Lincoln himself—help to explain why the signalman in *Gaslight* laughs aloud at the thought of Laura's stealing an axe from the shed. When Laura hears the train coming and calls to Snorkey from the locked shed, he yells back, "Is there nothing in there?—no hammer?—no crowbar?" The script indicates that Laura experiences momentary paralysis before exclaiming, "The axe!!!" The destructive American axe contrasts markedly with the hammer or crowbar that Snorkey requests. "Cut the woodwork!" he cries, and the audience hears Laura's physical exertion as she makes a spectacular racket. Playing the hero's part, Laura "mutilates" the door. Snorkey's cries of "Courage!" that culminate in the exultant statement "That's a true woman!" reflect his faith in the heroine's ability to destroy the door and save him from imminent death (43). And yet, Laura's employment of this masculine tool constitutes yet another instance of how she is "out of place," bucking traditional ideas regarding the separation of spheres at a time when suffrage was on the public mind.

Reports of spectators' reactions to the railroad rescue suggest that the heroine's use of an axe was a spectacle in and of itself. Three anecdotes, all of which underscore the rowdy character of nineteenth-century theatergoing as well as melodrama's tendency to invite participation, suggest that audience members had the axe firmly in mind when Laura used it to rescue the soldier-in-distress.[83] Rose Eytinge, the actress who originally played Laura, mentions the axe in her autobiography. She dedicates a mere two pages to *Under the Gaslight,* despite the popularity of the drama, and admits that her recollection of the play is hazy at best. But for a variety of reasons, she vividly remembers the axe.

> I confess I do not remember the story [of the play]. I only remember that the situation of the piece is where I break down a door with an axe which I opportunely find, and rescue somebody who is lashed down on a railroad track, and that this "business" was preceded by my frantic exclamation, "The axe, the axe!" This exclamation became a sort of catchword, and [A. H.] Davenport [originator of the Ray Trafford role], who was an incorrigible guyer, used to serve it up to me on all possible and impossible occasions, with the result that there was a great deal too much giggling and guying during the performance.[84]

It is unclear here whether "The axe, the axe!" was a catchword of the cast or if spectators also picked it up. But an anecdote from the *Daily Alta California* in San Francisco regarding a production of *Gaslight* at the Metropolitan Theatre (featuring Charles Wheatleigh as Snorkey) suggests that the audience did, in fact, take up the chant.

> "Under the Gaslight" drew another crowded house last night, and the audience were as much impressed with the sensation in the fourth act as on its first production; true, there was no *suggestion from the gallery* to aid Laura Courtland to burst open the door by *telling her of the axe,* but there was many a fair lady in the dress-circle who felt like hurrying up the release of the one-armed hero before the train could run over him.[85]

Here, the reporter notes the *absence* of a response that had occurred during a previous performance: noisy theatergoers in the gallery telling Laura of the axe. It seems that Daly's careful dramaturgy inspired the audience to call out helpfully to the heroine, "The axe! The axe!" as Eytinge remembered (perhaps because the signalman had pointed out the axes while locking Laura into the shed). When Snorkey cries out to the heroine, "Is there nothing in there?—no hammer?—no crowbar?" the spectators knew to "suggest" the axe. Indeed, Laura's next line seems to anticipate this response from the audience: after a moment, she, too, calls out, "The axe!!!"—in acknowledgment, perhaps, of the audience's cries.

Possibly, "The axe!" chant became a ritual, an opportunity for exchange between stage and auditorium within the fluid, unruly environment of nineteenth-century theater.[86] However, I admit I might not have noticed this passing reference in the *Alta* had it not been for an anecdote that theater historian Marvin Carlson once shared with me about his experience playing Snorkey in a 1957 production of *Under the Gaslight* at the University of Kansas. He reports that during some performances, the audience shouted "The axe! The axe!" during the same moment. They echoed the enthusiastic calls of the play's original spectators, even though they were separated from them by nearly a century. Admittedly, the vocalizations of this mid-twentieth-century audience were somewhat different, in that they exhibited a cheerful irony. Nevertheless, these anecdotes by Eytinge, the *Alta* reporter, and Carlson indicate that Laura's use of an American axe was sometimes foregrounded by the spectators themselves—inspired by either Daly's astute playwriting or the scene's poetics of endangerment, or simply a collective playfulness.[87]

Dénouement: The Railroad Rescue Revised and Reprised

When Snorkey conveyed his amazement in 1867 that women like Laura "ain't to have the vote" when African American men were about to gain that right, audiences may very well have perceived an activist statement. As anxieties over the rights and privileges of US citizenship increased during the postbellum years, Stanton and her fellow activists decried the injustice of granting suffrage to all men while denying it to white, taxpaying, native-born women. Meanwhile, the icon of the citizen-soldier, freshly popularized in illustrated media during the war, haunted discussions about the "woman question" by implicitly justifying black veterans' right to vote. Nightly at the Worrell Sisters' Theatre, actor J. K. Mortimer fleshed out the disabled yet lauded Civil War combatant only to be rescued, ironically, by a woman. Laura's use of the axe compounded this role reversal: by 1867, the tool had amassed considerable sociocultural meaning, weighed down not only by its history as a nativist, masculine object but also by its strong association with President Lincoln. By picking it up, Laura embodied the steadfastness, self-reliance, and independence of true womanhood as defined by suffragists. Three decades later, temperance advocate Carry A. Nation would also wield an axe in her famous "hatchetations"—utilizing, consciously or unconsciously, this iconic object for her own activist spectacles.[88] Although we can never truly know whether audiences who witnessed Daly's sensation scene perceived it as a critique of current events, the railroad rescue does seem to reflect its historical moment: a time of conflict, confusion, mixed messages, and mixed feelings regarding race, gender, and citizenship in the wake of a devastating war.

As I have argued throughout this book, the ubiquity of the spectacular instant during the nineteenth century, especially in the context of reform, signals the appeal of spectacle during an era when greater discipline and semblances of "normalcy" were also actively sought. Spectacle's role in shaping American culture seems all the more evident in light of sensation scenes that were reprised or revised in other times and contexts. Arguably, the railroad rescue is the most vivid example of this. But the division of labor in Daly's original sequence tends to surprise a contemporary reader encountering *Under the Gaslight* for the first time. Today, it is the vision of a *woman* tied to the train tracks, saved by the hero, that circulates in the collective imagination—operating as a kind of visual shorthand for the melodramatic genre itself. Schneider suggests that by considering immaterial evidence (or "residues") of performance, we can "articulate the ways in which performance, less bound to the ocular, 'sounds' (or begins again and again, as [Gertrude] Stein would have it), differently, via itself as repetition—like a copy or perhaps more like a ritual—like an echo in the ears of a confidence keeper, an audience member, a witness."[89] Clearly, the image lodged in our minds today is a distorted echo, ritual, and residue of the premier spectacular instant, repeated and re-formed over time.

The woman tied to the tracks is a spectacle inviting curiosity and contempt if there ever was one—and not merely because of its campy disempowerment of the heroine. Like Jean Baudrillard's simulacrum, it has no clearly identifiable progenitor; it is hyperreal, "generat[ed] by models of a real without origin or originality."

> it is the reflection of a profound reality;
> it masks and denatures a profound reality;
> it masks the *absence* of a profound reality;
> it has no relation to any reality whatsoever: it is its own pure simulacrum.[90]

The persistence of the woman-tied-to-the-tracks simulacrum, I argue, reveals the potency of Daly's rescue as originally conceived. It seems that at some point, America could no longer abide the spectacle of a woman rescuing a man, and everything that might mean. But it is not altogether clear when or how the scene's gender politics were "corrected." Although Boucicault's imitation of the scene in *After Dark* (1868) transformed Daly's heroine into a hero, the victim on the tracks was still a man.[91] Even in film serials from the early twentieth century, female protagonists who are tied to the railroad ties in *What Happened to Mary* (1912–13), *The Perils of Pauline* (1914), and *The Hazards of Helen* (1914–17) save themselves; they rarely need a rescuer, male or otherwise.[92] The modification had certainly occurred by the mid-twentieth century. For example, in the scenario that serves as the opening sequence of the *The Dudley Do-Right Show* (1969–70), Dudley Do-Right, a Canadian Mountie, arrives on horseback to save the writhing, wiggling Nell Fenwick from the train tracks. Of course, this animated cartoon series—with its tinny piano soundtrack and exaggerated stereotypes—is a proud parody of melodrama; as such, it derives its humor from the spectator's recognition of stock characters and familiar scenes. But the curious history of the railroad rescue suggests that even this antecedent is a simulacrum, inspired by other flawed fragments adrift in the public imagination.

If the iconic damsel-in-distress who struggles and awaits rescue is, to quote Baudrillard again, "no longer a question of imitation, nor duplication, nor even parody" but rather "a question of substituting signs of the real for the real," then her performative reiteration is historically significant.[93] She may have no material referent in the archive, but her endurance reveals the radical politics of her prototype. Although she exists now mainly as the super-sign of melodrama, she did have a forebear in Laura. The "true woman" that Laura represents was dramatically repressed and upended when she was transformed from savior to victim. As a result, the simulacrum inspires for me more questions than conclusions. Is it a reaction to or an antidote for the empowered heroines that appeared in turn-of-the-century melodramas and films, which Ben Singer examines at some length in *Melodrama and Modernity*? Was Laura troubling, culturally speaking, because she was *not* overtly aberrant, performing her role in a dress rather than trousers? (During the nineteenth century, "Representative cross-dressed theatrical women implied through their performance that power was not an essentially male privilege, and that gender was as artificial as the painted backdrop behind them," Elizabeth Reitz Mullenix asserts.)[94] And yet, the actress in drag is still a fiction, a stunt; Laura is a woman drawn from life, infused with Daly's signature realism: possible/plausible/probable. Is this why she had to be tied to the tracks, over the course of time and history? Is this why she had to take Snorkey's place?

As much as I would like to offer answers to these questions, provisional or otherwise, I will conclude instead by offering an anecdote of my own that, I think, underscores the peculiar significance of Daly's railroad rescue and its perseverance within US popular culture. While I was researching the history of the American axe, I happened across a televised rerun of James Cameron's cinematic melodrama *Titanic,* a film that broke worldwide box office records upon its release in 1997. Like *Under the Gaslight,* it is a story about the personal empowerment and liberation of a bourgeois woman. At a crucial moment, the heroine Rose (portrayed by Kate Winslet) abandons her spot in a lifeboat in order to seek out her hero, Jack (played by Leonardo DiCaprio), who has been handcuffed to a pipe in the bowels of the ship. Desperate to free him, Rose runs for help, but every man she encounters turns out to be a selfish coward, fleeing the rising water. Then suddenly, she sees (what else?) an axe. Despite her lack of strength and skill, she destroys Jack's handcuffs with one perfectly placed blow. Seeing this sensation anew—because, like so many others, I had already seen it before—I realized, immediately and viscerally, that this spectacular instant from a modern melodrama was yet another testament to the perpetual power, appeal, and political immanence of the sensation scene in American culture.

Afterword
Our Sensations, Our Heroes, Our Freaks

The spectator feels at home nowhere, for the spectacle is everywhere.

—GUY DEBORD, *THE SOCIETY OF THE SPECTACLE*[1]

This study explores how US citizens saw themselves and their world at pivotal moments during the nineteenth century, and how acts of seeing facilitated the circulation of ideas. A unique mode of communication employed by a wide range of producers, spectacle served as a conduit through which Americans engaged texts and products. Hoping to teach citizens correct and moral ways of living, reformers harnessed spectacle to advance their causes; at the same time, playwrights and theater managers looked to the hot topics of temperance, abolition, and women's suffrage for provocative source material. The ubiquity of sensational images in both theatrical performance and reform propaganda suggests there was some ambivalence about the ascendancy of the norm and the mandate for respectability during this century. The enactment of the spectacular instant in various media reveals a complex and paradoxical relationship between normalcy and excess, conformity and individuality, objectivity and subjectivity.

My fascination with the *opsis*-centricity of melodrama and my questions about the popularity of sensation scenes inspired me to investigate how readers and audiences developed viewing practices—ways of seeing—that constituted, for them, a kind of visual literacy. But one of the more surprising outcomes of this project is how it has transformed *my* way of seeing. As I learned more about the nineteenth-century obsession with spectacle, I began viewing today's America through a different lens. To my eye, the *delirium tremens*, Eliza's flight, and the railroad rescue are still everywhere, springing up in all sorts of places.

Sometimes, I see sensation scenes that are still intact (more or less), such as the blackface parody of Eliza's escape in the Mighty Mouse cartoon *Eliza on the Ice* (1944), or Will Smith's sloppy-but-successful rescue of Jason Bateman from an oncoming train in the summer blockbuster *Hancock* (2008), or the music video for the hit song "Mean" (2010), in which pop country singer Taylor Swift is tied to the railroad tracks (fig. 0.1). In other instances, I see a single element extracted from a canonical scenario—like the heroine's use of an axe in *Titanic* (1997), which seems haunted, somehow, by a long lineage of axe-wielding women, both fictional and factual: Laura Courtland begets Carry A. Nation begets Rose DeWitt Bukater.

Sensation scenes amuse and thrill, invigorating our senses and providing pleasant shocks of surprise and recognition. But entertainment is neither their only value nor their exclusive utility. In its classic form, the melodramatic sensation scene constitutes the best or worst moment in a character's life; as such, it instructs spectators how to behave during the best and the worst moments of their own lives. I venture that both the content and the dramaturgy of these sequences have become so embedded in the public imagination that they continue to serve a didactic function, teaching audiences how to be proper men, proper women, proper Americans. As relics of a prior but persistent visual vernacular, they implicitly train us how to be respectable denizens of the collective we.

In the twenty-first century, new media technologies have elevated the sensation scene to a new level, with actual people and real-life events transforming into spectacle—sometimes circulating so vigorously that they approach the mythic. Like their theatrical predecessors, these contemporary sensation scenes assault broad swaths of mesmerized, impressionable audiences. Even the nineteenth-century freak show seems to live on, in a subtle and insidious way, in broadcast news programs and so-called "reality TV" shows. We still want to see sensation, and cultural producers are still eager to profit from that desire.

Admittedly, the following observations about the enduring popularity of sensation scenes are speculative rather than conclusive. Nevertheless, they foreground issues and questions that deserve more investigation. Does spectacle still function as "a complex interplay of narrative and picture"?[2] What kind of cultural work occurs when, for example, an emergency water landing by an airplane pilot is reproduced to such an extent that it becomes spectacle, or a man who rescued someone from the subway tracks is paraded before the public, or an unemployed single mother of octuplets is transformed into a freak? How do these spectacles reflect, generate, or compose a contemporary expression of American reform culture?

Our Sensations

On January 15, 2009, US Airways Flight 1549 departed from New York City's LaGuardia Airport and began heading to Charlotte, North Carolina. Just a few minutes after takeoff, the plane struck a flock of geese, which caused a total engine failure. Knowing that a crash was imminent, the captain, Chesley B. Sullenberger III, made a quick decision to ditch the plane in the Hudson River along the west side of Manhattan rather than attempt an emergency landing at an airfield in New Jersey. Against all odds and expectations, Sullenberger was successful. All 155 passengers and crew survived, evacuating onto the wings and inflatable slides, where they were rescued by nearby watercraft (fig. A.1). David Paterson, then governor of New York, gave the incident a name: "a miracle on the Hudson." Almost immediately, this phrase began appearing in articles, broadcast news segments, and photo captions.

Images of the episode quickly became ubiquitous in the mainstream media as well as Internet collectives—Facebook, Flickr, Twitter, YouTube, blogs—maintained by people conventionally considered consumers, not producers. Jay Rosen calls this sprawling, amorphous, powerful community "the people formerly known as the audience." He observes that the availability of free or low-cost photography and communication technologies have democratized information to such an extent that twenty-first-century audiences are able to participate in the circulation of images and ideas more than ever before. As a result, they exert substantial influence on the framing and distribution of knowledge.

> Think of passengers on your ship who got a boat of their own. The writing readers. The viewers who picked up a camera. The formerly atomized listeners who with modest effort can connect with each other and gain the means to speak—to the world, as it were. . . . The people formerly known as the audience are those who were on the receiving end of a media system that ran one way . . . and who today are not in a situation like that at all.[3]

In effect, today's audiences are thoroughly involved in the reprise, recycling,

Figure A.1: The crash landing of US Airways Flight 1549 (2009). A bystander, Gregory Lam Pak Ng, took this photo moments after the crash and uploaded it to a photo-sharing website; the image began circulating worldwide when the Associated Press picked it up. Courtesy of the photographer.

and revision of sensational scenes. The transformation of Sullenberger's water landing (an incident) into "The Miracle on the Hudson" (a spectacle) is exemplary of this phenomenon. In a way, spectators are embedded in the formulation "Miracle on the Hudson" itself: a scene so extraordinary that it was not to be believed, except it was seen. Bystanders on bridges and riverbanks were the first to circulate reports via SMS messages, camera-equipped cellular phones, and social-networking websites. The involvement of the audience in the production, interpretation, and reception of the image increased its sense of scale, intensity, and excess, elevating the event into spectacle and blurring the line between record and representation, fact and fiction, real and unreal.

Our Heroes

The story of US Airways Flight 1549 epitomizes how real-life spectacles today are, in many respects, cocreated by audiences and producers. But another fascinating aspect of this event is how, after its spectacularization, it became associated with cultural ideals—in particular, that familiar melodramatic archetype, the hero. As images of the crashed airplane became a source of public obsession, so too did Sullenberger, who seemed unflappable in the face of disaster, and whose courage and leadership resulted in zero loss of life. He perfectly performed his role as pilot, exhibiting considerable technical skill in landing the plane safely; his performance was also affectively appropriate, since he remained calm and collected for the duration of the emergency. An exemplary captain, he was willing to put his passengers' safety before his own and, if necessary, go down with the ship (he checked the cabin twice for stray passengers before finally escaping the aircraft himself). These praiseworthy traits and actions received extensive attention in reports about the crash. Mayor Michael Bloomberg announced his intention to give the aviator a key to New York City because he had "inspired people around the city and millions more around the world." In the *Daily News,* Nancy Dillon called Sullenberger "a freshly minted legend" with "new superhero status," and reported that Governor Paterson had received a substantial donation to commission a statue of the pilot.[4] Yet, in stark contrast to the hypervisibility of his plane in the media, Sullenberger proved elusive, rendering himself invisible to the public eye—in part due to the requisite investigation by the National Transportation Safety Board; in part because, according to his friends and family, he was reluctant to be the center of attention. Testimonies about his humility contributed to his profile as a great American hero, a persona sculpted not by "Sully" himself, but by an admiring, fascinated public.

Most interesting of all is how readers and spectators saw Sullenberger and his Miracle on the Hudson through the lens of their historical moment. Sullenberger's spectacular deed occurred several months into a crisis that many eventually dubbed the Great Recession: a massive contraction in the global economy, caused in large part by risky lending practices and a bubble in the housing market, which began to be felt worldwide in 2008. In the months prior to this airplane crash, Americans watched a series of financial crashes, including the failure of the venerable Lehman Brothers banking firm; the government's bailout of corporations deemed "too big to fail," including the insurer American International Group, to the tune of hundreds of billions in public funds; and a dramatic increase in unemployment, with 2.6 million jobs lost in 2008, more than any other year since World War II. Almost $11 trillion in household wealth simply evaporated—the result of not only property foreclosures but also losses in personal investment accounts and retirement funds decimated by declines in the stock market.[5]

The sensational story of Flight 1549 punctured, for a moment, the disquiet and apprehension that had gripped the nation since the onset of the crisis. Ray Rivera reflected on this curious confluence of events in the *New York Times:* "Captain Sullenberger's efforts . . . emerged as singularly selfless leadership of a sort that seemed so removed from things like Ponzi schemes and subprime mortgages, corporate bailouts and deflected blame." Temporarily interrupting the relentless flow of news about the economic apocalypse, here was a miracle staged not by God but by Captain Sullenberger, whose valor and bravery immediately captured the collective imagination. Because the event occurred less than a week before the inauguration of the first African American president, Barack Obama (who many hoped would navigate the nation through financial peril), some commentators drew parallels between the captain and the president-elect; as a headline in the *Daily News* declared, everyone seemed to be "Praying Our New 'Pilot' Can Land Crisis as Safely."[6]

Like the breathlessly labeled Miracle on the Hudson, the nineteenth-century sensation scenes I investigate in this book became popular during moments of great national anxiety. In *The Drunkard,* Middleton suffered from the *delirium tremens* when a desire for stability and respectability obsessed men of every station. Audiences of *Uncle Tom's Cabin* cheered the runaway slaves Eliza and George when the excesses of the Fugitive Slave Act and the concomitant imminence of war were very much on the public mind. In *Under the Gaslight,* Laura saved a war veteran tied to the railroad tracks as the nation stood perched on the verge of incredible change: African American men, including those who had fought bravely in the Civil War, would soon become voters. In early 2009, US citizens worried about the elusiveness of the American dream, the disappearance of decadence, and the fragility of their class status; and they eagerly embraced Sullenberger as a selfless hero in a world overrun by selfish villains.

Another aspect of this story illuminates the didactic power of sensation scenes, both fictional and actual. On the surface, sensation scenes may seem devoid of cultural usefulness. But what if, through the power of repetition, they shape and train a citizenry? Heroes are often essentialized. For better or worse, many Americans believe that a person is born with a natural proclivity for doing good, that courage and derring-do are products of genetic inheritance. But heroes have a cultural inheritance, too. They are not born, but rather made—and spectacle plays a vital role in that making. Rivera, offering another astute observation about Sullenberger, writes, "Heroes are often born in an instant, the split second it takes to recognize a pending disaster and react, the blink of an eye it takes a Wesley Autrey to throw himself under a subway train to save a man fallen on the tracks."

Rivera's invocation here of another citizen-hero, Wesley Autrey, is significant. Two years prior to Sullenberger's water landing, Autrey, a construction worker and navy veteran, jumped into the path of a New York City subway train to assist Cameron Hollopeter, a film student who fell to the tracks while suffering from an epileptic seizure. Thanks to Autrey, Hollopeter survived. Among other accolades and acknowledgments, Autrey was awarded the Bronze Medallion, the city's highest award for citizenship; received multiple invitations to appear on television talk shows; and was offered gifts and money from admirers, including billionaire Donald Trump. Is it mere coincidence that, structurally and dramaturgically, Autrey's rescue mimicked the railroad sensation in *Under the Gaslight*—a scenario so unmoored from its source text that it is barely recognizable, now, as theater? In all likelihood, Autrey had never encountered Daly's play. But at some point in his life, he—like all of us—had probably seen an iteration of the railroad scene, whether in a film, an advertisement, or a *Rocky and Bullwinkle* cartoon. He was, unconsciously or not, reenacting that sensational scene. Autrey reported that his split-second decision to rescue Hollopeter derived from his sense of responsibility toward his fellow citizens: "If you see somebody in distress, do the right thing."[7] Did the railroad spectacle, popularized more than a century and a half ago by Daly, give Autrey faith in melodramatic rescues, spurring him to stage one himself?

Inevitably, whenever an event like this enthralls the public, some commentators wax cynical, wondering aloud who will ultimately profit from the heroics. Yet despite such immediate discounting, scenes like Autrey's subway rescue and the Miracle on the Hudson may have a certain efficacy. Sometimes, this efficacy is readily apparent, as in the case of Chad Lindsey, who told the *New York Times* that he thought of Autrey when he pulled an unconscious man from the subway tracks at Penn Station in March 2009.[8] In other cases, the effect may be less obvious but nevertheless possible. When boarding a plane, how many people picture, however briefly, the heavily circulated image of Flight 1549—perhaps even reminding themselves, in the event of an emergency, to let women and children go first, as Sullenberger and his crew told their frightened passengers?[9] To contribute to the survival of all instead of the survival of oneself? To be, like Sullenberger, the last to leave the ship?

In the midst of generalized anxiety, these sensational scenes offer a glimpse of utopia. In this sense, they are mass-media utopian performatives, leaping from their local three-dimensionality, exploding into popular culture, and stimulating our imagination. Jill Dolan argues that the utopian performative does not necessarily result in widespread activism, legislative action, or other wholesale signs of change.[10] But even though such instants are momentary and ephemeral, they change the individual spectators who experience them. Perhaps that is enough.

Our Freaks

Scholars have offered important insights about contemporary incarnations of the freak show, in which differently bodied people—such as "bearded lady" Jennifer Miller of Circus Amok, and Otis Jordan, the infamous "Frog Boy" of the 1984 New York State Fair—transform the nineteenth-century platform performance into a forum for empowerment, employment, and activism. In this context, the freak *stares back,* challenging and confronting the viewer in powerful ways. Performers with extraordinary bodies embrace the form as a way to short-circuit the dynamic of contempt and condescension fostered by the "traditional" freak show, and also to enjoy social and financial benefits from their time on stage. Michael M. Chemers argues that such performances establish "a totally new narrative of peculiarity as eminence, one particularly adapted to postmodern aesthetics." Both he and Rachel Adams underscore the agency seized by these performers who, in their everyday lives, struggle constantly with standards of normalcy. However, such shows are generally vanguard, experimental, fringy—taking place far from the mainstream—and as such, their reach is necessarily limited. To date, no one has seriously examined the places and stages where freaks of a more conventional sort are presented to the public.[11]

Take *Today,* NBC's flagship morning news program, for example. When it first aired in 1952, *Today* established the morning news show as a genre and has maintained its dominance for nearly sixty years. In December 2010, *Today* celebrated its fifteenth consecutive year as the highest-rated morning program on television.[12] Due to its reach and popularity, the show serves as a powerful, national, and communal text. As such, it harbors great potential to shape cultural idea(l)s about self-discipline and the socially acceptable limits of identity. Through sensational video footage, profiles of unusual people, and stories about celebrity misbehavior, *Today* helps to canonize norms through the exhibition of aberration—usually under the guise of "human interest." Obviously, there are many differences between a platform like *Today* and the nineteenth-century platform show. Yet striking similarities exist, both in terms of representation (strategies rooted in theatrical performance and dramaturgy) and processes of legitimation (specifically, the important role of "reality" in both the freak show and the modern news program).

Like all forms of popular culture, *Today* seeks to satisfy its audience's expectations—a tendency that Bruce A. McConachie, Jeffrey D. Mason, and Matthew Buckley have observed in melodrama as well.[13] *Today*'s conventions are revealed and enacted in miniature during the initial thirty seconds of the broadcast, during which three headlines are read by the cohosts. The first two usually relate to items of national or international significance, but almost always, the third story pertains to an exceptional individual or event: a drunken man driving his car into a swimming pool, captured on video; scratchy audio from a 911 emergency call made by a child trying to save her parent's life; or a story of unbearable excess, such as Nadya Suleman, a single mother of six who, with the help of fertility technology, gave birth to octuplets in January 2009. All of these stories harness the poetics of spectacle, whether visually (the car submerged in a pool), heroically (the child's uncharacteristic maturity under pressure), or morally (Suleman).

Indeed, Suleman is radically emblematic of the display of abnormality that is a hallmark of *Today* and its kin. The widespread use of the appellation "Octomom"—a kind of stage name for Suleman that was invented and disseminated by news outlets—underscores how she was constructed and consumed as a freak. In the immediate wake of her octuplets' birth, Suleman was rigorously exhibited on *Today* and in many other media, both professional and amateur.[14] Commentators routinely harnessed what Robert Bogdan describes as the "exotic mode" in their representations of her. Suleman's prolific childbearing evoked a more primitive, pre-birth-control era when American women bore many children in hopes that a few would survive to adulthood. The aesthetics of her face and body were visually and discursively exoticized as well. Photographs depicting her unusually large belly circulated in print, on television, and on the Internet—implicitly characterizing the contours of the maternal body more generally as freakish. Illustrators used the photos as source material for cartoons and visual humor, making grassroots contributions to the enfreakment of Suleman.[15]

Her facial features also became the subject of public commentary when media outlets (including *Today*) began discussing her resemblance to the film actress Angelina Jolie. Reporters, bloggers, and audiences compared photographs of the two women and wondered whether Suleman had undergone plastic surgery. The rumor became yet another opportunity to speculate about Suleman's pathological tendencies. *Life & Style,* a weekly tabloid, featured side-by-side photographs of Suleman and Jolie on its cover and declared, "Octuplets' Mom Obsessed with Angelina." Even this cover story became a story: Courtney Hazlett of *The Scoop, Today*'s celebrity news blog on MSNBC.com, posted a piece titled "Octuplet Mom Patterning Self on Jolie," accompanied by a picture of the *Life & Style* cover.[16] In addition to their faces, their apparent obsession with motherhood was a point of comparison. Prior to the Suleman sensation, Jolie had been subjected to public scrutiny because of her burgeoning family with actor Brad Pitt.

Suleman's freakish irresponsibility became an integral aspect of her story, deeply informing the ways in which her decisions and body were perceived, interpreted, and visually manipulated. One particular *Today* broadcast provides an intriguing case study of this dynamic. Financial questions swirled around Suleman almost from the moment of the octuplets' birth; six months later, these questions reached a new urgency when a court decided to regulate how she would financially benefit from her "excessive" childbearing. On July 28, 2009, *Today* reported that a California judge "appointed a guardian to oversee the estate of [Suleman's] octuplets to ensure they [wouldn't be] exploited by tabloid photo shoots and a planned reality show."[17] The judge's decision resulted from a lawsuit brought by Paul Petersen, former child star and proponent for children's rights in the entertainment industry, with the aid of attorney Gloria Allred. The broadcast also included a segment about congressional legislation to curb bonuses received by Wall Street bankers; an interview with Kurt Andersen about his book *Reset: How This Crisis Can Restore Our Values and Renew America* (2009); and a story about a New Jersey woman who attempted to stave off foreclosure by baking and selling cakes.[18] In 1860, Barnum's spectators could examine the "What Is It?" exhibit, featuring an African American man as a "missing link" between primates and humans, before or after watching Dion Boucicault's *The Octoroon,* a melodrama about slavery in Louisiana. In July 2009, a *Today* viewer could engage "Octomom" in a similar fashion—one moment, watching a story about bonuses received by employees of governmentally bailed-out banks; then, watching an interview with the author of a book on the financial crisis; then, taking in a story about Suleman, an unemployed mother of six who had possibly funded her fertility treatments with student loans and federal disability payments.

Public anxiety regarding the fate of Suleman's fourteen children was (and remains) genuine, and is probably warranted. But more interesting to me than the particulars of the public's concern is the *phenomenon* of its concern. Shaped by and through an excessive matrix of language, images, and interpersonal relations, freak shows show us what we ought not to be; what we should fear to be; what we must suppress (raging desire, wild truths, hyperbolic dreams) in order to conform, to approach the middle, to become middling. Reportage on *Today* and elsewhere emphasized Suleman's failure to adhere to a core value associated with US citizenship: to live within one's means. In the eyes of her critics, the irresponsibility she embodied was not just procreational but financial. Questions of fiscal discipline perpetually dogged Suleman—as freak, as abject, as reject.

Like heroes, freaks serve as cultural allegories, referencing questions and crises circulating during a given historical moment. In the same month that Sullenberger was hailed as a hero, Suleman emerged as his profound opposite. Both were transformed into public spectacles, but while "Sully" aroused curiosity, "Octomom" aroused contempt. Sullenberger embodied the mainstream norms that are implicitly privileged in US culture: white, male, married, employed, modest, selfless. Suleman embodied the Other, deviating in nearly every way from those desirable norms: racially ambiguous, female, unmarried, unemployed, immodest, selfish. While Sullenberger gave Americans an inspiring story as the Great Recession unfolded, Suleman gave Americans a reason to complain. And each was made into a morality tale for the masses.

Reform Culture, Re-Formed

The means of production and distribution have changed, but contemporary entertainment culture still harnesses the affective dynamism of spectacle to inspire and discipline US citizens. Every morning on *Today*, abnormality is put on display, bringing aberrant individuals before the public for examination and judgment. This also routinely occurs in the "reality TV" genre, on shows like *Big Brother* (CBS), *Project Runway* (Lifetime), and *The Biggest Loser* (NBC).[19] Many complain about these programs, which are obviously freak shows in everything but name. Yet producers continue to parade human curiosities before our eyes.

These bodies-*as*-spectacles simultaneously attract and repulse us, locking our gaze despite the insistent voice inside that admonishes our urge to stare.

Rosemarie Garland-Thomson writes that the stare, as the most intense mode of looking at another, "is an interpersonal action through which we act out who we imagine ourselves and others to be."[20] When extraordinary bodies or sensational scenes appear on film, television, and the Internet, we are invited to stare; and, staring, we make conclusions about life in general. Sensational entertainment invited nineteenth-century spectators to look differently at embodiment, thereby influencing how they read bodies in myriad contexts. I suspect that this is exponentially true today, due to the proliferation of opportunities to stare. What has changed, radically and irrevocably, are the contexts in which staring takes place. Now, we stare at screens. When in our homes, we enjoy considerably more privacy than audiences at Barnum's museum ever did. Nevertheless, in this age of "ambient television," to employ Anna McCarthy's phrase, a significant proportion of our consumption takes place in public.[21] Broadcasts, whether recorded or in real time, confront us at every turn—in restaurants and bars, supermarkets, waiting areas, and display windows. Moreover, the advent of video- and Internet-equipped smartphones has enabled us to put the spectacle in our pockets, allowing ever-more frequent and immediate access to sensational stories and images. Wherever we are, we stare, engaging in an interpersonal evaluation of who and what others are, and who and what we should be.

To be attuned to the dynamics of spectacle—its scale, its intensity, its excess, and its power—is to understand how we see. Yet most assume that spectacle's main function is to decorate and amuse, or believe that it is a voracious vacuum, robbing us of our ability to think, feel, or act. Probably, Aristotle's privileging of plot (which is, at its heart, a privileging of text) and his concomitant devaluing of spectacle (which fills our eyes, and perhaps our hearts) helped to establish this collective opinion about the relative emptiness of spectacle. Subsequently, theater critics and artists—ranging from Horace to Ben Jonson to George Bernard Shaw—helped to perpetuate it.[22] But spectacle is rarely empty. It is relational, working on scales both big and small. Because it comes into being through the vocabulary of norms, it is always already implicated in the establishment, perpetuation, and canonization of compulsory conventions.

As time passes, the issues change, but the aspirations remain. The American reform impulse began, many historians argue, as a tremendous faith in individual and social change generated by the Second Great Awakening. In the twenty-first century, the word *reform* appears less frequently in public discourse, but its fundamental energy is very much apparent. Efforts supporting or challenging affirmative action, gay marriage, reproductive freedom, gender expression, economic justice, universal health care, collective bargaining, the equal treatment of people with disabilities, and many other issues are generally termed *activism* today; but like the nineteenth-century reform movements that preceded them, these efforts comprise communities of individuals working toward the realization of their ideology in the world. As such, they are contemporary expressions of US reform culture, and therefore part of a long-lived tradition. People involved in these causes today face many of the dilemmas that advocates for temperance, abolition, and suffrage did. Is moral suasion the best way to create change, or is legislation the only answer? Who should be included in the effort, and who lacks the credentials or qualifications? How should I act—how should I perform? Should I appear "normal," adopting postures and poses of respectability, enabling others to see themselves in me? Or should I instead question the dominance of the norm by making a spectacle of myself, by letting my freak-flag fly? An examination of the use of spectacle in contemporary reform culture might reveal important similarities and differences between the past and the present.

But there is another kind of reform, hidden in plain sight, that also warrants our vigilance and our investigation. Organized political endeavors are relatively easy to examine, easy to see. But what about the everyday spectacles we consume via television and computer screens, often without our full awareness, let alone our permission? The narratives that become associated with sensational images like the Miracle on the Hudson and Nadya Suleman have the power to teach and shape us. They, too, remake—re-form—our beliefs, our ethics, our very bodies.

Notes

Introduction

1. Nan Enstad, "Dressed for Adventure: Working Women and Silent Movie Serials in the 1910s," *Feminist Studies* 21, no. 1 (Spring 1995): 90n44.

2. Nicholas Daly, *Literature, Technology, and Modernity, 1860–2000* (Cambridge: Cambridge University Press, 2004), 11–12.

3. Joseph Francis Daly, *The Life of Augustin Daly* (New York: Macmillan, 1917), 20.

4. Daniel C. Gerould and Marvin Carlson, eds., *Pixérécourt: Four Melodramas* (New York: Martin E. Segal Theatre Center, 2002), ix.

5. *Oxford English Dictionary,* 3rd ed. (online version September 2011), s.v. "normal" (A.I.2.a); Lennard J. Davis, *Enforcing Normalcy: Disability, Deafness, and the Body* (London: Verso, 1995), 24. As Davis points out, this definition of the word *normal* first became prevalent in the 1840s.

6. Baz Kershaw, *Theatre Ecology: Environments and Performance Events* (Cambridge: Cambridge University Press, 2007), 211 (emphasis in original); Rebecca Schneider, *Performing Remains: Art and War in Times of Theatrical Reenactment* (New York: Routledge, 2011), 37.

7. Rosemarie K. Bank, *Theatre Culture in America, 1825–1860* (Cambridge: Cambridge University Press, 1997); John W. Frick, *Theatre, Culture and Temperance Reform in Nineteenth-Century America* (Cambridge: Cambridge University Press, 2003); Jeffrey D. Mason, *Melodrama and the Myth of America* (Bloomington: Indiana University Press, 1993); Bruce A. McConachie, *Melodramatic Formations: American Theatre and Society, 1820–1870* (Iowa City: University of Iowa Press, 1992); Tice Miller, *Entertaining the Nation: American Drama in the Eighteenth and Nineteenth Centuries* (Carbondale: Southern Illinois University Press, 2007); Heather S. Nathans, *Early American Theatre from the Revolution to Thomas Jefferson: Into the Hands of the People* (Cambridge: Cambridge University Press, 2003); Heather

S. Nathans, *Slavery and Sentiment on the American Stage, 1787–1861: Lifting the Veil of Black* (Cambridge: Cambridge University Press, 2009); Peter P. Reed, *Rogue Performances: Staging the Underclasses in Early American Theatre Culture* (New York: Palgrave Macmillan, 2009); Jeffrey H. Richards, *Drama, Theatre, and Identity in the American New Republic* (Cambridge: Cambridge University Press, 2005); Jason Shaffer, *Performing Patriotism: National Identity in the Colonial and Revolutionary American Theater* (Philadelphia: University of Pennsylvania Press, 2007). I limit my discussion here to studies focusing on the United States because my project intervenes most assertively in that body of scholarship. Important examinations of Victorian theater or the melodramatic genre include, for example, Michael R. Booth, *English Melodrama* (London: Herbert Jenkins, 1965); Frank Rahill, *The World of Melodrama* (University Park: Pennsylvania State University Press, 1967); Robert Bechtold Heilman, *Tragedy and Melodrama: Versions of Experience* (Seattle: University of Washington Press, 1968); Daniel C. Gerould, ed., *Melodrama* (New York: New York Literary Forum, 1980); Peter Brooks, *The Melodramatic Imagination: Balzac, Henry James, Melodrama, and the Mode of Excess* (New York: Columbia University Press, 1985); Michael R. Booth, *Theatre in the Victorian Age* (Cambridge: Cambridge University Press, 1991); Michael Hays and Anastasia Nikolopoulou, eds., *Melodrama: The Cultural Emergence of a Genre* (New York: St. Martin's Press, 1996); and Tracy C. Davis and Peter Holland, eds., *The Performing Century: Nineteenth-Century Theatre's History* (Basingstoke, UK: Palgrave Macmillan, 2007).

8. Robert C. Allen, *Horrible Prettiness: Burlesque and American Culture* (Chapel Hill: University of North Carolina Press, 1991); Robin Bernstein, *Racial Innocence: Performing Childhood and Race from Slavery to Civil Rights* (New York: New York University Press, 2011); Faye E. Dudden, *Women in the American Theatre: Actresses and Audiences, 1790–1870* (New Haven: Yale University Press, 1994); Barbara Wallace Grossman, *A Spectacle of Suffering: Clara Morris on the American Stage* (Carbondale: Southern Illinois University Press, 2009); Eric Lott, *Love and Theft: Blackface Minstrelsy and the American Working Class* (New York: Oxford University Press, 1993); Kim Marra, *Strange Duets: Impresarios and Actresses in the American Theatre, 1865–1914* (Iowa City: University of Iowa Press, 2006); Lisa Merrill, *When Romeo Was a Woman: Charlotte Cushman and Her Circle of Female Spectators* (Ann Arbor: University of Michigan Press, 1999); Elizabeth Reitz Mullenix, *Wearing the Breeches: Gender on the Antebellum Stage* (New York: St. Martin's Press, 2000); Harvey Young, *Embodying Black Experience: Stillness, Critical Memory, and the Black Body* (Ann Arbor: University of Michigan Press, 2010).

9. Michael R. Booth, *Victorian Spectacular Theatre, 1850–1910* (Boston: Routledge and Kegan Paul, 1981); Michael Diamond, *Victorian Sensation, or, the Spectacular, the Shocking, and the Scandalous in Nineteenth-Century Britain* (London: Anthem Press, 2003); Martin Meisel, *Realizations: Narrative, Pictorial, and Theat-*

rical Arts in Nineteenth-Century England (Princeton: Princeton University Press, 1983); Lynn M. Voskuil, *Acting Naturally: Victorian Theatricality and Authenticity* (Charlottesville: University of Virginia Press, 2004).

10. David Grimsted, *Melodrama Unveiled: American Theater and Culture, 1800–1850* (Chicago: University of Chicago Press, 1968), 76–98; Joseph Roach, *Cities of the Dead: Circum-Atlantic Performance* (New York: Columbia University Press, 1996); Saidiya V. Hartman, *Scenes of Subjection: Terror, Slavery, and Self-Making in Nineteenth-Century America* (New York: Oxford University Press, 1997); Daphne A. Brooks, *Bodies in Dissent: Spectacular Performances of Race and Freedom, 1850–1910* (Durham: Duke University Press, 2006); Gay Gibson Cima, *Early American Women Critics: Performance, Religion, Race* (Cambridge: Cambridge University Press, 2006); Michael M. Chemers, *Staging Stigma: A Critical Examination of the American Freak Show* (New York: Palgrave Macmillan, 2008); Mark Cosdon, *The Hanlon Brothers: From Daredevil Acrobatics to Spectacle Pantomime, 1833–1931* (Carbondale: Southern Illinois University Press, 2009).

11. For an introduction to the notion of American reform culture, see T. Gregory Garvey, *Creating the Culture of Reform in Antebellum America* (Athens: University of Georgia Press, 2006).

12. Bruce A. McConachie, "New Historicism and American Theater History: Toward an Interdisciplinary Paradigm for Scholarship," in *The Performance of Power: Theatrical Discourse and Politics*, ed. Sue-Ellen Case and Janelle Reinelt (Iowa City: University of Iowa Press, 1991), 267.

13. Kershaw, *Theatre Ecology*, 208, 219–22. See also Kershaw, "Curiosity or Contempt: On Spectacle, the Human, and Activism," *Theatre Journal* 55, no. 4 (December 2003): 599.

14. Sarah Meer, *Uncle Tom Mania: Slavery, Minstrelsy, and Transatlantic Culture in the 1850s* (Athens: University of Georgia Press, 2005), 115.

15. Jacky Bratton, *New Readings in Theatre History* (Cambridge: Cambridge University Press, 2003), 12.

16. Smith argues that American plays have long been "shelved out of sight" for a variety of reasons, including an ongoing inferiority complex regarding the US's position within Western culture (especially in relation to Europe) and drama's mediocre status within the literary hierarchy. She asserts that in the academy, American drama has long been perceived "embarrassedly and fearfully" as "a vital manifestation of cultural provincialism, feminine emotion, and unstable radicalism"; as a result, "the critics approved and continue to uphold only those literary forms which were sanctioned by the propertied, patriarchal culture, a culture that necessarily had to value the containment and restraint of exuberance or subversiveness" (*American Drama: The Bastard Art* [Cambridge: Cambridge University Press, 1997], 3, 11).

17. Stanton B. Garner, *Bodied Spaces: Phenomenology and Performance in Contemporary Drama* (Ithaca: Cornell University Press, 1994), 3 (emphasis in original); Underwood quoted in Florine Thayer McCray, *The Life-Work of the Author of Uncle Tom's Cabin* (New York: Funk and Wagnalls, 1889), 122 (emphasis added).

18. *Oxford English Dictionary,* 2nd ed. (online version September 2011), s.v. "sense."

19. Throughout this book, I deliberately use the epithet *freak* in lieu of a more benign term because, as Rachel Adams observes, "like *queer,* [freak] is a concept that refuses the logic of identity politics, and the irreconcilable problems of inclusion and exclusion that necessarily accompany identitarian categories" (*Sideshow U.S.A.: Freaks and the American Cultural Imagination* [Chicago: University of Chicago Press, 2001], 10; emphasis added). For me, the word foregrounds the departures from normalcy that disabled performers embody—or rather, the departures from normalcy that they perform. The term *enfreakment,* which emphasizes that freaks are culturally constructed rather than born, is a coinage of David Hevey, *The Creatures That Time Forgot: Photography and Disability Imagery* (London: Routledge, 1992). David M. Henkin's *City Reading: Written Words and Public Spaces in Antebellum New York* (New York: Columbia University Press, 1998) has greatly influenced my thinking about the mediated aspects of nineteenth-century urban life.

20. Mason, *Melodrama,* 18.

21. Kershaw, "Curiosity or Contempt," 602.

22. In *Paper Money Men: Commerce, Manhood, and the Sensational Public Sphere in Antebellum America* (Columbus: Ohio State University Press, 2009), David Anthony has taken an important step toward theorizing the notion of a nineteenth-century American "sensational public sphere" (inspired by Jürgen Habermas's theory of the public sphere). He contends that the sensationalism of antebellum newspapers, novels, and plays offered "a kind of fantasy redress for the failed or imperiled manhood of the new paper economy" (27). However, a key difference between our projects is that Anthony focuses on the ways in which professional men were represented by and participated in the sensational sphere, whereas my study imagines and incorporates a much more diverse audience for spectacular aesthetics, including women.

23. Kershaw, *Theatre Ecology,* 216.

24. Jean Baudrillard, *Simulacra and Simulation* [1981], trans. Sheila Faria Glaser (Ann Arbor: University of Michigan Press, 1994), 1.

25. Numerous studies examine the historical and aesthetic relationship between melodrama and film. See, for example, Christine Gledhill, *Home Is Where the Heart Is: Studies in Melodrama and the Woman's Film* (London: BFI Publications, 1987); Robert Lang, *American Film Melodrama: Griffith, Vidor, Minnelli* (Princeton: Princeton University Press, 1989); Jacky Bratton, Jim Cook, and Christine Gledhill,

eds., *Melodrama: Stage Picture Screen* (London: British Film Institute, 1994); Nick Browne, ed., *Refiguring American Film Genres: History and Theory* (Berkeley: University of California Press, 1998); and Ben Singer, *Melodrama and Modernity: Early Sensational Cinema and Its Contexts* (New York: Columbia University Press, 2001).

Chapter 1

1. Peter Brooks, "Melodrama, Body, Revolution," in *Melodrama: Stage Picture Screen,* ed. Jacky Bratton, Jim Cook, and Christine Gledhill (London: British Film Institute, 1994), 18.

2. Martin Meisel, *Realizations: Narrative, Pictorial, and Theatrical Arts in Nineteenth-Century England* (Princeton: Princeton University Press, 1983), 39 (emphasis in original), 3; Tom Gunning, "The Horror of Opacity: The Melodrama of Sensation in the Plays of André De Lorde," in *Melodrama: Stage Picture Screen,* ed. Jacky Bratton, Jim Cook, and Christine Gledhill (London: British Film Institute, 1994), 52. Although the expression "sensation scene" was not widely used until the 1860s, I employ the phrase generically throughout this book because I appreciate how it emphasizes the provocative, memorable character of spectacular displays as well as spectators' somatic response to them.

3. Bernard Beckerman, "Spectacle in the Theatre," *Theatre Survey* 25, no. 1 (May 1984): 9–11. Baz Kershaw, acknowledging the relationship between spectacle and human proportion, argues that technological innovations in travel and communication since the mid-nineteenth century have steadily changed our sense of scale, thereby changing our perception of spectacle as well. See his *Theatre Ecology: Environments and Performance Events* (Cambridge: Cambridge University Press, 2007), 206–38; and "Curiosity or Contempt: On Spectacle, the Human, and Activism," *Theatre Journal* 55, no. 4 (December 2003): 591–611, especially 595–97.

4. Meisel, *Realizations,* 38; Charles Altieri, *The Particulars of Rapture: An Aesthetics of the Affects* (Ithaca: Cornell University Press, 2003), 187; Bert O. States, *Great Reckonings in Little Rooms: On the Phenomenology of Theater* (Berkeley: University of California Press, 1985), 153 (emphasis in original). Altieri describes intensity as having three dimensions, all of which are relational: magnitude, compression, and sharpness. Offering an example from the theatrical canon, he writes, "Think of the difference between hearing Lear's 'never, never, never' speech the first time one sees the play and hearing it with an awareness of the forces at work in the play as a whole. Or think of everything that comes to bear on Oedipus's blinding himself" (187).

5. Peter Brooks, *The Melodramatic Imagination: Balzac, Henry James, Melodrama, and the Mode of Excess* (New York: Columbia University Press, 1985), 41.

6. Kershaw, *Theatre Ecology,* 203; Kershaw, "Curiosity or Contempt."

7. The rise of melodrama and its tendency to "say everything" reflects, in some ways, the Second Great Awakening in the United States (roughly 1790–1840), which invited participants to express themselves performatively in spiritual conversion and religious practice. For more on this phenomenon, see Nathan O. Hatch, *The Democratization of American Christianity* (New Haven: Yale University Press, 1989); and Jon Butler, *Awash in a Sea of Faith: Christianizing the American People* (Cambridge: Harvard University Press, 1990).

8. Michel Foucault, *Discipline and Punish: The Birth of the Prison* [1975], trans. Alan Sheridan, 2nd ed. (New York: Vintage Books, 1995); Lennard J. Davis, *Enforcing Normalcy: Disability, Deafness, and the Body* (London: Verso, 1995), 24.

9. Foucault, *Discipline and Punish*, 193; Rodney Hessinger, "'The Most Powerful Instrument of College Discipline': Student Disorder and the Meritocracy in the Colleges of the Early American Republic," *History of Education Quarterly* 29, no. 3 (Autumn 1999): 237–62; Rodney Hessinger, *Seduced, Abandoned, and Reborn: Visions of Youth in Middle-Class America, 1780–1850* (Philadelphia: University of Pennsylvania Press, 2005); Davis, *Enforcing Normalcy*, 29–30 (quotation on 30). For more on the development and popularity of phrenology during the nineteenth century, see, for example, John Van Wyhe, *Phrenology and the Origins of Victorian Scientific Naturalism* (Aldershot, England: Ashgate, 2004); and Stephen Tomlinson, *Head Masters: Phrenology, Secular Education, and Nineteenth-Century Social Thought* (Tuscaloosa: University of Alabama Press, 2005).

10. Davis, *Enforcing Normalcy*, 34–35.

11. As Rosemarie Garland-Thomson has shown, by the turn of the twentieth century medical practitioners transformed impaired individuals into "disabled" people—pathologies instead of curiosities—and relegated them to hospitals; but until then, extraordinary bodies were frequently offered up as entertainment (*Extraordinary Bodies: Figuring Physical Disability in American Culture and Literature* [New York: Columbia University Press, 1997], 55–80). Although I focus on American freak shows, they did not originate in the United States and were popular elsewhere. Leslie Fiedler points out that the display of anomalous bodies for the purpose of amusement may be traced as far back as the second century CE (*Freaks: Myths and Images of the Secret Self* [New York: Simon and Schuster, 1978], 20). For more on freaks in earlier eras and other cultures, see, among others, Richard D. Altick, *The Shows of London* (Cambridge: Belknap Press of Harvard University Press, 1978); Marie-Hélène Huet, *Monstrous Imagination* (Cambridge: Cambridge University Press, 1993); Dudley Wilson, *Signs and Portents: Monstrous Births from the Middle Ages to the Enlightenment* (London: Routledge, 1993); and Paul Semonin, "Monsters in the Marketplace: The Exhibition of Human Oddities in Early Modern England," in *Freakery: Cultural Spectacles of the Extraordinary Body*, ed. Rosemarie Garland Thomson (New York: New York University Press, 1996), 69–81.

12. Meisel, *Realizations*, 141. Similarly, Michael Denning has shown that there was a reciprocal relationship between melodrama and the sensational dime novel, with authors re-creating popular plays in literary form and vice versa (*Mechanic Accents: Dime Novels and Working-Class Culture in America* [London: Verso, 1987], 24–25).

13. Robert Bogdan, *Freak Show: Presenting Human Oddities for Amusement and Profit* (Chicago: University of Chicago Press, 1988), 11, 25–68; Andrea Stulman Dennett, *Weird and Wonderful: The Dime Museum in America* (New York: New York University Press, 1997). See also Rachel Adams, *Sideshow U.S.A.: Freaks and the American Cultural Imagination* (Chicago: University of Chicago Press, 2001), 114–20.

14. Bluford Adams, *E Pluribus Barnum: The Great Showman and the Making of U.S. Popular Culture* (Minneapolis: University of Minnesota Press, 1997), 116–63; Matthew Rebhorn, "What Is It? The Frontier, Melodrama, and Boucicault's Amalgamated Drama," *Journal of American Drama and Theatre* 19, no. 3 (Fall 2007): 5–33.

15. David Hevey, *The Creatures That Time Forgot: Photography and Disability Imagery* (London: Routledge, 1992), 53; Bogdan, *Freak Show*, 105, 108.

16. "The inherently performative nature of live specimens veers exhibits of them strongly in the direction of spectacle," Barbara Kirshenblatt-Gimblett observes, "blurring still further the line between morbid curiosity and scientific interest, chamber of horrors and medical exhibition, circus and zoological garden, theater and living ethnographic display, scholarly lecture and dramatic monologue, cultural performance and staged re-creation" (*Destination Culture: Tourism, Museums, and Heritage* [Berkeley: University of California Press, 1998], 34).

17. William Wells Brown, *The Negro in the American Rebellion: His Heroism and His Fidelity* (Boston: Lee and Shepard, 1867); reprint, with an introduction and annotations by John David Smith (Athens: Ohio University Press, 2003), 42.

18. Carolyn Sorisio, *Fleshing Out America: Race, Gender, and the Politics of the Body in American Literature, 1833–1879* (Athens: University of Georgia Press, 2002), 28. See also Harvey Young, *Embodying Black Experience: Stillness, Critical Memory, and the Black Body* (Ann Arbor: University of Michigan Press, 2010).

19. Theodore Dwight Weld, *American Slavery as It Is: Testimony of a Thousand Witnesses* (New York: American Anti-Slavery Society, 1839); Stephen Browne, "'Like Gory Spectres': Representing Evil in Theodore Weld's *American Slavery as It Is*," *Quarterly Journal of Speech* 80 (August 1994): 277–92 (quotation on 277); Larry Gara, "The Professional Fugitive in the Abolition Movement," *Wisconsin Magazine of History* 48 (1965): 196–204. Lectures and performances by fugitive slaves operated intertextually with other antislavery spectacles, but I have elected not to explore this aspect of antebellum theater culture, given the limited scope of this study. For

more on that phenomenon, see Daphne A. Brooks, who offers important insights about the spectacular nature of Henry "Box" Brown's performances, in *Bodies in Dissent: Spectacular Performances of Race and Freedom, 1850–1910* (Durham: Duke University Press, 2006), 66–130; and Alison Piepmeier, who theorizes the corporeal politics of speeches attributed to Sojourner Truth, in *Out in Public: Configurations of Women's Bodies in Nineteenth-Century America* (Chapel Hill: University of North Carolina Press, 2004), 92–128. For more discussion of the role played by the black body in abolitionist discourse, especially the wounded bodies of slaves, see Jennifer Putzi, *Identifying Marks: Race, Gender, and the Marked Body in Nineteenth-Century America* (Athens: University of Georgia Press, 2006), 99–129.

20. Leslie A. Fiedler, foreword in *Freakery: Cultural Spectacles of the Extraordinary Body,* ed. Rosemarie Garland Thomson (New York: New York University Press, 1996), xiii; Adams, *Sideshow U.S.A.*, 7. See also Fiedler, *Freaks;* Rosemarie Garland Thomson, Introduction in *Freakery,* ed. Garland Thomson, 10; Garland Thomson, *Extraordinary Bodies;* Davis, *Enforcing Normalcy,* 2; Elizabeth Grosz, "Intolerable Ambiguity: Freaks as/at the Limit," in *Freakery,* ed. Garland Thomson, 55–66; Stuart Hall, ed., *Representation: Cultural Representations and Signifying Practices* (London: Sage, 1997), 223–90. In addition, Simi Linton offers a helpful discussion of how the normal body is canonized within contemporary rhetoric and discourse in *Claiming Disability: Knowledge and Identity* (New York: New York University Press, 1998), 8–33; and Michael Warner explores the politics of normalcy in relation to sexual identity in *The Trouble with Normal: Sex, Politics, and the Ethics of Queer Life* (New York: Free Press, 1999).

21. States, *Great Reckonings,* 154, 34. Jody Enders, offering an alternative view regarding the pleasure of such ruptures, calls them "dreaded moment[s] when theatrical events are not quite representation and not quite reality" (*Death by Drama and Other Medieval Urban Legends* [Chicago: University of Chicago Press, 2002], 66).

22. Hans Robert Jauss, *Toward an Aesthetic of Reception,* trans. Timothy Bahti (Minneapolis: University of Minnesota Press, 1982).

23. Marvin Carlson, *The Haunted Stage: The Theatre as Memory Machine* (Ann Arbor: University of Michigan Press, 2001), especially 52–95.

24. Michael L. Quinn, "Celebrity and the Semiotics of Acting," *New Theatre Quarterly* 4 (1990): 154–61.

25. "Scene in the Museum," *National Anti-Slavery Standard,* 24 September 1853, 70.

26. Rebecca Schneider, *Performing Remains: Art and War in Times of Theatrical Reenactment* (New York: Routledge, 2011), 109; Herbert Blau, *The Dubious Spectacle: Extremities of Theater, 1976–2000* (Minneapolis: University of Minnesota Press, 2002), 51. Some scholars, especially Philip Auslander, have questioned the way the-

ater aficionados tend to privilege "liveness." Auslander postulates that mediation profoundly impacts theatrical events, and that "the live" is always already influenced by "the recorded." But he also admits that these two types of performance are dissimilar phenomenologically, acknowledging, "live performance engages the senses *differently* than mediatized representations" (*Liveness: Performance in a Mediatized Culture* [London: Routledge, 1999], 2–3, 54, 55 [emphasis in original]). In accordance with Auslander's reasoning, I am interested in examining how the senses are *differently engaged* in the theater, and specifically, how moments of magnitude foster unique responses. For a provocative critique of Auslander's argument and the fetishization of liveness in theater studies, see chapter 3 of Schneider's *Performing Remains.*

27. States, *Great Reckonings,* 119. Terry Eagleton's notion of the "species-body," the abstract model of the body before its personalization, possibly illuminates how this aspect of performance operates; see *After Theory* (New York: Basic Books, 2003), 166.

28. Daphna Ben Chaim, drawing on Artaud's conception of theater as a "serious game," observes that the spectator's awareness of the play as a pretend event psychologically protects her from disturbing episodes enacted on stage (*Distance in the Theatre: The Aesthetics of Audience Response* [Ann Arbor, MI: UMI Research Press, 1984], 45). But Ben Chaim is referring to incidents suffered by characters, rather than hazards negotiated by actors.

29. Enders, *Death by Drama,* 11.

30. Even today, mechanical mishaps on stage inspire widespread discussion. This was the case when actress Idina Menzel fell through a trapdoor and broke a rib during one of her final performances in the Broadway musical *Wicked* (8 January 2005). More recently, injuries suffered by actors in Julie Taymor's production of the musical *Spider-Man: Turn Off the Dark* (2011), also on Broadway, have been heavily publicized and critiqued.

31. David Grimsted, *Melodrama Unveiled: American Theater and Culture, 1800–1850* (Chicago: University of Chicago Press, 1968), 76.

32. Ben Singer, *Melodrama and Modernity: Early Sensational Cinema and Its Contexts* (New York: Columbia University Press, 2001), 186. Singer's source for A. H. Woods's story is "Producing Spine-Thrillers," *Literary Digest* 45, no. 6 (10 August 1912): 222–23.

33. Piepmeier, *Out in Public,* 21.

34. Mary Grace Swift, "Dancers in Flames," *Dance Chronicle* 5, no. 1 (1982): 8. For more on the eroticism of the nineteenth-century ballet girl, see John Elsom, *Erotic Theatre* (New York: Taplinger Publishing, 1974); and Tracy C. Davis, "The Actress in Victorian Pornography," *Theatre Journal* 41, no. 3 (October 1989): 294–315.

35. Frederick Gleason, "Niblo's Garden," *Gleason's Pictorial Drawing-Room Companion* 2, no. 10 (1852): 1.

36. Sam Stockwell, letter to Moses Kimball, 12 October 1852, Moses Kimball Papers, Boston Athenaeum.

37. "Narrow Escape of Actors," *New York Times,* 21 March 1874, 10.

38. "Serious Accident," *Daily Alta California* (San Francisco), 29 November 1861, n.p. Russell Hartley Chronological Clipping Files, 1858–62 (folder: July–Dec. 1861), San Francisco Performing Arts Library and Museum.

39. René Wren, "Players Who Died Acting," *Theatre Magazine* 30, no. 9 (1919): 166. An earlier but similar chronicle of stage fatalities is William Bates, "Actors Who Have Died on the Stage," *Notes and Queries* 4, no. 278 (1873): 338–40.

40. Alan Read, *Theatre and Everyday Life: An Ethics of Performance* (London: Routledge, 1995), 216. See also Grimsted, *Melodrama Unveiled,* 77–78.

41. Frederick Gleason, "Burning of the National Theatre," *Gleason's Pictorial Drawing-Room Companion* 2, no. 19 (1852): 296.

42. Michael Booth suggests that the scale and complexity of sensation scenes distracted the audience and diminished the attention paid to actors (*Victorian Spectacular Theatre, 1850–1910* [Boston: Routledge and Kegan Paul, 1981], 27). Although this is a possibility, I believe it is not the case when the actor's safety seems to be at stake, because at such times a spectator's awareness shifts urgently from the actor-as-character toward the actor-as-human. These tensions are most likely to reach a fever pitch, I suggest, during a spectacular instant.

43. The Brooklyn Theatre disaster receives a lengthy mention in the biography of Augustin Daly written by his brother Joseph—suggesting that this incident specifically, and the threat of fire generally, haunted the collective memory. Joseph Francis Daly, *The Life of Augustin Daly* (New York: Macmillan, 1917), 223–24.

44. Box 7, scrapbook 8, vol. 2, Samuel Stark Scrapbook Collection, 1860–1950, Special Collections and University Archives, Stanford University. Unfortunately, the provenance of this scrapbook is uncertain, so it is not clear where the owner lived. However, a significant proportion of the playbills are from New York City theaters, suggesting that he or she saw performances there over a significant period of time.

45. Kershaw, *Theatre Ecology,* 218.

46. Jonathan Crary, *Techniques of the Observer: On Vision and Modernity in the Nineteenth Century* (Cambridge: MIT Press, 1990), 37, 24, 17. Although Crary focuses primarily on Europe, the technological devices and innovations he studies also circulated in the United States, suggesting that the "optical regime" he describes influenced Americans as well.

47. Patricia Crain, *The Story of A: The Alphabetization of America from* The New England Primer *to* The Scarlet Letter (Stanford: Stanford University Press, 2000), 7.

48. For more on the significant role played by *The New England Primer* in the education of American youths, see Daniel A. Cohen, "The Origin and Development of the *New England Primer*," *Children's Literature* 5 (1976): 52–57; Crain, *The Story of A;* and Patrick Spero, "The Revolution in Popular Publications: The Almanac and *New England Primer*, 1750–1800," *Early American Studies: An Interdisciplinary Journal* 8, no. 1 (Winter 2010): 41–74.

49. Jacob Abbott, *Rollo Learning to Talk* (Philadelphia: Hogan and Thompson, 1850), 6–7 (emphasis in original), 9–10. This book, first published as *The Little Scholar Learning to Talk: A Picture Book for Rollo* (1835), and others by Abbott were frequently reprinted during the nineteenth century.

50. Charles Jewett, *The Youth's Temperance Lecturer* (Boston: Whipple and Damrell, 1840), 6.

51. Garland-Thomson, *Staring*, 3.

52. Crain, *The Story of A*, 113.

53. Jacob Abbott, *Dialogues for the Amusement and Instruction of Young Persons* (New York: Harper & Brothers, 1856), 7.

54. Jacob Abbott, *The Alcove; Containing Some Further Account of Timboo, Mark, and Fanny* (New York: Harper & Brothers, 1856), 121–30. The strategy of comparison and contrast in Abbott's *The Alcove* is also apparent in prints and lithographs such as *The Drunkard's Progress* (1846) by Currier & Ives (see fig. 2.1), which depicts an inebriate in successive states of dissipation, and *The Bottle* (1847), George Cruikshank's famous graphic melodrama about the impact of alcohol on a middle-class family (see fig. 2.3), both of which I discuss in chapter 2.

55. M. L. Weems, *The Drunkard's Looking Glass, Reflecting a Faithful Likeness of the Drunkard, in Sundry Very Interesting Attitudes, with Lively Representations of the Many Strange Capers Which He Cuts at Different Stages of His Disease*, 6th ed. ([Philadelphia?]: Printed for the author, 1818), 4–5 (emphasis in original).

56. "Contented and Happy," *The Emancipator*, 7 March 1844, 4.

57. Heather S. Nathans, *Slavery and Sentiment on the American Stage, 1787–1861: Lifting the Veil of Black* (Cambridge: Cambridge University Press, 2009), 193; "Incendiary Pictures," *Anti-Slavery Record* 2, no. 8 (August 1836): 12; "The Moral Character of the Africo-Americans," *Anti-Slavery Record* 2, no. 4 (April 1836): 1–2; N. Southard, *Anti-Slavery Almanac for 1838* (Boston: D. K. Hitchcock, 1837), 17.

58. Guy Debord, *The Society of the Spectacle* (Detroit: Black & Red, 1977); Crary, *Techniques of the Observer*, 17–18.

59. Matthew S. Buckley, "Refugee Theatre: Melodrama and Modernity's Loss," *Theatre Journal* 61, no. 2 (2009): 187; Augusto Boal, *Games for Actors and Non-Actors* [1992], trans. Adrian Jackson, 2nd ed. (New York: Routledge, 2002); Bruce A. McConachie, "Catharsis and the Materiality of Spectatorship," *Assaph* 14 (1997): 96.

60. Kershaw, *Theatre Ecology,* 210, 211, 224. Lawrence W. Levine examines the transformation of American spectatorship over the course of the nineteenth century in *Highbrow/Lowbrow: The Emergence of Cultural Hierarchy in America* (Cambridge: Harvard University Press, 1988).

61. Stanton B. Garner, *Bodied Spaces: Phenomenology and Performance in Contemporary Drama* (Ithaca: Cornell University Press, 1994), 4 (emphasis in original).

62. *Daly v. Palmer et al.,* 6 F. Cas. 1132, 1134 and 1138 (emphasis added) (S. D. New York 1868). After the verdict, the *Times* published a sizable excerpt of Blatchford's decision: "Dramatic Copyright," *New York Times,* 18 December 1868, 2.

63. Schneider, *Performing Remains,* 36. My brief discussion here is by no means exhaustive, nor do I intend it to be. The "affective turn" in literary studies, cultural studies, and performance studies as well as the fields of psychology, biology, and anthropology is deep and vast. Several important examples, drawn from a wide range of disciplines, are anthologized in Melissa Gregg and Gregory J. Seigworth, eds., *The Affect Theory Reader* (Durham: Duke University Press, 2010).

64. Brian Massumi, *Parables for the Virtual: Movement, Affect, Sensation* (Durham: Duke University Press, 2002); Teresa Brennan, *The Transmission of Affect* (Ithaca: Cornell University Press, 2004), 2; Charles Altieri, *The Particulars of Rapture: An Aesthetics of the Affects* (Ithaca: Cornell University Press, 2003); Sara Ahmed, *The Cultural Politics of Emotion* (New York: Routledge, 2004), 6; Eve Kosofsky Sedgwick and Adam Frank, eds., *Shame and Its Sisters: A Silvan Tomkins Reader* (Durham: Duke University Press, 1995).

65. Ahmed, *Cultural Politics of Emotion,* 3.

66. Jill Dolan, *Utopia in Performance: Finding Hope at the Theater* (Ann Arbor: University of Michigan Press, 2005), 2, 6, 19; States, *Great Reckonings,* 37; Altieri, *Particulars,* 24. See also Marvin Carlson, "The Eternal Instant: Some Thoughts on Theatre and Religion," *Assaph* 14 (1997): 33–44.

67. Sedgwick and Frank, eds., *Shame and Its Sisters,* 38.

68. Gunning, "The Horror of Opacity," 52.

Chapter 2

1. John B. Gough, *Platform Echoes: Or, Living Truths for Head and Heart,* with an introduction by Rev. Lyman Abbott (Hartford, CT: A. D. Worthington, 1886), 83–84. Some printings of *Platform Echoes* feature an alternative subtitle, "Leaves from My Note-Book of Forty Years."

2. For more on Pierpont's possible involvement in *The Drunkard,* see John W. Frick, *Theatre, Culture and Temperance Reform in Nineteenth-Century America* (Cambridge: Cambridge University Press, 2003), 116–18; and Amy E. Hughes,

"Answering the Amusement Question: Antebellum Temperance Drama and the Christian Endorsement of Leisure," *New England Theatre Journal* 15 (2004): 1–19.

3. Frick, *Theatre, Culture, and Temperance Reform,* 64, 66; Michael R. Booth, "The Drunkard's Progress: Nineteenth-Century Temperance Drama," *Dalhousie Review* 44 (Summer 1964): 207; Judith N. McArthur, "Demon Rum on the Boards: Temperance Melodrama and the Tradition of Antebellum Reform," *Journal of the Early Republic* 9, no. 4 (Winter 1989): 536; Jeffrey D. Mason, *Melodrama and the Myth of America* (Bloomington: Indiana University Press, 1993), 83; Richard Moody, *Dramas from the American Theatre, 1762–1909* (Cleveland: World Publishing, 1966), 279–80. Similarly, Joan L. Silverman, in her unpublished dissertation "'I'll Never Touch Another Drop': Images of Alcoholism and Temperance in American Popular Culture, 1874–1919" (PhD diss., New York University, 1979), observes that in temperance dramaturgy "the hero's drinking intensifies after marriage and parenthood, culminating in delirium tremens" (37).

4. W. H. Sedley Smith, *The Drunkard; or, The Fallen Saved!* (Boston: Jones's Publishing House, 1847), 5. Subsequent page references will be indicated parenthetically.

5. Maud Skinner and Otis Skinner, *One Man in His Time: The Adventures of H. Watkins, Strolling Player, 1845–63, from His Journal* (Philadelphia: University of Pennsylvania Press, 1938), 70.

6. As I discuss in chapter 1, my analysis is informed by the work of Rachel Adams, Lennard J. Davis, Leslie A. Fiedler, Rosemarie Garland-Thomson, and others who have discussed the ways in which the disabled body canonizes the normal body.

7. Bruce A. McConachie, *Melodramatic Formations: American Theatre and Society, 1820–1870* (Iowa City: University of Iowa Press, 1992), 178.

8. As John W. Crowley has noted, the few extant biographies of Gough (all written before 1930) were intended for a popular audience and "are, in effect, hagiographies" ("Slaves to the Bottle: Gough's Autobiography and Douglass's Narrative," in *The Serpent in the Cup: Temperance in American Literature,* ed. David S. Reynolds and Debra J. Rosenthal [Amherst: University of Massachusetts Press, 1997], 135n38). To remedy this, Thomas Augst is developing a cultural biography of Gough (in progress). His scholarship on Gough includes "A Drunkard's Story," *Common-Place* 10, no. 3 (April 2010), http://www.common-place.org; and "Temperance, Mass Culture, and the Romance of Experience," *American Literary History* 19, no. 2 (Summer 2007): 297–323. See also Graham Warder, "Selling Sobriety: How Temperance Reshaped Culture in Antebellum America" (PhD diss., University of Massachusetts-Amherst, 2000), 108–220.

9. The literature on temperance reform is substantial, especially regarding

prohibitionist activity after the Civil War and during the early twentieth century. Since I am interested in early renditions of the *delirium tremens*, particularly during the 1840s, for the purposes of this study I concentrate on temperance activism during the antebellum period. Representative scholarship focusing (in whole or in part) on these early efforts includes Joseph R. Gusfield, *Symbolic Crusade: Status Politics and the American Temperance Movement* (Urbana: University of Illinois Press, 1963); W. J. Rorabaugh, *The Alcoholic Republic: An American Tradition* (New York: Oxford University Press, 1979); Ian R. Tyrrell, *Sobering Up: From Temperance to Prohibition in Antebellum America, 1800–1860* (Westport, CT: Greenwood Press, 1979); Mark Edward Lender and James Kirby Martin, *Drinking in America: A History* (New York: Free Press, 1982); Jack S. Blocker Jr., *American Temperance Movements: Cycles of Reform* (Boston: Twayne Publishers, 1989); Leonard U. Blumberg and William L. Pittman, *Beware the First Drink! The Washington Temperance Movement and Alcoholics Anonymous* (Seattle: Glen Abbey Books, 1991); and Steven Mintz, *Moralists and Modernizers: America's Pre-Civil War Reformers* (Baltimore: Johns Hopkins University Press, 1995).

10. The lithograph's title deliberately invokes *The Rake's Progress* (1732–33), a series of eight paintings by William Hogarth detailing a young man's escalating debauchery. For more on the mass-market influence of Currier & Ives, which proudly provided "Colored Engravings for the People," see Harry T. Peters, *Currier and Ives: Printmakers to the American People* (Garden City, NY: Doubleday, Doran, 1942); Bryan F. LeBeau, *Currier & Ives: America Imagined* (Washington, DC: Smithsonian Institution Press, 2001); and Peter C. Marzio, "Lithography as a Democratic Art: A Reappraisal," *Leonardo* 4, no. 1 (Winter 1971): 37–48.

11. Although now housed in the New-York Historical Society's ephemera collection, this particular card was probably distributed and signed outside of the United States. It is dated January 19, 1845, and Father Mathew's first visit to the US occurred in 1849.

12. Booth, "The Drunkard's Progress," 211; McArthur, "Demon Rum on the Boards," especially 533–39; McConachie, *Melodramatic Formations*, 184; Frick, *Theatre, Culture, and Temperance Reform*, 68–71.

13. Joel Bernard, "From Fasting to Abstinence: The Origins of the American Temperance Movement," in *Drinking: Behavior and Belief in Modern History*, ed. Susanna Barrows and Robin Room (Berkeley: University of California Press, 1991), 345.

14. Gerald N. Grob, introduction to Edward Jarvis, *Insanity and Idiocy in Massachusetts: Report of the Commission on Lunacy* (1855; reprint, Cambridge: Harvard University Press, 1971), 9. This rapid expansion did not go unnoticed in its time: Pliny Earle discusses the increasing number of asylums in the United States in his 1848 report on the Bloomingdale Insane Asylum in New York, attributing the

growth to "the attention of the community, in various parts of the country, [which] became awakened to the wants of that suffering class, and the efforts of many individuals [who] were actively directed to measures for their relief" (*History, Description and Statistics of the Bloomingdale Asylum for the Insane* [New York: Egbert, Hovey & King, 1848], 19–20).

15. Roger Bastide, *The Sociology of Mental Disorder* [1965], trans. Jean McNeil (New York: David McKay, 1972), 195.

16. See, for example, Norman Dain, *Concepts of Insanity in the United States, 1789–1865* (New Brunswick: Rutgers University Press, 1964); Mary Ann Jimenez, *Changing Faces of Madness: Early American Attitudes and Treatment of the Insane* (Hanover, NH: University Press of New England, 1987); David J. Rothman, *The Discovery of the Asylum: Social Order and Disorder in the New Republic*, rev. ed. (Piscataway, NJ: Aldine Transaction, 2002); and Andrew T. Scull, "Madness and Segregative Control: The Rise of the Insane Asylum," *Social Problems* 24, no. 3 (February 1977): 337–51.

17. Rorabaugh, *Alcoholic Republic*, 40–46; Tyrrell, *Sobering Up*, 17; Lender and Martin, *Drinking in America*, 37; Blocker, *American Temperance Movements*, 7–8; Mintz, *Moralists and Modernizers*, 72; Thomas R. Pegram, *Battling Demon Rum: The Struggle for a Dry America, 1800–1933* (Chicago: Ivan R. Dee, 1998), 13–15. In their history of the first inebriate asylum established in the United States (an institutional model originally advocated by Rush), John W. Crowley and William L. White assert, "The American temperance movement can rightly be said to have begun with the publication of [Rush's] *Inquiry*" (*Drunkard's Refuge: The Lessons of the New York State Inebriate Asylum* [Amherst: University of Massachusetts Press, 2004], 3). For more on Rush's influence, see Katherine H. Nelson, "The Temperance Physicians: Developing Concepts of Addiction" (PhD diss., American University, 2006), 48–58.

18. Jimenez, *Changing Faces of Madness*, 72.

19. Benjamin Rush, *Medical Inquiries and Observations Upon the Diseases of the Mind* (Philadelphia: Kimber & Richardson, 1812), 358, 164, 266–67 (emphasis in original).

20. Dimitrios Adamis et al., "A Brief Review of the History of Delirium as a Mental Disorder," *History of Psychiatry* 18, no. 4 (2007): 465.

21. Jimenez, *Changing Faces of Madness*, 88; Tyrrell, *Sobering Up*, 317. Jimenez's analysis of documents and reports from the State Lunatic Hospital in Worcester, Massachusetts, during the period 1837–1855 reveals that intemperance was the most common reason cited by family and friends who brought patients to the asylum (169n65).

22. Frick observes, "According to reformers and entrepreneurs alike, social progress demanded the adoption of an entirely new nexus of values—one that

stressed self-mastery, industry, thrift, self-denial and sobriety—as well as the eradication of traditional attitudes and behavior patterns that might be construed as obstacles to change" (*Theatre, Culture, and Temperance Reform,* 30). Tyrrell suggests that this attitude was particularly prevalent among the Washingtonians, who considered drunkenness to be a personal or moral failing rather than an inevitable effect of nurture or nature (*Sobering Up,* 170). For more discussion regarding the emphasis of social norms within the temperance movement, see Gusfield, *Symbolic Crusade,* 61–86.

23. For more on the advent of "moral treatment," which became the dominant therapeutic approach in lunatic asylums during the 1820s and 1830s, see Jimenez, *Changing Faces of Madness,* 111–23; and Rothman, *Discovery of the Asylum,* 130–54.

24. Earle, *History,* 24.

25. Robert H. Abzug, *Cosmos Crumbling: American Reform and the Religious Imagination* (New York: Oxford University Press, 1994); Mintz, *Moralists and Modernizers,* 11.

26. Earle, *History,* 26–35 (quotation on 26). Karen Halttunen points out that asylums depicted in literature during this period feature many of the sensational devices associated with gothic horror—in part because institutions for the mentally ill often failed to live up to their promise of benevolent treatment ("Gothic Mystery and the Birth of the Asylum: The Cultural Construction of Deviance in Early Nineteenth-Century America," in *Moral Problems in American Life: New Perspectives on Cultural History,* ed. Karen Halttunen and Lewis Perry [Ithaca: Cornell University Press, 1998], 41–57).

27. Earle, *History,* 49–50.

28. See figure 2.2 and Smith, *The Drunkard,* 40.

29. Earle, *History,* 39, 45–46, 50–51. Whether deliberately or not, Earle invokes the "sober house" here, a concept pioneered by Rush in 1812.

30. A notable exception is *Confessions of a Female Inebriate, or, Intemperance in High Life* (Boston: William Henshaw, 1842), an anonymous, Washingtonian-style temperance narrative written from the perspective of a woman. However, according to Crowley, the temperance activist Isaac F. Shepard probably wrote it. The narrative is anthologized in John W. Crowley, ed., *Drunkard's Progress: Narratives of Addiction, Despair, and Recovery* (Baltimore: Johns Hopkins University Press, 1999), 69–79. For more on the gender dynamics of drunkards and their victims, see, for example, Mary Ann Clawson, *Constructing Brotherhood: Class, Gender, and Fraternalism* (Princeton: Princeton University Press, 1989); Karen Sánchez-Eppler, "Temperance in the Bed of a Child: Incest and Social Order in Nineteenth-Century America," *American Quarterly* 47, no. 1 (March 1995): 1–33; and Ric N. Caric, "The Man with the Poker Enters the Room: Delirium Tremens and Popular Culture in Philadelphia, 1828–1850," *Pennsylvania History* 74, no. 4 (Autumn 2007): 452–91.

31. Earle, *History,* 43. This assertion is supported by Caric's study of records kept by the Philadelphia Alms House; he notes that the vast majority of documented DTs patients hailed from the working classes, even though rumors and stories circulating in popular culture tended to feature middle- and upper-class characters ("The Man with the Poker").

32. Edward Jarvis, *Insanity and Idiocy,* 55; Robert A. Gross, "Preserving Culture: Edward Jarvis and the Memory of Concord," in *Traditions and Reminiscences of Concord, Massachusetts, 1779–1878,* ed. Sarah Chapin (Amherst: University of Massachusetts Press, 1993), xxvi; William Sims Bainbridge, "Religious Insanity in America: The Official Nineteenth-Century Theory," *Sociological Analysis* 45, no. 3 (Fall 1984): 223–39. As Grob points out, Jarvis's views seem deeply informed by mainstream norms and middle-class values; his education at Harvard University at a time when reformist Unitarian liberalism dominated that institution may be one reason why self-improvement features so prominently in his writing (introduction to Jarvis, *Insanity and Idiocy,* 42).

33. William Henry Sedley Smith, Manuscript Side for Edward Middleton, 1844, Series III, Item 64, William Henry Sedley Smith Collection, Harvard Theatre Collection.

34. See, for example, Isaac Ray, *Mental Hygiene* (1863; reprint, with an introduction by Frank J. Curran, New York: Hafner Publishing, 1968), 243–44.

35. Ironically, Cribbs is the only one who actually experiences the horrors of institutionalization, when he is mistaken for Middleton and put in jail.

36. As the play progresses, Agnes's story is revealed: she went mad when her fiancé died of the *delirium tremens.* The villain Cribbs confesses in a soliloquy, "for my own purposes I ruined [him], I triumphed over him—he fell—died in a drunken fit, and she [Agnes] went crazy" (17).

37. Lawrence W. Levine, in *Highbrow/Lowbrow: The Emergence of Cultural Hierarchy in America* (Cambridge: Harvard University Press, 1988), argues that Shakespeare's plays made up a kind of shared vocabulary for nineteenth-century audiences, so the similarity between Agnes and the deranged heroine of *Hamlet* may not be coincidental. During this period, the portrayal of madness on American and British stages was deeply informed by long-standing theatrical conventions rooted in Shakespearean drama.

38. John Bouvé Clapp, "The First Dramatic Success," *Boston Evening Transcript,* 16 May 1903, n.p., Boston Museum Subject File, Charles E. Mason, Jr. Print Room, Boston Athenaeum.

39. Boston Museum Cast Lists, vol. 1 (1845–57), Harvard Theatre Collection. In playbills and cast lists from the early 1850s, Gann goes by her married name, Mrs. Wulf Fries. Incidentally, Gann originated Eliza in H. J. Conway's adaptation of *Uncle Tom's Cabin* at the museum in 1852.

40. Unidentified clipping, "Personalities: Tho" Clippings File, Harvard Theatre Collection; William Winter, *The Jeffersons* (Boston: James R. Osgood, 1881), 95; John Bouvé Clapp, "The First Star," *Boston Evening Transcript*, 9 May 1903, n.p., Boston Museum Subject File, Prints and Photographs Department, Boston Athenaeum. Playbills from the original run of *The Drunkard* indicate that the actress "Miss E. Coad" originated the role of Agnes (Boston Museum Playbills File, Harvard Theatre Collection). This might be Emily Coad, an actress and singer who debuted at the Chestnut Theatre in Philadelphia and eventually enjoyed a solid career in California during the Gold Rush era ("Drop-Curtain Monographs," *New York Times*, 3 July 1887, 16). The 1844 premiere of *The Drunkard* also featured Mrs. G. C. Germon (née Jane Anderson and a sister of Elizabeth Anderson/Mrs. J. W. Thoman) as Mary. As I discuss in the next chapter, Germon went on to originate Eliza Harris in the earliest presentations of George C. Aiken's version of *Uncle Tom's Cabin* (1852) at the Troy Museum (Troy, New York) and National Theatre (New York City).

41. McConachie, *Melodramatic Formations*, 184–85; Mason, *Melodrama*, 84–85; Frick, *Theatre, Culture, and Temperance Reform*, 123; Bastide, *Sociology of Mental Disorder*, 207. Although I argue that Agnes is an essential and meaningful character in Smith's play, it is important to keep in mind that scripts were frequently revised, shortened, or otherwise altered in production. For example, the actor Harry Watkins writes in his diary that when he performed the play, he often provided the company with an edited version, comprising four instead of five acts, that omitted Agnes altogether (entry dated 4 January 1851, Harry Watkins Diary, vol. 6, Skinner Family Papers, Harvard Theatre Collection). But even when Agnes was absent, other references to insanity likely remained intact—most obviously the DTs scene itself, the most vivid and spectacular reference of all.

42. It may also be that the *delirium tremens*—both in life and on stage—constitutes a sentimental response to economic crisis. See Joseph Fichtelberg, *Critical Fictions: Sentiment and the American Market, 1780–1870* (Athens: University of Georgia Press, 2003), and Caric, "The Man with the Poker."

43. For example, see Bluford Adams, *E Pluribus Barnum: The Great Showman and the Making of U.S. Popular Culture* (Minneapolis: University of Minnesota Press, 1997); Foster Rhea Dulles, *A History of Recreation: America Learns to Play* (New York: Appleton-Century-Crofts, 1965); Neil Harris, *Humbug: The Art of P. T. Barnum* (Boston: Little, Brown, 1973); Benjamin McArthur, *The Man Who Was Rip Van Winkle: Joseph Jefferson and Nineteenth-Century American Theatre* (New Haven: Yale University Press, 2007); McConachie, *Melodramatic Formations;* Geoffrey S. Proehl, *Coming Home Again: American Family Drama and the Figure of the Prodigal* (Madison: Fairleigh Dickinson University Press, 1997).

44. From entries dated 16 April 1849, 24 November 1849, 7 December 1849,

and 14 June 1850, in Harry Watkins Diary, vol. 4, Skinner Family Papers, Harvard Theatre Collection. In somewhat edited form, these entries may be consulted in Skinner and Skinner, *One Man in His Time,* 70, 82, 89.

45. Quotations from entries dated 17 April and 6 December 1849, Harry Watkins Diary, vol. 4. See also Skinner and Skinner, *One Man in His Time,* 71, 82, which is quoted in McConachie, *Melodramatic Formations,* 192.

46. McConachie suggests that, due to "the extreme physicality of the acting conventions" associated with the scene, "managers tried to cast the role with men who were in top physical condition" (*Melodramatic Formations,* 191, 192).

47. Michael L. Quinn, "Celebrity and the Semiotics of Acting," *New Theatre Quarterly* 4 (1990): 155.

48. McConachie, *Melodramatic Formations,* 176.

49. Proehl, *Coming Home Again,* 57.

50. Joseph Francis Daly, *The Life of Augustin Daly* (New York: Macmillan, 1917), 14–15. As I discuss later in this chapter, the temperance lecturer John B. Gough often cited his brief acting career as evidence of the depths to which he had sunk while he was a drinking man.

51. William Henry Sedley Smith, Diary, 1852–1854, Rare Books Department, Boston Public Library, Boston, Massachusetts. Other entries in which Smith describes his struggle with alcohol include 21–26 October 1852; and 25–26 November, 10–18 February, and 25–26 March 1853. For more on Smith's diary, particularly in regard to how it may contribute to our understanding of H. J. Conway's version *Uncle Tom's Cabin* (first presented at the Boston Museum in November 1852), see Edward Kahn, "Creator of Compromise: William Henry Sedley Smith and the Boston Museum's *Uncle Tom's Cabin,*" *Theatre Survey* 41, no. 2 (November 2000): 71–82.

52. Entry dated 16 April 1849, Harry Watkins Diary, vol. 4.

53. Mason, *Melodrama,* 65–66, 70; Frick, *Theatre, Culture, and Temperance Reform,* 32–35, 66, 121–23.

54. Tyrrell, *Sobering Up,* 159, 60, 73. For more on the Washingtonians, see Lender and Martin, *Drinking in America,* 75–79; Blocker, *American Temperance Movements,* 39–51; and Pegram, *Battling Demon Rum,* 24–31. Although the Washingtonians frequently criticized Gough after he achieved notoriety, Lyman Abbott, in his biographical introduction to a collection of Gough's stories and lectures, states, "If the Washingtonian movement had done the world no other service, the world would owe it a large debt for giving us John B. Gough" (Gough, *Platform Echoes,* 35).

55. Tyrrell, *Sobering Up,* 35–158. In this respect, *The Drunkard* seems to be very much a product of its time. In the second act, Stevens, a farmer, expresses concern that Middleton's casual drinking may transform into a persistent habit: "I don't say

that he does take too much liquor—but there's a great many that has began that way" (23). The principle underlying the total abstinence pledge was that moderate consumption of alcohol inevitably led to excessive consumption, and Stevens's comment reflects this belief. Moreover, in a conversation with Cribbs late in the fourth act, Mrs. Spindle alludes to the new vogue for teetotalism, asking him, "Do the 'stocracy go the hull temperance principle, and give their visitors nothing but ice water?" (43). The concept of teetotalism is highlighted most dramatically after Middleton's bout with the DTs, when Arden Rencelaw saves the protagonist from suicide by administering the pledge and putting him on the path of redemption. In true Washingtonian style, Rencelaw confesses that he himself suffered from habitual drinking for twenty years before being redeemed: "I am one of those, whose life and labors are passed in rescuing their fellow men from the abyss into which you have fallen. I administer the pledge of sobriety to those who would once more become an ornament to society. And a blessing to themselves, and to those around them. . . . come with me, we will restore you to society" (41).

56. Pegram, *Battling Demon Rum*, 29.

57. Heather S. Nathans, in *Slavery and Sentiment on the American Stage, 1787–1861: Lifting the Veil of Black* (Cambridge: Cambridge University Press, 2009), observes that this emphasis on performance can be traced back to the Great Awakening, which invited and embraced the performative contributions of individuals from all classes (17).

58. W. H. Daniels, *The Temperance Reform and Its Great Reformers* (New York: Nelson & Phillips, 1878), 99–108; Tyrrell, *Sobering Up*, 164.

59. Joseph Roach, *It* (Ann Arbor: University of Michigan Press, 2007), 1, 8.

60. John B. Gough, John B. Gough Papers (hereafter *JBGP*), folio vols. 1–19, American Antiquarian Society (AAS), Worcester, MA. The *JBGP* materials are grouped by size as well as content; Gough's scrapbooks are classified as "folio volumes" and the smaller bound manuscripts, such as his journals, are catalogued as "volumes." Given the limited scope of my project, I consulted the first three folios of the scrapbook collection, spanning the years 1842–45, 1845–48, and 1849–50. Unfortunately, the clippings are inconsistently dated; however, Gough seems to have placed them in chronological order. I offer approximate dates by taking into account their location in the scrapbook as well as information about Gough's whereabouts available in his lecture journal (JBG Journal, 1843–1858, *JBGP*, octavo vol. 6), in which he tracked the date, location, expenses incurred, compensation received, and number of pledge signatures collected at each engagement.

61. *Flushing Journal* (NY), n.d. (ca. April 1845), *JBGP*, folio vol. 1, n.p. (emphasis in original).

62. Baz Kershaw, "Curiosity or Contempt: On Spectacle, the Human, and Activism," *Theatre Journal* 55, no. 4 (December 2003): 591–611.

63. "Mr. Gough at the Carmine St. Church," *New-York Tribune,* n.d. (ca. December 1844); *Princeton Whig,* n.d. (ca. April 1845), emphasis in original; "Great Mass Temperance Meeting at Faneuil Hall—Mr. Gough, the Distinguished Washingtonian," *Boston Daily Mail,* n.d., *JBGP,* folio vol. 1, n.p.

64. "Mr. Gough at Hudson," *Columbia Washingtonian,* n.d. (ca. July 1844); "Great Meeting!" *Crystal Fount* (New York, NY), n.d. (ca. May 1844); "Great Meeting in the Prison," *White Mountain Torrent* (Concord, NH), n.d. (ca. February 1844); *JBGP,* folio vol. 1, n.p.

65. "John B. Gough," *Gloucester Telegraph* (MA), n.d. (ca. March 1844) and "Temperance," *Commercial Advertiser* (New York), n.d. (ca. late 1844), in *JBGP,* folio vol. 1, n.p.

66. This paradox is evident in T. Allston Brown, *A History of the New York Stage* (New York: Dodd, Mead, 1903), 1:255–56. Brown interrupts his narrative of theatrical facts and anecdotes with a paragraph about Gough: "During the season of 1835–36, John B. Gough appeared here [National Theatre] under the name of Gilbert. His stage career was a brief one, for he soon afterwards returned to his first trade of book-binding. He reappeared in 1837 as a low comedian at Providence, R. I., and he afterwards acted at the Old Lion Theatre, Boston. He traveled with a diorama and sang comic songs, and ultimately became famous as a temperance lecturer." The inclusion of Gough in Brown's narrative reveals that this famous solo performer was difficult to classify; Brown describes him neither as a "lecturer" nor as an "orator."

67. John B. Gough, *An Autobiography* (Boston: J. B. Gough, Gould, Kendall & Lincoln, 1848), 28–29.

68. John B. Gough, "I Have Often Been Asked Why I Did Not Adopt the Theatrical Profession," Lectures, *JBGP,* octavo vol. 3, n.p. (emphasis in original).

69. Gough, *An Autobiography,* 88.

70. JBG Journal, *JBGP,* 6–14.

71. Advertisement for *The Drunkard,* by W. H. Smith, Boston Museum, *Boston Evening Transcript,* 16 March 1864, 3; John B. Gough, Account Book (Roxbury, MA) 1843–1844, *JBGP,* octavo vol. 9; McConachie, *Melodramatic Formations,* 164. An advertisement in the *Transcript* the previous day indicates that the matinee was being offered "at the request of numerous families."

72. Spectators' fascination with Gough derived, in part, from his talent for speaking without a script.

73. "Mr. Gough—His Style of Speaking," *Princeton Whig,* n.d. (ca. April 1845); unidentified clipping (probably *National Intelligencer*), n.d. (ca. March 1845); *Pilot,* 28 September 1850; *JBGP,* folio vols. 1 and 3, n.p.

74. Gough, *Platform Echoes,* facing frontispiece (n.p.), list of illustrations (vii), 154–56.

75. Even today, total abstinence remains the recommended course for recover-

ing alcoholics. Most obviously, it is the central principle guiding Alcoholics Anonymous (AA), an organization that has much in common with the Washingtonian project of the 1840s. However, AA's emphasis on anonymity poses a stark contrast to nineteenth-century temperance activities, such as signing the pledge, that were usually performed in public.

76. Gough, *An Autobiography*, 75–86 (quotations on 76 and 81).

77. John B. Gough, "Statement of John B. Gough," 22 September 1845, *JBGP*, folio vol. 2, 9.

78. These quotations and subsequent ones in this section are from otherwise unidentified clippings (ca. late 1845) in *JBGP*, folio vol. 2 (emphasis in original). The *Christian World*, a short-lived Unitarian weekly in Boston, was published and edited by Rev. George G. Channing, a brother of the celebrated Rev. William Ellery Channing (1780–1842). Below this clipping in his scrapbook, Gough pasted a small slip of paper with the following verse, handwritten in pencil: "Should the great Channing from his grave arise / and on his brother's twaddle cast his eyes / How would he blush to think his honored name / Was borne by one who 's neither sense, nor shame."

79. "Gough's Case—Moral Obliquity," *New York Herald*, n.d. (ca. December 1845); *Goffiana; a Review of the Life and Writings of John B. Gough* (Boston: Ruggles, 1846), 38, 39.

80. Quotation is from an otherwise unidentified clipping in *JBGP*, folio vol. 2, 6.

81. Roach, *It*, 8.

82. Gough, JBG Journal, *JBGP*, 47.

83. McConachie, *Melodramatic Formations*, 175.

84. Ibid., 162.

85. Mason, *Melodrama*, 10, 11, 62, 67.

86. Frick, *Theatre, Culture, and Temperance Reform*, 13 (emphasis added), 60. Frick reiterates this assertion in John W. Frick, "'Not from the Drowsy Pulpit!': Moral Reform Melodrama on the Nineteenth-Century Stage," *Theatre Symposium* 15 (2007): 41–51.

87. Richard Hofstadter, *The Age of Reform: From Bryan to F.D.R.* (New York: Random House, 1955); Gusfield, *Symbolic Crusade*. The endurance of the arguments advanced by these scholars is evident in later studies. For example, Blocker writes in his preface, "Gusfield's *Symbolic Crusade* played a large part in defining issues of modern temperance research; although I disagree with Gusfield on many points, this book enters a debate that he more than anyone else began" (*American Temperance Movements*, ix).

88. Tyrrell, *Sobering Up*, 6; Blocker, *American Temperance Movements*, 161; Mintz, *Moralists and Modernizers*, xxii.

89. Bernard, "From Fasting to Abstinence," 337.

90. Jessica Warner and Janine Riviere, "Why Abstinence Matters to Americans," *Addiction* 102, no. 4 (April 2007): 502–5.

91. Of course, Haidt's framework is neither the only nor necessarily the best strategy for understanding the ideological underpinnings of activist movements. But it helpfully reveals points of overlap and contention across groups and collectives.

92. This brief summary is based on Jonathan Haidt and Jesse Graham, "When Morality Opposes Justice: Conservatives Have Moral Intuitions That Liberals May Not Recognize," *Social Justice Research* 20 (2007): 98–116. Quotation is from Haidt and Craig Joseph, "Intuitive Ethics: How Innately Prepared Intuitions Generate Culturally Variable Virtues," *Daedalus* 55 (Fall 2004): 56, an article that describes an earlier incarnation of the theory based on four moral intuitions. See also Haidt and Joseph, "The Moral Mind: How Five Sets of Innate Moral Intuitions Guide the Development of Many Culture-Specific Virtues, and Perhaps Even Modules," in *The Innate Mind: Foundations and the Future,* ed. Peter Carruthers, Stephen Laurence, and Stephen P. Stich (New York: Oxford University Press, 2008), 367–92. Haidt summarizes his findings in *The Righteous Mind: Why Good People Are Divided by Politics and Religion* (New York: Pantheon Books, 2012), which was not yet available at the time of this writing.

93. Haidt and Graham, "When Morality Opposes Justice," 106.

94. Gough, *Platform Echoes,* 83–84.

Chapter 3

1. William Wells Brown, *A Lecture Delivered before the Female Anti-Slavery Society of Salem* (Boston: Massachusetts Anti-Slavery Society, 1847), 4.

2. Saidiya V. Hartman, *Scenes of Subjection: Terror, Slavery, and Self-Making in Nineteenth-Century America* (New York: Oxford University Press, 1997), 62.

3. Leslie A. Fiedler, *The Inadvertent Epic: From Uncle Tom's Cabin to Roots* (New York: Simon and Schuster, 1979), 25.

4. Lauren Berlant, *The Female Complaint: The Unfinished Business of Sentimentality in American Culture* (Durham: Duke University Press, 2008), 44–46; Sarah Meer, *Uncle Tom Mania: Slavery, Minstrelsy, and Transatlantic Culture in the 1850s* (Athens: University of Georgia Press, 2005), 118–19; Hartman, *Scenes of Subjection,* 27. I acknowledge that in most *Uncle Tom* melodramas, Eliza and George are "whitened" racially (through cues like speech and social behavior) and dramaturgically (aggressively encoded as romantic protagonists). But they are also outlaws, and their status as such was repeatedly underscored: a playbill for Aiken's *Uncle Tom's Cabin* at the National Theatre, for example, lists the characters as "George Harris,

a Fugitive" and "Eliza, the Fugitive's Wife." Eliza's designation as "wife" simultaneously highlights and obfuscates the fact that slaves could not legally marry—one of George's motives for escaping. Playbill for *Uncle Tom's Cabin,* National Theatre (New York), 16 February 1854, Harvard Theatre Collection.

5. Claire Parfait, *The Publishing History of* Uncle Tom's Cabin, *1852–2002* (Burlington, VT: Ashgate, 2007), 14–15.

6. Meer, *Uncle Tom Mania;* Robin Bernstein, *Racial Innocence: Performing Childhood and Race from Slavery to Civil Rights* (New York: New York University Press, 2011); Jo-Ann Morgan, *Uncle Tom's Cabin as Visual Culture* (Columbia: University of Missouri Press, 2007); Patricia A. Turner, "The Rise and Fall of Eliza Harris: From Novel to Tom Shows to Quilts," 2007, Stephen Railton, ed., *Uncle Tom's Cabin and American Culture* (hereafter *UTC and American Culture*), University of Virginia, http://utc.iath.virginia.edu/interpret/exhibits/turner/turner.html; Patricia A. Turner, *Crafted Lives: Stories and Studies of African American Quilters* (Jackson: University Press of Mississippi, 2009), 160–62. See also Harry Birdoff, *The World's Greatest Hit: Uncle Tom's Cabin* (New York: S. F. Vanni, 1947); Fiedler, *Inadvertent Epic;* and Thomas F. Gossett, *Uncle Tom's Cabin and American Culture* (Dallas: Southern Methodist University Press, 1985), among many others. Exemplars of the tendency to treat *Uncle Tom's Cabin* as a kind of nineteenth-century urtext include Jane Tompkins, *Sensational Designs: The Cultural Work of American Fiction, 1790–1860* (New York: Oxford University Press, 1985), 122–46; Linda Williams, *Playing the Race Card: Melodramas of Black and White from Uncle Tom to O. J. Simpson* (Princeton: Princeton University Press, 2002); and Berlant, *Female Complaint,* 33–67.

7. Harriet Beecher Stowe, *Uncle Tom's Cabin; or, Life among the Lowly* (Boston: John P. Jewett, 1852); Harriet Beecher Stowe, *Uncle Tom's Cabin; or, Life among the Lowly,* illustrated ed. (Boston: John P. Jewett, 1853). See also Morgan, *Uncle Tom's Cabin as Visual Culture,* 22–26; Parfait, *Publishing History,* 67–89, 212–14.

8. Morgan observes that Billings's illustration of Eliza's escape "resembles a stage tableau" and that this "is no coincidence" in light of the prolific stage adaptations produced after the novel's publication (*Uncle Tom's Cabin as Visual Culture,* 86). Bernstein notes that George L. Aiken capitalized on the popularity of Billings's images by dramatizing all six plates from the first edition: "The correspondence between the first set of Billings images and the Aiken script is one hundred percent, and there is no noticeable correspondence between the Aiken script and Billings's second set of images [in the Illustrated Edition], . . . which was published after Aiken completed his script" (*Racial Innocence,* 118). Presumably, Aiken's choices regarding which other sensation scenes to include were guided by other criteria: What would move and enthrall his audience? What would work well on stage? Among many other possibilities in the novel, Aiken selected Eliza's flight, suggest-

ing that he believed the scene would fulfill such criteria. Other early adapters, such as C. W. Taylor, also chose to dramatize the scene.

9. George L. Aiken, *Uncle Tom's Cabin; or, Life among the Lowly* (New York: Samuel French, 1858). As Birdoff notes, many changes were made to Aiken's play during its run at the National Theatre in New York City during 1853–54 (*World's Greatest Hit,* 101–2). It seems likely that the 1858 Samuel French edition incorporates those changes. Because I am interested in audiences' reception of the play in the wake of improvements made to the Fugitive Slave Act, I also consult newspaper advertisements, reviews, and playbills from the years 1852 to 1854.

10. Several scholars have characterized Conway's *Uncle Tom* as politically conservative, among them Bruce A. McConachie, "Out of the Kitchen and into the Marketplace: Normalizing *Uncle Tom's Cabin* for the Antebellum Stage," *Journal of American Drama and Theatre* 3, no. 1 (Winter 1991): 5–28; and Bluford Adams, *E Pluribus Barnum: The Great Showman and the Making of U.S. Popular Culture* (Minneapolis: University of Minnesota Press, 1997). See also Robert C. Toll, *Blacking Up: The Minstrel Show in Nineteenth Century America* (New York: Oxford University Press, 1974), 88–97; Loren Kruger, "Our Theater? Stages in an American Cultural History," *American Literary History* 8, no. 4 (1996): 708–11; and John W. Frick, "'Not from the Drowsy Pulpit!': Moral Reform Melodrama on the Nineteenth-Century Stage," *Theatre Symposium* 15 (2007): 48–49. In contrast, Jeffrey D. Mason, in *Melodrama and the Myth of America* (Bloomington: Indiana University Press, 1993), argues that Aiken's version is equally conservative in its politics (89–126); and Edward Kahn asserts that the political position of Conway's script was "one of compromise" ("Creator of Compromise: William Henry Sedley Smith and the Boston Museum's *Uncle Tom's Cabin,*" *Theatre Survey* 41, no. 2 [November 2000]: 71). Historians disagree about which play was most popular. For example, Judith Williams asserts that Conway's was ("*Uncle Tom*'s Women," in *African American Performance and Theater History: A Critical Reader,* ed. Harry J. Elam and David Krasner [New York: Oxford University Press, 2001], 21), whereas Thomas L. Riis asserts the opposite ("The Music and Musicians in Nineteenth-Century Productions of *Uncle Tom's Cabin,*" *American Music* 4, no. 3 [Autumn 1986]: 269). See also Toll, *Blacking Up,* 88–97; and Bruce A. McConachie, "H. J. Conway's Dramatization of *Uncle Tom's Cabin:* A Previously Unpublished Letter," *Theatre Journal* 34, no. 2 (May 1982): 49.

11. "*Uncle Tom's Cabin* at the National Theatre" (unsigned; likely James Gordon Bennett), review of *Uncle Tom's Cabin,* by C. W. Taylor, National Theatre (New York), *New York Herald,* 3 September 1852, 4; advertisement for *Uncle Tom's Cabin,* National Theatre (New York), *New York Herald,* 2 September 1852, 6.

12. Playbill for *Uncle Tom's Cabin,* National Theatre (New York), 30 August 1852, Harry Birdoff Collection, Harriet Beecher Stowe Center, Hartford, CT; play-

bill for *Uncle Tom's Cabin,* Eagle Theatre (Boston), 16 October 1852, Harvard Theatre Collection; both playbills available at Railton, ed., *UTC and American Culture.* Meer, too, observes that surviving records indicate "Taylor made a feature of his 'Floating Ice'" (*Uncle Tom Mania,* 117).

13. Benjamin Quarles, *Black Abolitionists* (New York: Oxford University Press, 1969), 226–28; Birdoff, *World's Greatest Hit,* 46, 48, 51, 54.

14. "'Uncle Tom' among the Bowery Boys," review of *Uncle Tom's Cabin,* by George L. Aiken, National Theatre (New York), *New York Times,* 27 July 1853, 1 (emphasis in original).

15. Playbill for *Uncle Tom's Cabin,* National Theatre (New York), 16 February 1854; and playbill for *Uncle Tom's Cabin,* Bowery Theatre (New York), 10 February 1854, both at Harvard Theatre Collection. See also Birdoff, *World's Greatest Hit,* 100.

16. Birdoff, *World's Greatest Hit,* 44; review of *Uncle Tom's Cabin,* by George L. Aiken, Troy Museum, *Northern Budget* (Troy, NY), 7 October 1852, and playbill for *Uncle Tom's Cabin,* National Theatre (New York), 26 July 1853, both available at Railton, ed., *UTC and American Culture;* advertisement for *Uncle Tom's Cabin,* by C. W. Taylor, National Theatre (New York), *New York Herald,* 2 September 1852, 6. According to William Winter in *The Jeffersons* (Boston: James R. Osgood, 1881), Mrs. Germon was the sister of Elizabeth Anderson, later Mrs. J. W. Thoman (95).

17. T. Allston Brown, *A History of the New York Stage* (New York: Dodd, Mead, 1903), 1:309; "'Uncle Tom' among the Bowery Boys"; Joseph Norton Ireland, *Records of the New York Stage* (New York: T. H. Morrell, 1867), 1:620; Henry F. Stone, "Memories of *Uncle Tom's Cabin,*" *Dramatic Mirror,* 25 March 1901, n.p., available at Railton, ed., *UTC and American Culture.*

18. Marvin Carlson, *The Haunted Stage: The Theatre as Memory Machine* (Ann Arbor: University of Michigan Press, 2001), 52–95.

19. Stowe herself "whitened" Eliza after the story's original serialization in the *National Era;* she changed the heroine from a mulatto to a quadroon in the novel published by Jewett (Parfait, *Publishing History,* 83).

20. "'Uncle Tom' among the Bowery Boys"; Turner, "Rise and Fall of Eliza Harris"; Mason, *Melodrama,* 120. However, Mason does not take into account that *Uncle Tom's Cabin* constituted Stowe's response to the Compromise of 1850. Clearly, Bennett of the *New York Herald* and other critics did not believe slavery was a "background" issue in the play; their anxieties about the FSA help to explain why they considered *Uncle Tom* melodramas not only inappropriate but also incendiary.

21. Birdoff, *World's Greatest Hit,* 69, 74–75. Commenting on this review, Meer observes, "The moment of shared feeling is transmuted into evidence of *Uncle Tom*'s miraculous powers of spiritual enlightenment" (*Uncle Tom Mania,* 115).

22. "A Lecture by Lucy Stone," *New-York Tribune,* 4 February 1854, 7.

23. H. J. Conway, *Uncle Tom's Cabin* (1876 Promptbook), Howard Collection, Harry Ransom Humanities Research Center, University of Texas, Austin, 50–53; available at Railton, ed., *UTC and American Culture.* Unfortunately, the only known copy of Conway's script dates from after the Civil War, making it a somewhat tricky source for scholars interested in antebellum presentations of the play. However, as McConachie observes, it follows the outline of scenes in playbills for early productions, suggesting that the promptbook generally resembles the original text (*Melodramatic Formations: American Theatre and Society, 1820–1870* [Iowa City: University of Iowa Press, 1992], 289n31).

24. H. J. Conway, letter to Moses Kimball, 1 June 1852, Moses Kimball Papers, Boston Athenaeum.

25. McConachie, "H. J. Conway's Dramatization," 151.

26. Conway, *Uncle Tom's Cabin,* 43, 46. The presence of bloodhounds is significant for several reasons. In the popular imagination, dogs have long been associated with Eliza's flight, in large part because post–Civil War "Tom Shows" frequently featured them. But bloodhounds were not used in antebellum productions. Dogs are invoked metaphorically in Aiken's *Uncle Tom's Cabin*—for example, Eliza likens her pursuers to animals, saying, "How shall I escape these human blood-hounds?" (12)—but they do not appear on stage. The Conway promptbook suggests that live animals were not deployed in the Harrises' escape scene; instead, actors barked from the wings. Interestingly, a similar scenario is invoked in *The Hunted Slaves* (1861), an oil painting by Richard Ansdell that depicts a male fugitive slave wielding a hatchet to protect his female companion from a pack of dogs. The painting demonstrates that images of bloodhounds pursuing runaways circulated transatlantically at this time; also, given the medium (oil painting), it suggests that such representations were encountered and consumed by diverse audiences, including elites.

27. Conway, *Uncle Tom's Cabin,* 44, 46, 48.

28. Advertisements for *Uncle Tom's Cabin,* American Museum (New York), in *New York Times,* 22 November 1853, 5 (emphasis in original); and *New York Herald,* 29 November 1853, 5; both available at Railton, ed., *UTC and American Culture.*

29. Bernstein, *Racial Innocence,* 14. Here, Bernstein invokes both Diana Taylor, *The Archive and the Repertoire: Performing Cultural Memory in the Americas* (Durham: Duke University Press, 2003), and Fiedler, *Inadvertent Epic.*

30. Howard Thurman, *Deep River: Reflections on the Religious Insight of Certain of the Negro Spirituals* (Port Washington, NY: Kennikat Press, 1969), 66. For more on the music culture of slaves during the antebellum era, see Dena J. Epstein, *Sinful Tunes and Spirituals: Black Folk Music to the Civil War* (Urbana: University

of Illinois Press, 1977). Underscoring the association between rivers and freedom, Vincent Harding uses the river as an ongoing metaphor in his study *There Is a River: The Black Struggle for Freedom in America* (San Diego: Harcourt Brace, 1981).

31. Tompkins, *Sensational Designs,* 138. In the novel, Stowe makes some of these connections explicit—when Eliza first glimpses the Ohio River, for example: "Her first glance was at the river, which lay, like Jordan, between her and the Canaan of liberty on the other side" (*Uncle Tom's Cabin* [1852], 1:82–83).

32. M. A. Collier and E. J. Loder, "Eliza's Flight, A Scene from Uncle Tom's Cabin" (Boston: Oliver Ditson, 1852).

33. *Pictures and Stories from Uncle Tom's Cabin* (Boston: John P. Jewett, 1853), cover, title page, 8–9; Stephen Railton, "*Uncle Tom* as Children's Book," n.d., available at Railton, ed., *UTC and American Culture.*

34. Paul Holzwarth, undated transcription of grave markers in Oxford South Congregational Church Cemetery (Oxford, MA), USGenWeb Project, http://usgwarchives.net/ma/mafiles.htm; Benjamin S. Jones, *Abolitionrieties: Or, Remarks on Some of the Members of the Pennsylvania State Anti-Slavery Society for the Eastern District, and the American Anti-Slavery Society* (n.p., 1840[?]).

35. Jill Weitzman Fenichell, "Fragile Lessons: Ceramic and Porcelain Representations of *Uncle Tom's Cabin,*" in *Ceramics in America 2006,* ed. Robert Hunter (Hanover: Chipstone Foundation, 2006), 41. Louise L. Stevenson argues, however, that we should bear in mind that the inclusion of *Uncle Tom's Cabin* objects in American art collections "reflects more about the taste of professional and amateur collectors from the late nineteenth century onward than about the preference of nineteenth-century consumers who lived through the rage for the novel" ("Virtue Displayed: The Tie-Ins of *Uncle Tom's Cabin,*" 2007, in Railton, ed., *UTC and American Culture*). On the other hand, collectors who preserved these objects after the Civil War were motivated to do so, in part, because they understood them to be culturally and historically significant.

36. Hartman, *Scenes of Subjection,* 22.

37. "*Uncle Tom's Cabin* at the National Theatre."

38. Leonard Cassuto, *The Inhuman Race: The Racial Grotesque in American Literature and Culture* (New York: Columbia University Press, 1997), 86–87, 101, 102 (emphasis in original). It is noteworthy that the first play by an African American to be published in the United States, William Wells Brown's *The Escape; or, A Leap for Freedom* (Boston: R. F. Wallcut, 1858), centered precisely on this topic. Wells was a fugitive slave who achieved recognition on both sides of the Atlantic as a writer and lecturer. Meer observes that the fugitive slave also looms large in "anti-*Tom* novels" penned by proslavery writers; these texts "return obsessively to the subject of runaways, and in the frequency of their references they point to the impact fugitive slaves were themselves making upon the argument" (*Uncle Tom Mania,* 76). Daniel

S. Whitney, among others, wrote plays dramatizing the possibility that free men and women, including whites, could be kidnapped and enslaved under the revived FSA. For more discussion about Whitney's *Warren, A Tragedy in Five Acts* (1850) and other dramas featuring fugitive or kidnapped slaves, see Amy E. Hughes, "Defining Faith: Theatrical Reactions to Pro-Slavery Christianity in Antebellum America," in *Interrogating America through Theatre and Performance*, ed. William Demastes and Iris Smith Fischer (New York: Palgrave Macmillan, 2007), 29–45; and Heather S. Nathans, *Slavery and Sentiment on the American Stage, 1787–1861: Lifting the Veil of Black* (Cambridge: Cambridge University Press, 2009), 80–85.

39. For more on the Fugitive Slave Act and its history, see Larry Gara, "The Fugitive Slave Law: A Double Paradox," *Civil War History* 10 (1964): 229–40; and Stanley W. Campbell, *The Slave Catchers: Enforcement of the Fugitive Slave Law, 1850–1860* (Chapel Hill: University of North Carolina Press, 1970), 3–25. For more on the perceptions and pursuits of runaway slaves, see, among others, Herbert Aptheker, "Slave Resistance in the United States," in *Key Issues in the Afro-American Experience*, ed. Nathan I. Huggins, Martin Kilson, and Daniel M. Fox (New York: Harcourt Brace Jovanovich, 1971), 161–73; Paul Finkelman, ed., *Articles on American Slavery*, vol. 6, *Fugitive Slaves* (New York: Garland Publishing, 1989); Freddie L. Parker, *Running for Freedom: Slave Runaways in North Carolina, 1775–1840* (New York: Garland Publishing, 1993); Freddie L. Parker, ed., *Stealing a Little Freedom: Advertisements for Slave Runaways in North Carolina, 1791–1840* (New York: Garland Publishing, 1994); and John Hope Franklin and Loren Schweninger, *Runaway Slaves: Rebels on the Plantation* (New York: Oxford University Press, 1999).

40. US Constitution, art. IV, sec. 2, par. 3.

41. Campbell, *Slave Catchers*, 49; Jane H. Pease and William H. Pease, "Confrontation and Abolition in the 1850s," *Journal of American History* 58, no. 4 (March 1972): 923–37; David R. Maginnes, "The Case of the Court House Rioters in the Rendition of the Fugitive Slave Anthony Burns, 1854," *Journal of Negro History* 56, no. 1 (1971): 31–42.

42. Frederick Douglass, *My Bondage and My Freedom* (New York: Miller, Orton & Mulligan, 1855), 431. By the time installments of *Uncle Tom's Cabin* began appearing in the *National Era* in 1851, Stowe had changed her subtitle to "Life among the Lowly"—an adjustment that "shift[ed] the focus from the specific category of slaves to the universal one of the poor and downtrodden" (Parfait, *Publishing History*, 21).

43. Cassuto, *Inhuman Race*, 80. For a discussion of the long-term ramifications of antebellum laws reducing slaves to property, see Stephen M. Best, *The Fugitive's Properties: Law and the Poetics of Possession* (Chicago: University of Chicago Press, 2004).

44. *Anti-Slavery Almanac for 1846* (New York: Finch & Weed, [1845]), n.p. (emphasis in original).

45. For more on how literacy played a role in Douglass's self-actualization, see Lucinda H. MacKethan, "From Fugitive Slave to Man of Letters: The Conversion of Frederick Douglass," *Journal of Narrative Technique* 16, no. 1 (Winter 1986): 55–71.

46. Douglass, *My Bondage and My Freedom*, 146, 157, 159, 161 (emphasis in original). *My Bondage and My Freedom* is a revision of Douglass's original narrative, first published in 1845; as John Sekora and Peter A. Dorsey argue, this version seems to represent Douglass's thoughts and reflections most faithfully (John Sekora, "'Mr. Editor, If You Please': Frederick Douglass, *My Bondage and My Freedom*, and the End of the Abolitionist Imprint," *Callaloo* 17, no. 2 [Spring 1994]: 608–26; Peter A. Dorsey, "Becoming the Other: The Mimesis of Metaphor in Douglass's *My Bondage and My Freedom*," *PMLA* 111, no. 3 [May 1996]: 435–50).

47. In addition, when Eliza "steals" Harry, she saves him from a routine performance of oppression: the first time he appears in Aiken's play, Harry does not speak or otherwise express his personality but rather embodies a generic type—Jim Crow—by dancing a "breakdown" at Mr. Shelby's command (6). This moment enacts what Hartman calls the "innocent amusements" of the plantation, when slaves performed for the master's edification (*Scenes of Subjection*, 17–48). Despite the carefree character of such performances, they reinforced the relation between dominator and dominated.

48. Harriet Beecher Stowe, *A Key to Uncle Tom's Cabin* (Boston: John P. Jewett, 1853), 48. In 1835, the *Anti-Slavery Record* pictorially reenacted a similar incident, two decades before Margaret Garner's infamous infanticide: "The Desperation of a Mother," *Anti-Slavery Record* 1, no. 9 (September 1835): 1.

49. Stowe, *A Key*, 67–123 (quotation on 72; emphasis in original).

50. For more discussion about runaways who found refuge in swamps, especially their influence on antebellum literature, see William Tynes Cowan, *The Slave in the Swamp: Disrupting the Plantation Narrative* (New York: Routledge, 2005); and Lisa Whitney, "In the Shadow of *Uncle Tom's Cabin:* Stowe's Vision of Slavery from the Great Dismal Swamp," *New England Quarterly* 66, no. 4 (December 1993): 552–69.

51. Jennifer Putzi, *Identifying Marks: Race, Gender, and the Marked Body in Nineteenth-Century America* (Athens: University of Georgia Press, 2006), 104.

52. Stowe, *A Key*, 5. Stowe extensively cites and reproduces advertisements in her *Key*, even though she also says "they are less common now, [which] is a matter of hope and gratulation" (21).

53. Ibid., 13, 175–83 (quotations on 78–79 and 81).

54. *Oxford English Dictionary*, 2nd ed. (online version September 2011), s.v. "chattel" (especially I.1 and I.3) and "cattle" (I and II).

55. Jean Baudrillard, *Simulacra and Simulation* [1981], trans. Sheila Faria Glaser (Ann Arbor: University of Michigan Press, 1994), 18–19.

56. Playbill, *Uncle Tom's Cabin,* National Theatre (New York), 30 August 1852, Harry Birdoff Collection, Harriet Beecher Stowe Center; available at Railton, ed., *UTC and American Culture;* "*Uncle Tom's Cabin* at the National Theatre."

57. Conway, *Uncle Tom's Cabin,* 41–42.

58. Bertram Wyatt-Brown, "Modernizing Southern Slavery: The Proslavery Argument Reinterpreted," in *Region, Race, and Reconstruction: Essays in Honor of C. Vann Woodward,* ed. J. Morgan Krousser and James M. McPherson (New York: Oxford University Press, 1982), 27–49.

59. "'Uncle Tom' among the Bowery Boys." Cited in Meer, *Uncle Tom Mania,* 108. See also Birdoff, *World's Greatest Hit,* 77. In light of the audience's supposed support of the mulatto "freeman," it is tempting to wonder why images of Eliza were more widespread than those of George. Both Conway and Aiken retained the Harrises' sensational escape on the craggy ravine, when the family flees the slave catchers while under gunfire. Morgan speculates that its relative absence in American visual culture reveals the limits of abolitionist sentiment during the 1850s: a mulatto fugitive turning pistols on his pursuers was, perhaps, unpalatable for all but the most ardent abolitionists (*Uncle Tom's Cabin as Visual Culture,* 26). If this is true, then it helps to explain why Northerners would embrace the mother's dash for freedom in lieu of the more radical "Freeman's Defense."

60. Campbell, *Slave Catchers,* 49.

61. Brown, *A Lecture,* 4 (emphasis added).

62. Berlant, *Female Complaint,* 48.

63. Michel de Certeau, *The Practice of Everyday Life* (Berkeley: University of California Press, 1984), 165–76.

64. *A Grand Slave Hunt, or Trial of Speed for the Presidency,* unsigned lithograph, ca. 1852–56, American Antiquarian Society. In this cartoon, Webster and other politicians chase a runaway slave mother and her children; in Webster's hand is a paper labeled "Fugitive Slave Law."

65. Birdoff, *World's Greatest Hit,* 92–93; Meer, *Uncle Tom Mania,* 111–12.

66. Meer, *Uncle Tom Mania,* 118–19; Hartman, *Scenes of Subjection,* 27.

67. Tompkins, *Sensational Designs,* xvi.

68. Railton makes this observation in "*UTC* as Magic Lantern Show," 2007, available at Railton, ed., *UTC and American Culture.* Railton's online archive also features a digital reenactment of the show.

69. Berlant, *Female Complaint,* 47.

Chapter 4

1. Elizabeth Cady Stanton, "'Reconstruction': Lecture by ECS in Brooklyn, New York [19 February 1867]," in *The Selected Papers of Elizabeth Cady Stanton and*

Susan B. Anthony, ed. Ann D. Gordon (New Brunswick: Rutgers University Press, 2000), 2:28.

2. Augustin Daly, *Under the Gaslight: A Totally Original and Picturesque Drama of Life and Love in These Times, in Five Acts* (New York: W. C. Wemyss, 1867), 43. Subsequent page references will be indicated parenthetically.

3. Marvin Felheim, *The Theater of Augustin Daly* (New York: Greenwood Press, 1956), 51–55. Although it remains the definitive biography of Daly, Felheim's study lacks documentation and bibliographic references, so in this chapter I sometimes refer to the doctoral dissertation upon which the book is based: Marvin Felheim, "The Career of Augustin Daly" (PhD diss., Harvard University, 1948).

4. Advertisements for *Under the Gas-Light*, by Augustin Daly, Worrell Sisters' New-York Theatre, *New York Times*, 30 September 1867, 7; 2 October 1867, 7; 11 December 1867, 7. The production was also presented for a short time at the Brooklyn Academy of Music (*New York Times*, 8 October 1867, 7). Felheim's production history indicates that from 1867 to 1869, multiple theaters in New York City, Brooklyn, and England presented *Gaslight*; see "Career of Augustin Daly," 15–19; and *Theater of Augustin Daly*, 51–53. He claims that a production of the play was presented in Brooklyn or Manhattan nearly every year until the 1880s—further testament to its popularity.

5. Felheim, *Theater of Augustin Daly*, 49. As Nicholas Daly points out in *Literature, Technology, and Modernity, 1860–2000* (Cambridge: Cambridge University Press, 2004), 11–12, the railroad sensation in *Under the Gaslight* was not the first example of a scene involving trains and tracks, but it was the first to become popular in the United States.

6. Bruce A. McConachie, *Melodramatic Formations: American Theatre and Society, 1820–1870* (Iowa City: University of Iowa Press, 1992), 297n33.

7. Emma Dassori, "Performing the Woman Question: The Emergence of Anti-Suffrage Drama," *ATQ* (*American Transcendental Quarterly*) 19, no. 4 (December 2005): 301. For several examples, see Bettina Friedl, ed., *On to Victory: Propaganda Plays of the Woman Suffrage Movement* (Boston: Northeastern University Press, 1987).

8. Robert Darnton, *The Great Cat Massacre and Other Episodes in French Cultural History* (New York: Basic Books, 1984). I join Andrew Sofer (*The Stage Life of Props* [Ann Arbor: University of Michigan Press, 2003]), among others, in endeavoring to show how individual elements of the mise-en-scène operate in tandem to convey meaning. In some respects, my method mirrors the "thick description" of anthropologist Clifford Geertz, who attempts to "draw large conclusions from small, but very densely textured facts; to support broad assertions about the role of culture in the construction of collective life by engaging them exactly with complex specifics" (*The Interpretation of Cultures: Selected Essays by Clifford Geertz* [New

York: Basic Books, 1973], 28). Heeding Patrice Pavis's warning in *Languages of the Stage: Essays in the Semiology of the Theatre* (New York: Performing Arts Journal Publications, 1982) that an "object-bound and concrete conception of the theatrical relationship is dangerous" (71), I acknowledge that not all audience members may have perceived the connotations I attribute to various components in Daly's railroad rescue. Pavis recommends that the scholar take "two historicities" into account: "that of the work within its literary and social context, and that of the receiver in his own time and within a system of ideological and aesthetic expectations" (72); this is what I endeavor to do.

9. Peggy Phelan, "Feminist Theory, Poststructuralism, and Performance," *TDR: The Drama Review* 32, no. 1 (Spring 1988): 122; Rebecca Schneider, *Performing Remains: Art and War in Times of Theatrical Reenactment* (New York: Routledge, 2011), 6. Interestingly, in *Unmarked: The Politics of Performance* (London: Routledge, 1993), Phelan revises the phrase I quote here from her *TDR* article; in *Unmarked,* it reads, "the epitome of cross-cutting neck-wrenching cartoon drama" (160)—perhaps referring to Nell Fenwick in the animated cartoon *The Dudley Do-Right Show,* who is tied to the railroad tracks by the villainous Snidely Whiplash and saved by Dudley Do-Right, her hero. Phelan's generalization in the article, along with her inclination to be more specific in the revision (transforming "melodrama" to "cartoon drama"), reveals the strong cultural association of the damsel-in-distress with melodrama.

10. For more on the notion of separate spheres, see, among others, Nancy F. Cott, *The Bonds of Womanhood: "Woman's Sphere" in New England, 1780–1835* (New Haven: Yale University Press, 1977); Ann Douglas, *The Feminization of American Culture* (New York: Avon Books, 1977); Keith E. Melder, *Beginnings of Sisterhood: The American Woman's Rights Movement, 1800–1850* (New York: Schocken Books, 1977), 1–11; and Lori D. Ginzberg, *Women in Antebellum Reform* (Wheeling, IL: Harlan Davidson, 2000), 8–14. For alternative views, see Cathy N. Davidson, "Preface: No More Separate Spheres!," *American Literature* 70, no. 3 (September 1998): 443–63, and other articles in that issue critiquing the concept. Two discussions regarding the impact of separate-spheres ideology on women's moral reform activity include Melder, *Beginnings of Sisterhood,* 1–11; and Ginzberg, *Women in Antebellum Reform,* 8–14.

11. Melder, *Beginnings of Sisterhood,* 53; Karlyn Kohrs Campbell, ed., *Women Public Speakers in the United States, 1800–1925* (Westport, CT: Greenwood Press, 1993), xi, xii; Gay Gibson Cima, *Early American Women Critics: Performance, Religion, Race* (Cambridge: Cambridge University Press, 2006). Several scholars have examined women's involvement in the temperance movement as a precursor to their work for abolition and suffrage. See, for example, Barbara Leslie Epstein, *The Politics of Domesticity: Women, Evangelism, and Temperance in Nineteenth-*

Century America (Middletown, CT: Wesleyan University Press, 1981); Ian R. Tyrrell, "Women and Temperance in Antebellum America, 1830–1860," *Civil War History* 28, no. 2 (June 1982): 128–52; and Janet Zollinger Giele, *Two Paths to Women's Equality: Temperance, Suffrage, and the Origins of Modern Feminism* (New York: Twayne Publishers, 1995).

12. Suzanne M. Marilley, *Woman Suffrage and the Origins of Liberal Feminism in the United States, 1820–1920* (Cambridge: Harvard University Press, 1996), 16, 20.

13. Aileen S. Kraditor, *Means and Ends in American Abolitionism: Garrison and His Critics on Strategy and Tactics, 1834–1850* (New York: Pantheon Books, 1969), 41–62; Melder, *Beginnings of Sisterhood,* 147; Marilley, *Woman Suffrage,* 43. For more on Douglass's support of universal suffrage before the Civil War and his eventual abandonment of that position, see Benjamin Quarles, "Frederick Douglass and the Woman's Rights Movement," *Journal of Negro History* 25, no. 1 (January 1940): 35–44.

14. *Lily,* 15 February 1856, 28; Lori D. Ginzberg, "'Moral Suasion Is Moral Balderdash': Women, Politics, and Social Activism in the 1850s," *Journal of American History* 73, no. 3 (December 1986): 603–5.

15. Wendy Hamand Venet, *Neither Ballots nor Bullets: Women Abolitionists and the Civil War* (Charlottesville: University Press of Virginia, 1991), 94–122.

16. Elizabeth Cady Stanton, Susan B. Anthony, and Matilda Joslyn Gage, eds., *History of Woman Suffrage,* 3 vols. (New York: Fowler and Wells, 1882; reprint, Salem, NH: Ayer Company Publishers, 1985), 2:57n, 2:65. A political manifesto as well as a work of historiography, the *History* illuminates how nineteenth-century suffragists conceived and remembered their activities before, during, and after the war.

17. Carolyn Summers Vacca in *A Reform against Nature: Woman Suffrage and the Rethinking of American Citizenship, 1840–1920* (New York: Peter Lang, 2004) states that "women's rights activists subsumed their agenda to the war efforts and the plight of slaves" (45); but her study does not address the suffrage rhetoric deployed by leaders of the Woman's National Loyal League.

18. Ibid., 45–46.

19. "Resolutions of the Equal Rights Convention in New York City [12 December 1866]," in *The Selected Papers of Elizabeth Cady Stanton and Susan B. Anthony,* ed. Ann D. Gordon (New Brunswick: Rutgers University Press, 2000), 2:6–7. Incidentally, many of the commodities described in this passage—"bread, education, intelligence, self-protection, self-reliance and self-respect," and so forth—are, for the most part, successfully obtained by Laura in *Under the Gaslight* when she is forced to live on her own.

20. Marilley, *Woman Suffrage,* 71–80; Vacca, *A Reform against Nature,* 46–52; Quarles, "Frederick Douglass," 41.

21. Linda K. Kerber, *No Constitutional Right to Be Ladies: Women and the Obligations of Citizenship* (New York: Hill and Wang, 1998), 146. Here, Kerber is acknowledging Elizabeth Blackmar, *Manhattan for Rent, 1785–1850* (Ithaca: Cornell University Press, 1989), 117. See also Linda K. Kerber, *Women of the Republic: Intellect and Ideology in Revolutionary America* (Chapel Hill: University of North Carolina Press, 1980); and Marilley, *Woman Suffrage.*

22. Luce Irigaray, *This Sex Which Is Not One* [1977], trans. Catherine Porter with Carolyn Burke (Ithaca: Cornell University Press, 1985), 127. See also Vacca, *A Reform against Nature,* 6.

23. Interestingly, this publication was founded in 1851, at the dawn of the decade when female reformers began emphasizing electoral action in lieu of moral suasion (Ginzberg, "Moral Suasion").

24. Sarah Josepha Hale, "Editor's Table," *Godey's Lady's Book and Magazine* 75 (October 1867): 354 (emphasis in original); Horace Bushnell, *Women's Suffrage: The Reform against Nature* (New York: Charles Scribner, 1869).

25. *An Appeal against Anarchy of Sex to the Constitutional Convention and the People of the State of New-York by a Member of the Press* (New York: John A. Gray & Green Printers, 1867), 8 (emphasis added). See also Vacca, *A Reform against Nature,* 54.

26. Stanton, Anthony, and Gage, eds., *History,* 2:60–61 (emphasis in original).

27. Stanton, "'Reconstruction,'" 36.

28. Given the limited scope of this chapter, I have chosen to concentrate on how Laura seems to embody a prosuffrage model of womanhood, rather than on how she fits into the long tradition of melodramatic stage heroines. Discussions of the stock figures associated with the genre may be found in David Grimsted, *Melodrama Unveiled: American Theater and Culture, 1800–1850* (Chicago: University of Chicago Press, 1968), 171–203; and Lyn Stiefel Hill, "Heroes, Heroines, and Villains in English and American Melodrama, 1850–1900" (PhD diss., CUNY Graduate Center, 1981), among others.

29. Dion Boucicault, *The Octoroon; or, Life in Louisiana* [1859], in *Major Voices: The Drama of Slavery,* ed. Eric Gardner (New Milford, CT: Toby Press, 2005), 485–553.

30. It seems this line resonates deeply with McConachie because it serves as the title of his chapter on sensation drama (*Melodramatic Formations,* 215, 198–230).

31. Advertisement for *Under the Gas-Light,* by Augustin Daly, at Worrell Sisters' New-York Theatre, *New York Times,* 30 September 1867, 7.

32. According to a newspaper account published forty years later, the train effect was created and patented by John (Jack) Denham, a stage machinist. Apparently, the train "dash[ed] across the stage" and featured smoke and fire effects ("the engine snorted and hissed steam and puffed . . . fireworks from the smoke-stack").

Hugh O'Donnell, "Sophie Worrell: Responsible for Frou-Frou in America," unidentified press clipping (stamped 22 July 1900), William Worrell and Worrell Sisters Clippings File, Harvard Theatre Collection. See also T. Allston Brown, *A History of the New York Stage* (New York: Dodd, Mead, 1903), 2:385. The opinion written by Samuel Blatchford, the presiding judge of *Daly v. Palmer et al.*, 6 F. Cas. 1132 (S. D. New York 1868), describes the railroad rescue in *Under the Gaslight* as follows: "She takes an axe and strikes the door. The whistle is heard again, with the rumble of the approaching train. She gives more blows on the door with the axe, it opens, she runs and unfastens Snorkey, the lights of the engine appear, and she moves Snorkey's head from the track as the train rushes past."

33. Grimsted, *Melodrama Unveiled,* 174.

34. McConachie (citing Hill, "Heroes, Heroines, and Villains") underplays Laura's actions in the railroad sequence, asserting that "courageous heroines were fairly common in English and American melodramas after 1850" (*Melodramatic Formations,* 298n33). However, I would counter that these heroines probably reflect emergent ideas regarding the social and political advancement of women: after all, the first major US women's rights convention took place in Seneca Falls in 1848.

35. Lewis C. Strang, *Players and Plays of the Last Quarter Century* (Boston: L. C. Page, 1902), 103–4; Rose Eytinge, *The Memories of Rose Eytinge* (New York: Frederick A. Stokes, 1905), 85–86 (quotations on 86); "Amusements," *New York Times,* 13 August 1867, 5 (emphasis added); obituary for Rose Eytinge, *Boston Evening Transcript,* 20 December 1911, n.p., Rose Eytinge Clippings File, Harvard Theatre Collection.

36. McConachie, *Melodramatic Formations,* 297n33.

37. Joseph Francis Daly, *The Life of Augustin Daly* (New York: Macmillan, 1917), 75.

38. Felheim, *Theater of Augustin Daly,* 48; McConachie, *Melodramatic Formations,* 224, 221.

39. Brown, *History of the New York Stage,* 515. Felheim observes that Mortimer "had just made a hit as Badger" and that Badger's "function in uniting the principle characters and his general attitude are similar to Snorkey's" ("Career of Augustin Daly," 15n2).

40. "Amusements," *New York Times,* 13 August 1867, 5.

41. In *Protecting Soldiers and Mothers: The Political Origins of Social Policy in the United States* (Cambridge: Belknap Press of Harvard University Press, 1992), Theda Skocpol describes the human impact of the Civil War this way: "Overall, the Union side in the Civil War suffered 364,511 mortal casualties (including 140,414 battle deaths and 224,097 other deaths, mostly from disease). These numbers translate into a ratio of 18 (17.95) northerners killed per thousand in the population, whereas only 1.31 Americans per thousand were to die in World War I, and 3.14

per thousand in World War II. As for the Union military's wounded who survived, they numbered some 281,881, or about 14 (13.88) per thousand in the northern population" (103–4).

42. Jim Cullen, "'I's a Man Now': Gender and African American Men," in *Divided Houses: Gender and the Civil War,* ed. Catherine Clinton and Nina Silber (New York: Oxford University Press, 1992), 79.

43. For a general introduction to the notion of the citizen-soldier and how it permeates debates about citizenship, see R. Claire Snyder, *Citizen-Soldiers and Manly Warriors: Military Service and Gender in the Civic Republic Tradition* (Lanham, MD: Rowman & Littlefield, 1999).

44. Mark E. Neely Jr. and Harold Holzer, *The Union Image: Popular Prints of the Civil War North* (Chapel Hill: University of North Carolina Press, 2000).

45. Neely and Holzer analyze several other Civil War era illustrations featuring women, home, and hearth in *The Union Image,* 84–107. See also Bryan F. LeBeau, *Currier & Ives: America Imagined* (Washington, DC: Smithsonian Institution Press, 2001), 98–103. Neely and Holzer point out that surviving copyright registry books for Currier & Ives indicate that the proportion of war-themed prints decreased over the course of the conflict (*The Union Image,* 87–88). Although this possibly reflects a lessening appetite for pictures of soldiers, it seems equally likely that prints purchased by consumers early in the war had a long-term presence in domestic spaces, which may account for the decline in consumption.

46. *Soldier's Memorial* (1863), Sarony, Major & Knapp [lithographers], Print Collections, American Antiquarian Society, Worcester, MA.

47. Examples of these envelopes are available in the John A. McAllister Collection, Library Company of Philadelphia; and the Civil War Envelopes Collection, American Antiquarian Society.

48. William F. Thompson, *The Image of War: The Pictorial Reporting of the American Civil War* (1960; reprint, Baton Rouge: Louisiana State University Press, 1994), 104.

49. In "Warwork and the Crisis of Domesticity in the North," in *Divided Houses: Gender and the Civil War,* ed. Catherine Clinton and Nina Silber (New York: Oxford University Press, 1992), Jeanie Attie offers a contrasting view, arguing that "the antebellum ideology of gender spheres faced one of its first crises" during the war (248). Although women supported the Union cause in valuable ways, I would counter that the proliferation of Civil War images depicting women in domestic spaces, paired with the marked absence of prints featuring women working in male-dominated professions (such as clerking) during the war, suggests that "progressive" depictions of women were either unmarketable or unwelcome. See Neely and Holzer, *The Union Image,* 100; and William Fletcher Thompson Jr., "Pictorial Propaganda and the Civil War," *Wisconsin Magazine of History* 46, no. 1 (Autumn 1962): 24.

50. Simone de Beauvoir, *The Second Sex*, trans. H. M. Parshley (1949; reprint, New York: Alfred A. Knopf, 1983), 255.

51. Robert Bogdan, *Freak Show: Presenting Human Oddities for Amusement and Profit* (Chicago: University of Chicago Press, 1988), 108, 147–75.

52. De Beauvoir, *The Second Sex,* 267. Of course, other feminists, especially Judith Butler in *Gender Trouble: Feminism and the Subversion of Identity* (New York: Routledge, 1990; reprint, New York: Routledge, 1999) and *Bodies That Matter: On the Discursive Limits of "Sex"* (New York: Routledge, 1993), have augmented and updated de Beauvoir's idea; but I appreciate how de Beauvoir's phrasing, in particular, is invoked by scholars working within disability studies.

53. Kerber, *No Constitutional Right,* 224.

54. Complicating this view, Venet notes that radical Republicans pursued universal male suffrage "for both humanitarian and tactical reasons. They needed the votes of Southern blacks to ensure their dominance in the South and their national political hegemony" (*Neither Ballots nor Bullets,* 151).

55. Skocpol, *Protecting Soldiers and Mothers,* 149, 51 (emphasis in original).

56. Marilley, *Woman Suffrage,* 66–71.

57. Quoted in Melder, *Beginnings of Sisterhood,* 148.

58. Parker Pillsbury, *The Mortality of Nations: An Address Delivered before the American Equal Rights Association, in New York, Thursday Evening, May 9, 1867* (New York: Robert J. Johnston, 1867), 9, 10–11.

59. George William Curtis, *Equal Rights for Women. A Speech by George William Curtis in the Constitutional Convention of New York at Albany, July 19, 1867* (New York: American Equal Rights Association, 1867), 22.

60. Stanton, Anthony, and Gage, eds., *History,* 2:1, 2:19–20, 2:88. Contemporary scholars have verified that hundreds of women fought in the Civil War, almost always in disguise. See, for example, Elizabeth D. Leonard, *All the Daring of the Soldier: Women of the Civil War Armies* (New York: Penguin Books, 1999); and DeAnne Blanton and Lauren M. Cook, *They Fought Like Demons: Women Soldiers in the American Civil War* (Baton Rouge: Louisiana State University Press, 2002).

61. Abraham Lincoln, "Emancipation Proclamation," American Treasures of the Library of Congress, 2 December 2002, http://www.loc.gov/exhibits/treasures/trt026.html.

62. Kerber, *No Constitutional Right,* 243.

63. William Fletcher Thompson Jr., "Pictorial Images of the Negro during the Civil War," *Wisconsin Magazine of History* 48, no. 4 (Summer 1965): 285–88.

64. Thompson, *Image of War,* 172. See also LeBeau, *Currier & Ives,* 222.

65. *Major Martin R. Delany U.S.A.: Promoted on the Battle Field for Bravery,* lithograph by John Smith (Philadelphia), ca. 1865, National Portrait Gallery, Smithsonian Institution, Washington, DC (reproduced in Neely and Holzer, *The Union*

Image, 233); Cullen, "'I's a Man Now,'" 77. See also LeeAnn Whites, "The Civil War as a Crisis in Gender," in *Divided Houses: Gender and the Civil War,* ed. Catherine Clinton and Nina Silber (New York: Oxford University Press, 1992), 3–21.

66. Jennifer Putzi, *Identifying Marks: Race, Gender, and the Marked Body in Nineteenth-Century America* (Athens: University of Georgia Press, 2006).

67. Megan Kate Nelson, *Ruin Nation: Destruction and the American Civil War* (Athens: University of Georgia Press, 2012), 186.

68. Quoted in Frances Clarke, "'Honorable Scars': Northern Amputees and the Meaning of Civil War Injuries," in *Union Soldiers and the Northern Home Front: Wartime Experiences, Postwar Adjustments,* ed. Paul A. Cimbala and Randall M. Miller (New York: Fordham University Press, 2002), 379.

69. Putzi, *Identifying Marks,* 118.

70. Nelson, *Ruin Nation,* 193. See also Megan Kate Nelson, "Looking for Limbs in all the Right Places: Retrieving the Civil War's Broken Bodies," *Common-Place* 12, no. 1 (October 2011), http://www.common-place.org.

71. Ronald Jager, "Tool and Symbol: The Success of the Double-Bitted Axe in North America," *Technology and Culture* 40, no. 4 (1999): 858.

72. Henry J. Kauffman, *American Axes: A Survey of Their Development and Their Makers* (Brattleboro, VT: Stephen Greene Press, 1972), 17–18; Gary Kulik, "American Difference Revisited: The Case of the American Axe," in *American Material Culture: The Shape of the Field,* ed. Ann Smart Martin and J. Ritchie Garrison (Winterthur, DE: Winterthur Museum, 1997), 22, 29, 31; Charles A. Heavrin, *The Axe and Man: The History of Man's Early Technology as Exemplified by His Axe* (Mendham, NJ: Astragal Press, 1998), 110; David E. Nye, *America as Second Creation: Technology and Narratives of New Beginnings* (Cambridge: MIT Press, 2003), 44. See also Carroll W. Pursell, *The Machine in America: A Social History of Technology* (Baltimore: Johns Hopkins University Press, 1995), 14.

73. "Progress of Agriculture," *The Cultivator* (Albany, NY), January 1851, 33; "Raising the Hatchet," *Vanity Fair,* 20 April 1861, 185; D. W. Lothrop, "Legislative Agricultural Society," *New England Farmer,* May 1862, 211 (emphasis in original). Jager notes that Europe increasingly adopted the American axe in its forestry operations, implicitly acknowledging the superiority of the US version over the Continental original ("Tool and Symbol," 851).

74. Barbara Novak, "The Double-Edged Axe," *Art in America* 64, no. 1 (January–February 1976): 46. Novak discusses how the tree stump, in particular, symbolizes the tool's destructive power.

75. Unknown artist, *The Clearing of Paris* (ca. 1805), Hamlin Memorial Library and Museum, Paris Hill, ME; Kulik, "American Difference Revisited," 26.

76. Thomas Cole, *River in the Catskills* (1843), Museum of Fine Arts, Boston, MA; Tony Tanner, *Scenes of Nature, Signs of Men* (Cambridge: Cambridge Univer-

sity Press, 1987), 7–8; Alan Wallach, "Thomas Cole's *River in the Catskills* as Anti-pastoral," *Art Bulletin* 84, no. 2 (June 2002): 341–42.

77. Heavrin, *The Axe and Man,* 110, 20; Jager, "Tool and Symbol," 852; Kulik, "American Difference Revisited," 33–35.

78. D. W. Bartlett, *Life and Public Services of Hon. Abraham Lincoln* (New York: H. Dayton, 1860), 17. These are Lincoln's own words, part of an autobiography he wrote during his presidential campaign; see Don E. Fehrenbacher, ed., *Abraham Lincoln: Speeches and Writings, 1859–1865* (New York: Library of America, 1989), 160–67.

79. Gary L. Bunker, *From Rail-Splitter to Icon: Lincoln's Image in Illustrated Periodicals, 1860–1865* (Kent, OH: Kent State University Press, 2001), 16.

80. Harold Holzer, *Lincoln Seen and Heard* (Lawrence: University of Kansas Press, 2000), 75.

81. Bartlett, *Life and Public Services,* 109. For more about how axes and rails figured in Lincoln's first presidential campaign, particularly in illustrated periodicals, see Bunker, *From Rail-Splitter to Icon,* 31–66.

82. Lincoln Presidential Library and Museum, "A Presidential Discovery: Presidential Library Discovers Original Axe Lincoln Used to 'Show Off' for Wounded Soldiers a Week before His Assassination," news release, 16 February 2008. According to this news release, the axe was long thought to be one of the "numerous 'Lincoln axes' that have turned up through the years . . . [with] no proof . . . that Lincoln actually held and used them" (2); but documents recently discovered in the library's archives suggest that the tool is, indeed, the one used by Lincoln in Virginia on 8 April 1865.

83. In *New Readings in Theatre History* (Cambridge: Cambridge University Press, 2003), Jacky Bratton asserts that memoirs and anecdotes "have not often been read for what their writers or their subjects seem to stress," but they are nevertheless "important as a control of social resources through the making of myth and legend." In other words, individual accounts of an event are valuable not only for their content but also for the mythic, even flamboyant, qualities perpetuated through the act of storytelling. Errors, omissions, and hyperbole are inevitable by-products of the process; but the stories curated by the narrator, by virtue of *being* selective, tend to be noteworthy (95, 103).

84. Eytinge, *Memories of Rose Eytinge,* 116. It is interesting to note that Eytinge describes the railroad sequence here as a "situation" rather than a "sensation scene," even though her autobiography was published long after the latter phrase entered general usage in the 1860s. This provides further evidence that the concept of the "situation" resembles the later coinage "sensation scene," as I argue in the first chapter.

85. "Amusements, Etc.," *Daily Alta California,* 27 November 1867, 1 (emphasis

added). The *Alta* critic further observes that some middle-class female spectators in the dress circle were so moved by the sensations generated by the railroad scene that they attempted to rush the stage and rescue Snorkey themselves—in all likelihood, an instance of hyperbolic puffery, but nevertheless interesting due to its emphasis on female heroics.

86. Lawrence W. Levine, *Highbrow/Lowbrow: The Emergence of Cultural Hierarchy in America* (Cambridge: Harvard University Press, 1988), 178–92.

87. Moreover, I personally witnessed this phenomenon while watching *Under the Gaslight,* directed by Michael Hardart, at the Metropolitan Playhouse in New York City in 2009. During the railroad scene, I noted that a single spectator—restrained, perhaps, by the relatively small size of the venue as well as the conventions governing contemporary theatergoing—suggested, almost inaudibly, "The axe!" at the precise moment that nineteenth-century spectators apparently did.

88. For more on Nation, see Fran Grace, *Carry A. Nation: Retelling the Life* (Bloomington: Indiana University Press, 2001). Nation was widely criticized for her "unwomanly" behavior, which she exhibited most sensationally during her hatchetations.

89. Schneider, *Performing Remains,* 105.

90. Jean Baudrillard, *Simulacra and Simulation* [1981], trans. Sheila Faria Glaser (Ann Arbor: University of Michigan Press, 1994), 1, 6.

91. For more discussion about Boucicault's play, especially its presentation in England, see Nicholas Daly, *Literature, Technology, and Modernity,* 10–33.

92. Nan Enstad, "Dressed for Adventure: Working Women and Silent Movie Serials in the 1910s," *Feminist Studies* 21, no. 1 (Spring 1995): 83 and 90n44.

93. Baudrillard, *Simulacra and Simulation,* 2.

94. Ben Singer, *Melodrama and Modernity: Early Sensational Cinema and Its Contexts* (New York: Columbia University Press, 2001), 221–62; Elizabeth Reitz Mullenix, *Wearing the Breeches: Gender on the Antebellum Stage* (New York: St. Martin's Press, 2000), 90. Mullenix argues that women in breeches roles challenged conventional models of womanhood, especially during the early suffrage and dress-reform movements. Several other scholars have examined nineteenth-century actresses whose appeal and popularity centered on drag performances or "trouser roles" (e.g., Lydia Thompson, Charlotte Cushman, Adah Isaacs Menken); see, for example, Robert C. Allen, *Horrible Prettiness: Burlesque and American Culture* (Chapel Hill: University of North Carolina Press, 1991); Faye E. Dudden, *Women in the American Theatre: Actresses and Audiences, 1790–1870* (New Haven: Yale University Press, 1994); Lisa Merrill, *When Romeo Was a Woman: Charlotte Cushman and Her Circle of Female Spectators* (Ann Arbor: University of Michigan Press, 1999); and Daphne A. Brooks, *Bodies in Dissent: Spectacular Performances of Race and Freedom, 1850–1910* (Durham: Duke University Press, 2006), 131–206.

Afterword

1. Guy Debord, *The Society of the Spectacle* (Detroit: Black & Red, 1977), 23.

2. Martin Meisel, *Realizations: Narrative, Pictorial, and Theatrical Arts in Nineteenth-Century England* (Princeton: Princeton University Press, 1983), 3.

3. Jay Rosen, "The People Formerly Known as the Audience," *PressThink* (blog), 27 June 2006, http://archive.pressthink.org/2006/06/27/ppl_frmr.html. Rosen acknowledges Dan Gillmor, *We the Media: Grassroots Journalism by the People, for the People* (Sebastopol, CA: O'Reilly, 2004), for coining the phrase "former audience," which encapsulates the same concept.

4. Audrey Hudson, "Officials Probe How Crash 'So Survivable,'" *Washington Times*, 17 January 2009, A03; Nancy Dillon, "Sully's Got 'No Idea' He's a Star," *New York Daily News*, 17 January 2009, 6.

5. Financial Crisis Inquiry Commission, *The Financial Crisis Inquiry Report: Final Report of the National Commission on the Causes of the Financial and Economic Crisis in the United States* (Washington, DC: US Government Printing Office, January 2011), xv, 309–52; David Goldman, "Worst Year for Jobs Since '45," CNNMoney.com, 9 January 2009, http://money.cnn.com/2009/01/09/news/economy/jobs_december. The severity of the global recession, which is still in progress at this writing, makes it extremely difficult to estimate its cost to American taxpayers and citizens around the world. In many respects, the costs are incalculable, due to the recession's complex causes and enormous scope.

6. Ray Rivera, "A Pilot Becomes a Hero Years in the Making," *New York Times*, 16 January 2009, A21; Mike Lupica, "Praying Our New 'Pilot' Can Land Crisis as Safely," *New York Daily News*, 19 January 2009, 6.

7. Trymaine Lee and Cassi Feldman, "Construction Worker One Day, Subway Hero the Next," *New York Times*, 4 January 2007, B1; Diane Cardwell, "Subway Rescuer Receives the City's Highest Award," *New York Times*, 5 January 2007, B6; Robin Shulman, "Subway Samaritan Now Must Survive Onrushing Media; New York City Embraces Man Who Saved Stranger on Tracks," *Washington Post*, 5 January 2007, A03.

8. Michael Wilson, "Leap to Track. Rescue Man. Clamber Up. Catch a Train," *New York Times*, 17 March 2009, A20.

9. Dennis Murphy, Hoda Kotb, Peter Greenberg, and Chris Hansen, "Miracle on the Hudson," *Dateline*, NBC, 16 January 2009, NBC News Transcripts, Lexis-Nexis Academic.

10. Jill Dolan, *Utopia in Performance: Finding Hope at the Theater* (Ann Arbor: University of Michigan Press, 2005).

11. Michael M. Chemers, *Staging Stigma: A Critical Examination of the American Freak Show* (New York: Palgrave Macmillan, 2008), 103–30 (quotation on 105);

Rachel Adams, *Sideshow U.S.A.: Freaks and the American Cultural Imagination* (Chicago: University of Chicago Press, 2001), 210–28.

12. Chris Ariens, "'Today' Poised to Mark 15 Years as Nation's #1 Morning Show," 9 December 2010, MediaBistro.com, http://www.mediabistro.com/tvnewser.

13. Bruce A. McConachie, *Melodramatic Formations: American Theatre and Society, 1820–1870* (Iowa City: University of Iowa Press, 1992); Jeffrey D. Mason, *Melodrama and the Myth of America* (Bloomington: Indiana University Press, 1993); Matthew S. Buckley, "Refugee Theatre: Melodrama and Modernity's Loss," *Theatre Journal* 61, no. 2 (October 2009): 175–90.

14. As of September 2010, Suleman had been featured on more than thirty-five broadcasts. RenLai Merrill, BurrellesLuce (news transcript service), e-mail message to author, 22 September 2010.

15. See, for example, David Gilmore's caricature based on a photograph of Suleman during her final days of pregnancy, titled "Please Don't Pay the Crazy Lady," *Pretty on the Outside* (blog), 12 February 2009, http://prettyontheoutside.typepad.com/gilmore/2009/02/nadya-suleman-wants-to-get-paid.html.

16. Courtney Hazlett, "Octuplet Mom Patterning Self on Jolie," *The Scoop* (blog), *Today* (NBC), 11 February 2009, http://today.msnbc.msn.com/id/29125355.

17. Michael Okwu and Meredith Vieira, "Guardian Appointed to Oversee Finances of Nadya Suleman's Children," *Today*, NBC, 28 July 2009, NBC News Transcripts, LexisNexis Academic.

18. Ann Curry, Lisa Myers, and Brian Williams, "House Begins Work on Legislation to Rein in Huge Corporate Bonuses"; Meredith Vieira, "Kurt Andersen Discusses His Book, *Reset: How This Crisis Can Restore Our Values and Renew America*"; Al Roker, Kathie Lee Gifford, Natalie Morales, and Hoda Kotb, "Angela Logan and Josh Kaye Discuss How Angela Made Cakes to Save Her House from Foreclosure"; *Today*, NBC, 28 July 2009, NBC News Transcripts, LexisNexis Academic.

19. As Andy Lavender has argued, the presentational techniques and overall dramaturgy of most reality TV shows seem deeply indebted to the theater ("Pleasure, Performance and the *Big Brother* Experience," *Contemporary Theatre Review* 13, no. 2 [2003]: 15–23).

20. Rosemarie Garland-Thomson, *Staring: Why We Look* (New York: Oxford University Press, 2009), 14.

21. Anna McCarthy, *Ambient Television: Visual Culture and Public Space* (Durham: Duke University Press, 2001).

22. Baz Kershaw, *Theatre Ecology: Environments and Performance Events* (Cambridge: Cambridge University Press, 2007), 219.

Bibliography

Primary Sources

Newspapers and Serials Cited

Anti-Slavery Almanac
Anti-Slavery Record
Boston Evening Transcript
Christian World
Columbia Washingtonian
Commercial Advertiser (New York)
Crystal Fount (New York)
Cultivator (Albany)
Daily Alta California (San Francisco)
Daily Mail (Boston)
Dramatic Mirror (New York)
The Emancipator
Flushing Journal (New York)
Frank Leslie's Illustrated
Gleason's Pictorial Drawing-Room Companion
Gloucester Telegraph (MA)
Godey's Lady's Book and Magazine
Harper's Weekly
National Anti-Slavery Standard
New England Farmer
New York Herald
New York Sun
New York Times
New-York Tribune

Northern Budget (Troy, NY)
Pilot (Boston)
Pittsfield Washingtonian (MA)
Police Gazette (New York)
Princeton Whig
Vanity Fair
White Mountain Torrent (Concord, NH)
Worcester County Cataract (MA)

Manuscripts, Graphic Materials, and Archival Collections

Afro-Americana Collection, Library Company of Philadelphia
Bella C. Landauer Collection, Department of Prints, Photographs & Architectural Collections, New-York Historical Society
Billy Rose Theatre Collection, Performing Arts Library, New York Public Library
Boston Museum Cast Lists, 1845–1898, Harvard Theatre Collection, Houghton Library, Harvard University
Boston Museum Subject File, Charles E. Mason, Jr. Print Room, Boston Athenaeum
Cabinet Photos Collection, Harvard Theatre Collection, Houghton Library, Harvard University
Charles Phillips California Dramatic Collection, Bancroft Library, University of California–Berkeley
Clippings Files, Harvard Theatre Collection, Houghton Library, Harvard University
Clippings Files, San Francisco Performing Arts Library and Museum
Correspondence Files, Skinner Family Papers, Harvard Theatre Collection, Houghton Library, Harvard University
Diary of Harry Watkins, Skinner Family Papers, Harvard Theatre Collection, Houghton Library, Harvard University
Diary of William Henry Sedley Smith, 1852–1854, Rare Books and Manuscripts Department, Boston Public Library
Harry T. Peters Collection, Department of Prints, Photographs & Architectural Collections, New-York Historical Society
John A. McAllister Collection, Library Company of Philadelphia
John B. Gough Papers, American Antiquarian Society (Worcester, MA)
Moses Kimball Papers, Boston Athenaeum
Oversize Theatre Miscellaneous Files, California Historical Society (San Francisco)
Playbills Files, Harvard Theatre Collection, Houghton Library, Harvard University
Portrait Prints Collection, Harvard Theatre Collection, Houghton Library, Harvard University

Print Collection, Charles E. Mason, Jr. Print Room, Boston Athenaeum
Print Collections, American Antiquarian Society (Worcester, MA)
Print and Graphic Collections, Department of Prints, Photographs & Architectural Collections, New-York Historical Society
Printed Ephemera Collection, Historical Society of Pennsylvania
Prints and Photographs Collection, Library Company of Philadelphia
Prints and Photographs Division, Library of Congress
Russell Hartley Chronological Clipping Files, San Francisco Performing Arts Library and Museum
Samuel Stark Scrapbook Collection, 1860–1950, Special Collections and University Archives, Stanford University
Transparency Files, Department of Prints, Photographs & Architectural Collections, New-York Historical Society
William Henry Sedley Smith Collection of Prompt Books, Marked Editions, and Manuscript Sides, Harvard Theatre Collection, Houghton Library, Harvard University

Texts, Documents, and Published Anthologies

Aiken, George L. *Uncle Tom's Cabin; or, Life among the Lowly.* 1852–53. New York: Samuel French, 1858.

Abbott, Jacob. *The Alcove; Containing Some Further Account of Timboo, Mark, and Fanny.* New York: Harper & Brothers, 1856.

Abbott, Jacob. *Dialogues for the Amusement and Instruction of Young Persons.* New York: Harper & Brothers, 1856.

Abbott, Jacob. *Rollo Learning to Talk.* Philadelphia: Hogan and Thompson, 1850.

An Appeal against Anarchy of Sex to the Constitutional Convention and the People of the State of New-York by a Member of the Press. New York: John A. Gray & Green Printers, 1867.

Bartlett, D. W. *Life and Public Services of Hon. Abraham Lincoln.* New York: H. Dayton, 1860.

Boucicault, Dion. *The Octoroon; or, Life in Louisiana.* 1859. In *Major Voices: The Drama of Slavery,* edited by Eric Gardner, 485–553. New Milford, CT: Toby Press, 2005.

Brown, William Wells. *The Escape; or, A Leap for Freedom.* Boston: R. F. Wallcut, 1858.

Brown, William Wells. *A Lecture Delivered before the Female Anti-Slavery Society of Salem.* Boston: Massachusetts Anti-Slavery Society, 1847.

Brown, William Wells. *The Negro in the American Rebellion: His Heroism and His*

Fidelity. Boston: Lee and Shepard, 1867. Reprint, with an introduction and annotations by John David Smith, Athens: Ohio University Press, 2003.

Bushnell, Horace. *Women's Suffrage: The Reform against Nature.* New York: Charles Scribner, 1869.

Confessions of a Female Inebriate, or, Intemperance in High Life. Boston: William Henshaw, 1842.

Conway, H. J. *Uncle Tom's Cabin.* 1876 Promptbook. Howard Collection, Harry Ransom Humanities Research Center, University of Texas, Austin. Transcription available at Stephen Railton, ed., *Uncle Tom's Cabin and American Culture* (online archive), University of Virginia. http://www.iath.virginia.edu/utc/onstage/scripts/conwayhp.html.

Curtis, George William. *Equal Rights for Women. A Speech by George William Curtis in the Constitutional Convention of New York at Albany, July 19, 1867.* New York: American Equal Rights Association, 1867.

Cruikshank, George. *The Bottle in Eight Plates.* London: National Temperance Publication Depot, 1881.

Daly, Augustin. *Under the Gaslight: A Totally Original and Picturesque Drama of Life and Love in These Times, in Five Acts.* New York: W. C. Wemyss, 1867.

Daly, Joseph Francis. *The Life of Augustin Daly.* New York: Macmillan, 1917.

Daly v. Palmer et al. 6 F. Cas. 1132 (S. D. New York 1868).

Daniels, W. H. *The Temperance Reform and Its Great Reformers.* New York: Nelson & Phillips, 1878.

Dorchester, Daniel. *The Liquor Problem in All Ages.* New York: Phillips & Hunt, 1884. Reprint, New York: Arno Press, 1981.

Douglass, Frederick. *My Bondage and My Freedom.* New York: Miller, Orton & Mulligan, 1855.

Earle, Pliny. *History, Description and Statistics of the Bloomingdale Asylum for the Insane.* New York: Egbert, Hovey & King, 1848.

Eytinge, Rose. *The Memories of Rose Eytinge.* New York: Frederick A. Stokes, 1905.

Fehrenbacher, Don E., ed. *Abraham Lincoln: Speeches and Writings, 1859–1865.* New York: Library of America, 1989.

Friedl, Bettina, ed. *On to Victory: Propaganda Plays of the Woman Suffrage Movement.* Boston: Northeastern University Press, 1987.

Goffiana; A Review of the Life and Writings of John B. Gough. Boston: Ruggles, 1846.

Gordon, Ann D., ed. *The Selected Papers of Elizabeth Cady Stanton and Susan B. Anthony.* Vol. 2, *Against an Aristocracy of Sex: 1866 to 1873.* New Brunswick: Rutgers University Press, 2000.

Gough, John B. *An Autobiography.* Boston: J. B. Gough, Gould, Kendall & Lincoln, 1848.

Gough, John B. *Platform Echoes: Or, Living Truths for Head and Heart.* With an introduction by Rev. Lyman Abbott. Hartford, CT: A. D. Worthington, 1886.

Jarvis, Edward. *Insanity and Idiocy in Massachusetts: Report of the Commission on Lunacy.* 1855. Reprint, with a critical introduction by Gerald N. Grob, Cambridge: Harvard University Press, 1971.

Jewett, Charles. *The Youth's Temperance Lecturer.* Boston: Whipple and Damrell, 1840.

Jones, Benjamin S. *Abolitionrieties: Or, Remarks on Some of the Members of the Pennsylvania State Anti-Slavery Society for the Eastern District, and the American Anti-Slavery Society.* N.p., 1840[?].

Lincoln, Abraham. "Emancipation Proclamation." American Treasures of the Library of Congress. http://www.loc.gov/exhibits/treasures/trto26.html.

Moody, Richard. *Dramas from the American Theatre, 1762–1909.* Cleveland: World Publishing, 1966.

Parker, Freddie L., ed. *Stealing a Little Freedom: Advertisements for Slave Runaways in North Carolina, 1791–1840.* New York: Garland Publishing, 1994.

Pictures and Stories from Uncle Tom's Cabin. Boston: John P. Jewett, 1853.

Pillsbury, Parker. *The Mortality of Nations: An Address Delivered before the American Equal Rights Association, in New York, Thursday Evening, May 9, 1867.* New York: Robert J. Johnston, 1867.

Ray, Isaac. *Mental Hygiene.* 1863. Reprint, with an introduction by Frank J. Curran, New York: Hafner Publishing, 1968.

Rush, Benjamin. *An Inquiry into the Effects of Ardent Spirits upon the Human Body and Mind.* 6th ed. with additions. New York: Cornelius Davis, 1811.

Rush, Benjamin. *Medical Inquiries and Observations Upon the Diseases of the Mind.* Philadelphia: Kimber & Richardson, 1812.

Smith, W. H. *The Drunkard; or, The Fallen Saved!* 1844. Boston: Jones's Publishing House, 1847.

Stanton, Elizabeth Cady, Susan B. Anthony, and Matilda Joslyn Gage, eds. *History of Woman Suffrage.* 3 vols. New York: Fowler and Wells, 1882. Reprint, Salem, NH: Ayer Company Publishers, 1985.

Stowe, Harriet Beecher. *A Key to Uncle Tom's Cabin.* Boston: John P. Jewett, 1853.

Stowe, Harriet Beecher. *Uncle Tom's Cabin; or, Life among the Lowly.* 2 vols. Boston: John P. Jewett, 1852.

Stowe, Harriet Beecher. *Uncle Tom's Cabin; or, Life among the Lowly.* Illustrated ed. Boston: John P. Jewett, 1853.

Weld, Theodore Dwight. *American Slavery as It Is: Testimony of a Thousand Witnesses.* New York: American Anti-Slavery Society, 1839.

Secondary Sources

Books, Articles, and Chapters

Abzug, Robert H. *Cosmos Crumbling: American Reform and the Religious Imagination.* New York: Oxford University Press, 1994.

Adamis, Dimitrios, Adrian Treloar, Finbarr C. Martin, and Alastair J. D. MacDonald. "A Brief Review of the History of Delirium as a Mental Disorder." *History of Psychiatry* 18, no. 4 (December 2007): 459–69.

Adams, Bluford. *E Pluribus Barnum: The Great Showman and the Making of U.S. Popular Culture.* Minneapolis: University of Minnesota Press, 1997.

Adams, Rachel. *Sideshow U.S.A.: Freaks and the American Cultural Imagination.* Chicago: University of Chicago Press, 2001.

Ahmed, Sara. *The Cultural Politics of Emotion.* New York: Routledge, 2004.

Allen, Robert C. *Horrible Prettiness: Burlesque and American Culture.* Chapel Hill: University of North Carolina Press, 1991.

Altick, Richard D. *The Shows of London.* Cambridge: Belknap Press of Harvard University Press, 1978.

Altieri, Charles. *The Particulars of Rapture: An Aesthetics of the Affects.* Ithaca: Cornell University Press, 2003.

Anthony, David. *Paper Money Men: Commerce, Manhood, and the Sensational Public Sphere in Antebellum America.* Columbus: Ohio State University Press, 2009.

Aptheker, Herbert. "Slave Resistance in the United States." In *Key Issues in the Afro-American Experience,* vol. 1, *To 1877,* edited by Nathan I. Huggins, Martin Kilson, and Daniel M. Fox, 161–73. New York: Harcourt Brace Jovanovich, 1971.

Attie, Jeanie. "Warwork and the Crisis of Domesticity in the North." In *Divided Houses: Gender and the Civil War,* edited by Catherine Clinton and Nina Silber, 247–59. New York: Oxford University Press, 1992.

Augst, Thomas. "A Drunkard's Story." *Common-Place* 10, no. 3 (April 2010). http://www.common-place.org.

Augst, Thomas. "Temperance, Mass Culture, and the Romance of Experience." *American Literary History* 19, no. 2 (Summer 2007): 297–323.

Auslander, Philip. *Liveness: Performance in a Mediatized Culture.* London: Routledge, 1999.

Bainbridge, William Sims. "Religious Insanity in America: The Official Nineteenth-Century Theory." *Sociological Analysis* 45, no. 3 (Fall 1984): 223–39.

Bank, Rosemarie K. *Theatre Culture in America, 1825–1860.* Cambridge: Cambridge University Press, 1997.

Bastide, Roger. *The Sociology of Mental Disorder.* 1965. Translated by Jean McNeil. New York: David McKay, 1972.

Bates, William. "Actors Who Have Died on the Stage." *Notes and Queries* 4, no. 278 (1873): 338–40.
Baudrillard, Jean. *Simulacra and Simulation.* 1981. Translated by Sheila Faria Glaser. Ann Arbor: University of Michigan Press, 1994.
de Beauvoir, Simone. *The Second Sex.* 1949. Translated by H. M. Parshley. Reprint, New York: Alfred A. Knopf, 1983.
Beckerman, Bernard. "Spectacle in the Theatre." *Theatre Survey* 25, no. 1 (May 1984): 1–13.
Ben Chaim, Daphna. *Distance in the Theatre: The Aesthetics of Audience Response.* Ann Arbor, MI: UMI Research Press, 1984.
Berlant, Lauren. *The Female Complaint: The Unfinished Business of Sentimentality in American Culture.* Durham: Duke University Press, 2008.
Bernard, Joel. "From Fasting to Abstinence: The Origins of the American Temperance Movement." In *Drinking: Behavior and Belief in Modern History,* edited by Susanna Barrows and Robin Room, 337–53. Berkeley: University of California Press, 1991.
Bernstein, Robin. *Racial Innocence: Performing Childhood and Race from Slavery to Civil Rights.* New York: New York University Press, 2011.
Best, Stephen M. *The Fugitive's Properties: Law and the Poetics of Possession.* Chicago: University of Chicago Press, 2004.
Birdoff, Harry. *The World's Greatest Hit: Uncle Tom's Cabin.* New York: S. F. Vanni, 1947.
Blanton, DeAnne, and Lauren M. Cook. *They Fought Like Demons: Women Soldiers in the American Civil War.* Baton Rouge: Louisiana State University Press, 2002.
Blau, Herbert. *The Dubious Spectacle: Extremities of Theater, 1976–2000.* Minneapolis: University of Minnesota Press, 2002.
Blocker, Jack S., Jr. *American Temperance Movements: Cycles of Reform.* Boston: Twayne Publishers, 1989.
Blumberg, Leonard U., and William L. Pittman. *Beware the First Drink! The Washington Temperance Movement and Alcoholics Anonymous.* Seattle: Glen Abbey Books, 1991.
Boal, Augusto. *Games for Actors and Non-Actors.* 1992. Translated by Adrian Jackson. 2nd ed. New York: Routledge, 2002.
Bogdan, Robert. *Freak Show: Presenting Human Oddities for Amusement and Profit.* Chicago: University of Chicago Press, 1988.
Booth, Michael R. "The Drunkard's Progress: Nineteenth-Century Temperance Drama." *Dalhousie Review* 44 (Summer 1964): 205–12.
Booth, Michael R. *English Melodrama.* London: Herbert Jenkins, 1965.

Booth, Michael R. *Theatre in the Victorian Age.* Cambridge: Cambridge University Press, 1991.

Booth, Michael R. *Victorian Spectacular Theatre, 1850–1910.* Boston: Routledge & Kegan Paul, 1981.

Bratton, Jacky. *New Readings in Theatre History.* Cambridge: Cambridge University Press, 2003.

Bratton, Jacky, Jim Cook, and Christine Gledhill, eds. *Melodrama: Stage Picture Screen.* London: British Film Institute, 1994.

Brennan, Teresa. *The Transmission of Affect.* Ithaca: Cornell University Press, 2004.

Brooks, Daphne A. *Bodies in Dissent: Spectacular Performances of Race and Freedom, 1850–1910.* Durham: Duke University Press, 2006.

Brooks, Peter. "Melodrama, Body, Revolution." In *Melodrama: Stage Picture Screen,* edited by Jacky Bratton, Jim Cook, and Christine Gledhill, 11–24. London: British Film Institute, 1994.

Brooks, Peter. *The Melodramatic Imagination: Balzac, Henry James, Melodrama, and the Mode of Excess.* New York: Columbia University Press, 1985.

Brown, T. Allston. *A History of the New York Stage.* 3 vols. New York: Dodd, Mead, 1903.

Browne, Nick, ed. *Refiguring American Film Genres: History and Theory.* Berkeley: University of California Press, 1998.

Browne, Stephen. "'Like Gory Spectres': Representing Evil in Theodore Weld's *American Slavery as It Is.*" *Quarterly Journal of Speech* 80 (August 1994): 277–92.

Buckley, Matthew S. "Refugee Theatre: Melodrama and Modernity's Loss." *Theatre Journal* 61, no. 2 (October 2009): 175–90.

Bunker, Gary L. *From Rail-Splitter to Icon: Lincoln's Image in Illustrated Periodicals, 1860–1865.* Kent, OH: Kent State University Press, 2001.

Butler, Jon. *Awash in a Sea of Faith: Christianizing the American People.* Cambridge: Harvard University Press, 1990.

Butler, Judith. *Bodies That Matter: On the Discursive Limits of "Sex."* New York: Routledge, 1993.

Butler, Judith. *Gender Trouble: Feminism and the Subversion of Identity.* New York: Routledge, 1990. Reprint, with a new preface, New York: Routledge, 1999.

Campbell, Karlyn Kohrs, ed. *Women Public Speakers in the United States, 1800–1925.* Westport, CT: Greenwood Press, 1993.

Campbell, Stanley W. *The Slave Catchers: Enforcement of the Fugitive Slave Law, 1850–1860.* Chapel Hill: University of North Carolina Press, 1970.

Caric, Ric N. "The Man with the Poker Enters the Room: Delirium Tremens and Popular Culture in Philadelphia, 1828–1850." *Pennsylvania History* 74, no. 4 (Autumn 2007): 452–91.

Carlson, Marvin. "The Eternal Instant: Some Thoughts on Theatre and Religion." *Assaph* 14 (1997): 33–44.

Carlson, Marvin. *The Haunted Stage: The Theatre as Memory Machine.* Ann Arbor: University of Michigan Press, 2001.

Cassuto, Leonard. *The Inhuman Race: The Racial Grotesque in American Literature and Culture.* New York: Columbia University Press, 1997.

de Certeau, Michel. *The Practice of Everyday Life.* Berkeley: University of California Press, 1984.

Cima, Gay Gibson. *Early American Women Critics: Performance, Religion, Race.* Cambridge: Cambridge University Press, 2006.

Clarke, Frances. "'Honorable Scars': Northern Amputees and the Meaning of Civil War Injuries." In *Union Soldiers and the Northern Home Front: Wartime Experiences, Postwar Adjustments,* edited by Paul A. Cimbala and Randall M. Miller, 361–94. New York: Fordham University Press, 2002.

Clawson, Mary Ann. *Constructing Brotherhood: Class, Gender, and Fraternalism.* Princeton: Princeton University Press, 1989.

Cohen, Daniel A. "The Origin and Development of the *New England Primer.*" *Children's Literature* 5 (1976): 52–57.

Cosdon, Mark. *The Hanlon Brothers: From Daredevil Acrobatics to Spectacle Pantomime, 1833–1931.* Carbondale: Southern Illinois University Press, 2009.

Cott, Nancy F. *The Bonds of Womanhood: "Woman's Sphere" in New England, 1780–1835.* New Haven: Yale University Press, 1977.

Cowan, William Tynes. *The Slave in the Swamp: Disrupting the Plantation Narrative.* New York: Routledge, 2005.

Crain, Patricia. *The Story of A: The Alphabetization of America from* The New England Primer *to* The Scarlet Letter. Stanford: Stanford University Press, 2000.

Crary, Jonathan. *Techniques of the Observer: On Vision and Modernity in the Nineteenth Century.* Cambridge: MIT Press, 1990.

Crowley, John W. "Slaves to the Bottle: Gough's Autobiography and Douglass's Narrative." In *The Serpent in the Cup: Temperance in American Literature,* edited by David S. Reynolds and Debra J. Rosenthal, 115–35. Amherst: University of Massachusetts Press, 1997.

Crowley, John W., ed. *Drunkard's Progress: Narratives of Addiction, Despair, and Recovery.* Baltimore: Johns Hopkins University Press, 1999.

Crowley, John W., and William L. White. *Drunkard's Refuge: The Lessons of the New York State Inebriate Asylum.* Amherst: University of Massachusetts Press, 2004.

Cullen, Jim. "'I's a Man Now': Gender and African American Men." In *Divided Houses: Gender and the Civil War,* edited by Catherine Clinton and Nina Silber, 76–91. New York: Oxford University Press, 1992.

Dain, Norman. *Concepts of Insanity in the United States, 1789–1865*. New Brunswick: Rutgers University Press, 1964.

Daly, Nicholas. *Literature, Technology, and Modernity, 1860–2000*. Cambridge: Cambridge University Press, 2004.

Darnton, Robert. *The Great Cat Massacre and Other Episodes in French Cultural History*. New York: Basic Books, 1984.

Dassori, Emma. "Performing the Woman Question: The Emergence of Anti-Suffrage Drama." *ATQ (American Transcendental Quarterly)* 19, no. 4 (December 2005): 301–17.

Davidson, Cathy N. "Preface: No More Separate Spheres!" *American Literature* 70, no. 3 (September 1998): 443–63.

Davis, Lennard J. *Enforcing Normalcy: Disability, Deafness, and the Body*. London: Verso, 1995.

Davis, Tracy C. "The Actress in Victorian Pornography." *Theatre Journal* 41, no. 3 (October 1989): 294–315.

Davis, Tracy C., and Peter Holland, eds. *The Performing Century: Nineteenth-Century Theatre's History*. Basingstoke, UK: Palgrave Macmillan, 2007.

Debord, Guy. *The Society of the Spectacle*. 1967. Detroit: Black & Red, 1977.

Dennett, Andrea Stulman. *Weird and Wonderful: The Dime Museum in America*. New York: New York University Press, 1997.

Denning, Michael. *Mechanic Accents: Dime Novels and Working-Class Culture in America*. London: Verso, 1987.

Diamond, Michael. *Victorian Sensation, or, the Spectacular, the Shocking, and the Scandalous in Nineteenth-Century Britain*. London: Anthem Press, 2003.

Dolan, Jill. *Utopia in Performance: Finding Hope at the Theater*. Ann Arbor: University of Michigan Press, 2005.

Dorsey, Peter A. "Becoming the Other: The Mimesis of Metaphor in Douglass's *My Bondage and My Freedom*." *PMLA* 111, no. 3 (May 1996): 435–50.

Douglas, Ann. *The Feminization of American Culture*. New York: Avon Books, 1977.

Dudden, Faye E. *Women in the American Theatre: Actresses and Audiences, 1790–1870*. New Haven: Yale University Press, 1994.

Dulles, Foster Rhea. *A History of Recreation: America Learns to Play*. New York: Appleton-Century-Crofts, 1965.

Eagleton, Terry. *After Theory*. New York: Basic Books, 2003.

Elsom, John. *Erotic Theatre*. New York: Taplinger Publishing, 1974.

Enders, Jody. *Death by Drama and Other Medieval Urban Legends*. Chicago: University of Chicago Press, 2002.

Enstad, Nan. "Dressed for Adventure: Working Women and Silent Movie Serials in the 1910s." *Feminist Studies* 21, no. 1 (Spring 1995): 67–90.

Epstein, Barbara Leslie. *The Politics of Domesticity: Women, Evangelism, and Tem-*

perance in Nineteenth-Century America. Middletown, CT: Wesleyan University Press, 1981.

Epstein, Dena J. *Sinful Tunes and Spirituals: Black Folk Music to the Civil War.* Urbana: University of Illinois Press, 1977.

Felheim, Marvin. "The Career of Augustin Daly." PhD diss., Harvard University, 1948.

Felheim, Marvin. *The Theater of Augustin Daly.* New York: Greenwood Press, 1956.

Fenichell, Jill Weitzman. "Fragile Lessons: Ceramic and Porcelain Representations of *Uncle Tom's Cabin.*" In *Ceramics in America 2006,* edited by Robert Hunter, 40–57. Hanover: Chipstone Foundation, 2006.

Fichtelberg, Joseph. *Critical Fictions: Sentiment and the American Market, 1780–1870.* Athens: University of Georgia Press, 2003.

Fiedler, Leslie A. Foreword to *Freakery: Cultural Spectacles of the Extraordinary Body,* edited by Rosemarie Garland Thomson. New York: New York University Press, 1996.

Fiedler, Leslie A. *Freaks: Myths and Images of the Secret Self.* New York: Simon and Schuster, 1978.

Fiedler, Leslie A. *The Inadvertent Epic: From Uncle Tom's Cabin to Roots.* New York: Simon and Schuster, 1979.

Financial Crisis Inquiry Commission. *The Financial Crisis Inquiry Report: Final Report of the National Commission on the Causes of the Financial and Economic Crisis in the United States.* Washington, DC: US Government Printing Office, January 2011.

Finkelman, Paul, ed. *Articles on American Slavery.* Vol. 6, *Fugitive Slaves.* New York: Garland Publishing, 1989.

Foucault, Michel. *Discipline and Punish: The Birth of the Prison.* 1975. Translated by Alan Sheridan. 2nd ed. New York: Vintage Books, 1995.

Franklin, John Hope, and Loren Schweninger. *Runaway Slaves: Rebels on the Plantation.* New York: Oxford University Press, 1999.

Frick, John W. "'Not from the Drowsy Pulpit!': Moral Reform Melodrama on the Nineteenth-Century Stage." *Theatre Symposium* 15 (2007): 41–51.

Frick, John W. *Theatre, Culture and Temperance Reform in Nineteenth-Century America.* Cambridge: Cambridge University Press, 2003.

Gara, Larry. "The Fugitive Slave Law: A Double Paradox." *Civil War History* 10, no. 3 (September 1964): 229–40.

Gara, Larry. "The Professional Fugitive in the Abolition Movement." *Wisconsin Magazine of History* 48, no. 3 (Spring 1965): 196–204.

Garland-Thomson, Rosemarie. *Extraordinary Bodies: Figuring Physical Disability in American Culture and Literature.* New York: Columbia University Press, 1997.

Garland-Thomson, Rosemarie. Introduction to *Freakery: Cultural Spectacles of the*

Extraordinary Body, edited by Rosemarie Garland Thomson, 1–19. New York: New York University Press, 1996.

Garland-Thomson, Rosemarie. *Staring: Why We Look.* New York: Oxford University Press, 2009.

Garner, Stanton B. *Bodied Spaces: Phenomenology and Performance in Contemporary Drama.* Ithaca: Cornell University Press, 1994.

Garvey, T. Gregory. *Creating the Culture of Reform in Antebellum America.* Athens: University of Georgia Press, 2006.

Geertz, Clifford. *The Interpretation of Cultures: Selected Essays by Clifford Geertz.* 1973. Reprint, with a new introduction, New York: Basic Books, 2000.

Gerould, Daniel C. "The Americanization of Melodrama." In *American Melodrama,* edited by Daniel C. Gerould, 7–29. New York: Performing Arts Journal Publications, 1983.

Gerould, Daniel C., ed. *Melodrama.* New York: New York Literary Forum, 1980.

Gerould, Daniel C. "Representations of Melodramatic Performance." In *Browning Institute Studies,* vol. 18, edited by Adrienne Auslander Munich, 49–66. New York: Browning Institute, 1990.

Gerould, Daniel C., and Marvin Carlson, eds. Introduction to *Pixérécourt: Four Melodramas.* New York: Martin E. Segal Theatre Center, 2002.

Giele, Janet Zollinger. *Two Paths to Women's Equality: Temperance, Suffrage, and the Origins of Modern Feminism.* New York: Twayne Publishers, 1995.

Ginzberg, Lori D. "'Moral Suasion Is Moral Balderdash': Women, Politics, and Social Activism in the 1850s." *Journal of American History* 73, no. 3 (December 1986): 601–22.

Ginzberg, Lori D. *Women in Antebellum Reform.* Wheeling, IL: Harlan Davidson, 2000.

Gledhill, Christine. *Home Is Where the Heart Is: Studies in Melodrama and the Woman's Film.* London: BFI Publications, 1987.

Glenn, Susan A. *Female Spectacle: The Theatrical Roots of Modern Feminism.* Cambridge: Harvard University Press, 2000.

Gossett, Thomas F. *Uncle Tom's Cabin and American Culture.* Dallas: Southern Methodist University Press, 1985.

Grace, Fran. *Carry A. Nation: Retelling the Life.* Bloomington: Indiana University Press, 2001.

Gregg, Melissa, and Gregory J. Seigworth, eds. *The Affect Theory Reader.* Durham: Duke University Press, 2010.

Grimsted, David. *Melodrama Unveiled: American Theater and Culture, 1800–1850.* Chicago: University of Chicago Press, 1968.

Grob, Gerald N. Introduction to Edward Jarvis, *Insanity and Idiocy in Massachu-*

setts: Report of the Commission on Lunacy (1855), 1–71. Cambridge: Harvard University Press, 1971.

Gross, Robert A. "Preserving Culture: Edward Jarvis and the Memory of Concord." In *Traditions and Reminiscences of Concord, Massachusetts, 1779–1878,* edited by Sarah Chapin, xv–xliv. Amherst: University of Massachusetts Press, 1993.

Grossman, Barbara Wallace. *A Spectacle of Suffering: Clara Morris on the American Stage.* Carbondale: Southern Illinois University Press, 2009.

Grosz, Elizabeth. "Intolerable Ambiguity: Freaks as/at the Limit." In *Freakery: Cultural Spectacles of the Extraordinary Body,* edited by Rosemarie Garland Thomson, 55–66. New York: New York University Press, 1996.

Gunning, Tom. "The Horror of Opacity: The Melodrama of Sensation in the Plays of André de Lorde." In *Melodrama: Stage Picture Screen,* edited by Jacky Bratton, Jim Cook, and Christine Gledhill, 50–61. London: British Film Institute, 1994.

Gusfield, Joseph R. *Symbolic Crusade: Status Politics and the American Temperance Movement.* Urbana: University of Illinois Press, 1963.

Haidt, Jonathan. *The Righteous Mind: Why Good People Are Divided by Politics and Religion.* New York: Pantheon Books, 2012.

Haidt, Jonathan, and Jesse Graham. "When Morality Opposes Justice: Conservatives Have Moral Intuitions That Liberals May Not Recognize." *Social Justice Research* 20 (2007): 98–116.

Haidt, Jonathan, and Craig Joseph. "Intuitive Ethics: How Innately Prepared Intuitions Generate Culturally Variable Virtues." *Daedalus* 133, no. 4 (Fall 2004): 55–66.

Haidt, Jonathan, and Craig Joseph. "The Moral Mind: How Five Sets of Innate Moral Intuitions Guide the Development of Many Culture-Specific Virtues, and Perhaps Even Modules." In *The Innate Mind,* vol. 3, *Foundations and the Future,* edited by Peter Carruthers, Stephen Laurence, and Stephen P. Stich, 367–91. New York: Oxford University Press, 2008.

Hall, Stuart, ed. *Representation: Cultural Representations and Signifying Practices.* London: Sage, 1997.

Halttunen, Karen. "Gothic Mystery and the Birth of the Asylum: The Cultural Construction of Deviance in Early Nineteenth-Century America." In *Moral Problems in American Life: New Perspectives on Cultural History,* edited by Karen Halttunen and Lewis Perry, 41–57. Ithaca: Cornell University Press, 1998.

Harding, Vincent. *There Is a River: The Black Struggle for Freedom in America.* San Diego: Harcourt Brace, 1981.

Harris, Neil. *Humbug: The Art of P. T. Barnum.* Boston: Little, Brown, 1973.

Hartman, Saidiya V. *Scenes of Subjection: Terror, Slavery, and Self-Making in Nineteenth-Century America.* New York: Oxford University Press, 1997.

Hatch, Nathan O. *The Democratization of American Christianity.* New Haven: Yale University Press, 1989.

Hays, Michael, and Anastasia Nikolopoulou, eds. *Melodrama: The Cultural Emergence of a Genre.* New York: St. Martin's Press, 1996.

Heavrin, Charles A. *The Axe and Man: The History of Man's Early Technology as Exemplified by His Axe.* Mendham, NJ: Astragal Press, 1998.

Heilman, Robert Bechtold. *Tragedy and Melodrama: Versions of Experience.* Seattle: University of Washington Press, 1968.

Henkin, David M. *City Reading: Written Words and Public Spaces in Antebellum New York.* New York: Columbia University Press, 1998.

Hessinger, Rodney. "'The Most Powerful Instrument of College Discipline': Student Disorder and the Meritocracy in the Colleges of the Early American Republic." *History of Education Quarterly* 29, no. 3 (Autumn 1999): 237–62.

Hessinger, Rodney. *Seduced, Abandoned, and Reborn: Visions of Youth in Middle-Class America, 1780–1850.* Philadelphia: University of Pennsylvania Press, 2005.

Hevey, David. *The Creatures That Time Forgot: Photography and Disability Imagery.* London: Routledge, 1992.

Hill, Lyn Stiefel. "Heroes, Heroines, and Villains in English and American Melodrama, 1850–1900." PhD diss., Graduate Center, City University of New York, 1981.

Hofstadter, Richard. *The Age of Reform: From Bryan to F.D.R.* New York: Random House, 1955.

Holzer, Harold. *Lincoln Seen and Heard.* Lawrence: University of Kansas Press, 2000.

Holzwarth, Paul. Transcription of Grave Markers in Oxford South Congregational Church Cemetery, Oxford, Worcester County, Massachusetts. N.d. *USGenWeb Project.* http://usgwarchives.net/ma/mafiles.htm.

Huet, Marie-Hélène. *Monstrous Imagination.* Cambridge: Harvard University Press, 1993.

Hughes, Amy E. "Answering the Amusement Question: Antebellum Temperance Drama and the Christian Endorsement of Leisure." *New England Theatre Journal* 15 (2004): 1–19.

Hughes, Amy E. "Defining Faith: Theatrical Reactions to Pro-Slavery Christianity in Antebellum America." In *Interrogating America through Theatre and Performance,* edited by William Demastes and Iris Smith Fischer, 29–45. New York: Palgrave Macmillan, 2007.

Ireland, Joseph Norton. *Records of the New York Stage.* Vol. 1, *1759 to 1860.* New York: T. H. Morrell, 1867.

Irigaray, Luce. *This Sex Which Is Not One.* 1977. Translated by Catherine Porter with Carolyn Burke. Ithaca: Cornell University Press, 1985.

Jager, Ronald. "Tool and Symbol: The Success of the Double-Bitted Axe in North America." *Technology and Culture* 40, no. 4 (October 1999): 833–60.

Jauss, Hans Robert. *Toward an Aesthetic of Reception.* Translated by Timothy Bahti. Minneapolis: University of Minnesota Press, 1982.

Jimenez, Mary Ann. *Changing Faces of Madness: Early American Attitudes and Treatment of the Insane.* Hanover, NH: University Press of New England, 1987.

Kahn, Edward. "Creator of Compromise: William Henry Sedley Smith and the Boston Museum's *Uncle Tom's Cabin.*" *Theatre Survey* 41, no. 2 (November 2000): 71–82.

Kauffman, Henry J. *American Axes: A Survey of Their Development and Their Makers.* Brattleboro, VT: Stephen Greene Press, 1972.

Kerber, Linda K. *No Constitutional Right to Be Ladies: Women and the Obligations of Citizenship.* New York: Hill and Wang, 1998.

Kerber, Linda K. *Women of the Republic: Intellect and Ideology in Revolutionary America.* Chapel Hill: University of North Carolina Press, 1980.

Kershaw, Baz. "Curiosity or Contempt: On Spectacle, the Human, and Activism." *Theatre Journal* 55, no. 4 (December 2003): 591–611.

Kershaw, Baz. *Theatre Ecology: Environments and Performance Events.* Cambridge: Cambridge University Press, 2007.

Kirshenblatt-Gimblett, Barbara. *Destination Culture: Tourism, Museums, and Heritage.* Berkeley: University of California Press, 1998.

Kraditor, Aileen S. *Means and Ends in American Abolitionism: Garrison and His Critics on Strategy and Tactics, 1834–1850.* New York: Pantheon Books, 1969.

Kruger, Loren. "Our Theater? Stages in an American Cultural History." *American Literary History* 8, no. 4 (1996): 699–714.

Kulik, Gary. "American Difference Revisited: The Case of the American Axe." In *American Material Culture: The Shape of the Field,* edited by Ann Smart Martin and J. Ritchie Garrison, 21–36. Winterthur, DE: Winterthur Museum, 1997.

Lang, Robert. *American Film Melodrama: Griffith, Vidor, Minnelli.* Princeton: Princeton University Press, 1989.

Lavender, Andy. "Pleasure, Performance and the *Big Brother* Experience." *Contemporary Theatre Review* 13, no. 2 (2003): 15–23.

LeBeau, Bryan F. *Currier & Ives: America Imagined.* Washington, DC: Smithsonian Institution Press, 2001.

Lender, Mark Edward, and James Kirby Martin. *Drinking in America: A History.* New York: Free Press, 1982.

Leonard, Elizabeth D. *All the Daring of the Soldier: Women of the Civil War Armies.* New York: Penguin Books, 1999.

Levine, Lawrence W. *Highbrow/Lowbrow: The Emergence of Cultural Hierarchy in America.* Cambridge: Harvard University Press, 1988.

Lincoln Presidential Library and Museum. "A Presidential Discovery: Presidential Library Discovers Original Axe Lincoln Used to 'Show Off' for Wounded Soldiers a Week before His Assassination." News release. 16 February 2008.

Linton, Simi. *Claiming Disability: Knowledge and Identity.* New York: New York University Press, 1998.

Lott, Eric. *Love and Theft: Blackface Minstrelsy and the American Working Class.* New York: Oxford University Press, 1993.

MacKethan, Lucinda H. "From Fugitive Slave to Man of Letters: The Conversion of Frederick Douglass." *Journal of Narrative Technique* 16, no. 1 (Winter 1986): 55–71.

Maginnes, David R. "The Case of the Court House Rioters in the Rendition of the Fugitive Slave Anthony Burns, 1854." *Journal of Negro History* 56, no. 1 (January 1971): 31–42.

Marilley, Suzanne M. *Woman Suffrage and the Origins of Liberal Feminism in the United States, 1820–1920.* Cambridge: Harvard University Press, 1996.

Marra, Kim. *Strange Duets: Impresarios and Actresses in the American Theatre, 1865–1914.* Iowa City: University of Iowa Press, 2006.

Marzio, Peter C. "Lithography as a Democratic Art: A Reappraisal." *Leonardo* 4, no. 1 (Winter 1971): 37–48.

Mason, Jeffrey D. *Melodrama and the Myth of America.* Bloomington: Indiana University Press, 1993.

Massumi, Brian. *Parables for the Virtual: Movement, Affect, Sensation.* Durham: Duke University Press, 2002.

McArthur, Benjamin. *The Man Who Was Rip Van Winkle: Joseph Jefferson and Nineteenth-Century American Theatre.* New Haven: Yale University Press, 2007.

McArthur, Judith N. "Demon Rum on the Boards: Temperance Melodrama and the Tradition of Antebellum Reform." *Journal of the Early Republic* 9, no. 4 (Winter 1989): 517–40.

McCarthy, Anna. *Ambient Television: Visual Culture and Public Space.* Durham: Duke University Press, 2001.

McConachie, Bruce A. "Catharsis and the Materiality of Spectatorship." *Assaph* 14 (1997): 95–100.

McConachie, Bruce A. "H. J. Conway's Dramatization of *Uncle Tom's Cabin:* A Previously Unpublished Letter." *Theatre Journal* 34, no. 2 (May 1982): 149–54.

McConachie, Bruce A. *Melodramatic Formations: American Theatre and Society, 1820–1870.* Iowa City: University of Iowa Press, 1992.

McConachie, Bruce A. "New Historicism and American Theater History: Toward an Interdisciplinary Paradigm for Scholarship." In *The Performance of Power: Theatrical Discourse and Politics,* edited by Sue-Ellen Case and Janelle Reinelt, 265–71. Iowa City: University of Iowa Press, 1991.

McConachie, Bruce A. "Out of the Kitchen and into the Marketplace: Normalizing *Uncle Tom's Cabin* for the Antebellum Stage." *Journal of American Drama and Theatre* 3, no. 1 (Winter 1991): 5–28.

McCray, Florine Thayer. *The Life-Work of the Author of Uncle Tom's Cabin.* New York: Funk & Wagnalls, 1889.

Meer, Sarah. *Uncle Tom Mania: Slavery, Minstrelsy, and Transatlantic Culture in the 1850s.* Athens: University of Georgia Press, 2005.

Meisel, Martin. *Realizations: Narrative, Pictorial, and Theatrical Arts in Nineteenth-Century England.* Princeton: Princeton University Press, 1983.

Melder, Keith E. *Beginnings of Sisterhood: The American Woman's Rights Movement, 1800–1850.* New York: Schocken Books, 1977.

Merrill, Lisa. *When Romeo Was a Woman: Charlotte Cushman and Her Circle of Female Spectators.* Ann Arbor: University of Michigan Press, 1999.

Miller, Tice. *Entertaining the Nation: American Drama in the Eighteenth and Nineteenth Centuries.* Carbondale: Southern Illinois University Press, 2007.

Mintz, Steven. *Moralists and Modernizers: America's Pre-Civil War Reformers.* Baltimore: Johns Hopkins University Press, 1995.

Moody, Richard. Introduction to *The Drunkard.* In *Dramas from the American Theatre, 1762–1909,* edited by Richard Moody, 277–80. Cleveland: World Publishing, 1966.

Morgan, Jo-Ann. *Uncle Tom's Cabin as Visual Culture.* Columbia: University of Missouri Press, 2007.

Mullenix, Elizabeth Reitz. *Wearing the Breeches: Gender on the Antebellum Stage.* New York: St. Martin's Press, 2000.

Nathans, Heather S. *Early American Theatre from the Revolution to Thomas Jefferson: Into the Hands of the People.* Cambridge: Cambridge University Press, 2003.

Nathans, Heather S. *Slavery and Sentiment on the American Stage, 1787–1861: Lifting the Veil of Black.* Cambridge: Cambridge University Press, 2009.

Neely, Mark E., Jr., and Harold Holzer. *The Union Image: Popular Prints of the Civil War North.* Chapel Hill: University of North Carolina Press, 2000.

Nelson, Katherine H. "The Temperance Physicians: Developing Concepts of Addiction." PhD diss., American University, 2006.

Nelson, Megan Kate. "Looking for Limbs in All the Right Places: Retrieving the Civil War's Broken Bodies." *Common-Place* 12, no. 1 (October 2011). http://www.common-place.org.

Nelson, Megan Kate. *Ruin Nation: Destruction and the American Civil War.* Athens: University of Georgia Press, 2012.

Novak, Barbara. "The Double-Edged Axe." *Art in America* 64, no. 1 (January–February 1976): 44–50.

Nye, David E. *America as Second Creation: Technology and Narratives of New Beginnings.* Cambridge: MIT Press, 2003.

Parfait, Claire. *The Publishing History of* Uncle Tom's Cabin, *1852–2002*. Burlington, VT: Ashgate, 2007.

Parker, Freddie L. *Running for Freedom: Slave Runaways in North Carolina, 1775–1840*. New York: Garland Publishing, 1993.

Pavis, Patrice. *Languages of the Stage: Essays in the Semiology of the Theatre.* New York: Performing Arts Journal Publications, 1982.

Pease, Jane H., and William H. Pease. "Confrontation and Abolition in the 1850s." *Journal of American History* 58, no. 4 (March 1972): 923–37.

Pegram, Thomas R. *Battling Demon Rum: The Struggle for a Dry America, 1800–1933*. Chicago: Ivan R. Dee, 1998.

Peters, Harry T. *Currier and Ives: Printmakers to the American People.* Garden City, NY: Doubleday, Doran, 1942.

Phelan, Peggy. "Feminist Theory, Poststructuralism, and Performance." *TDR: The Drama Review* 32, no. 1 (Spring 1988): 107–27.

Phelan, Peggy. *Unmarked: The Politics of Performance.* London: Routledge, 1993.

Piepmeier, Alison. *Out in Public: Configurations of Women's Bodies in Nineteenth-Century America.* Chapel Hill: University of North Carolina Press, 2004.

Proehl, Geoffrey S. *Coming Home Again: American Family Drama and the Figure of the Prodigal.* Madison, NJ: Fairleigh Dickinson University Press, 1997.

Pursell, Carroll W. *The Machine in America: A Social History of Technology.* Baltimore: Johns Hopkins University Press, 1995.

Putzi, Jennifer. *Identifying Marks: Race, Gender, and the Marked Body in Nineteenth-Century America.* Athens: University of Georgia Press, 2006.

Quarles, Benjamin. *Black Abolitionists.* New York: Oxford University Press, 1969.

Quarles, Benjamin. "Frederick Douglass and the Woman's Rights Movement." *Journal of Negro History* 25, no. 1 (January 1940): 35–44.

Quinn, Michael L. "Celebrity and the Semiotics of Acting." *New Theatre Quarterly* 4 (1990): 154–61.

Rahill, Frank. *The World of Melodrama.* University Park: Pennsylvania State University Press, 1967.

Railton, Stephen, ed. *Uncle Tom's Cabin and American Culture.* Online archive. University of Virginia. http://www.iath.virginia.edu/utc.

Read, Alan. *Theatre and Everyday Life: An Ethics of Performance.* London: Routledge, 1995.

Rebhorn, Matthew. "What Is It? The Frontier, Melodrama, and Boucicault's Amalgamated Drama." *Journal of American Drama and Theatre* 19, no. 3 (Fall 2007): 5–33.

Reed, Peter P. *Rogue Performances: Staging the Underclasses in Early American Theatre Culture.* New York: Palgrave Macmillan, 2009.

Richards, Jeffrey H. *Drama, Theatre, and Identity in the American New Republic.* Cambridge: Cambridge University Press, 2005.

Riis, Thomas L. "The Music and Musicians in Nineteenth-Century Productions of *Uncle Tom's Cabin.*" *American Music* 4, no. 3 (Autumn 1986): 268–86.

Roach, Joseph. *Cities of the Dead: Circum-Atlantic Performance.* New York: Columbia University Press, 1996.

Roach, Joseph. *It.* Ann Arbor: University of Michigan Press, 2007.

Rorabaugh, W. J. *The Alcoholic Republic: An American Tradition.* New York: Oxford University Press, 1979.

Rothman, David J. *The Discovery of the Asylum: Social Order and Disorder in the New Republic.* 1971. Rev. ed., Piscataway, NJ: Aldine Transaction, 2002.

Sánchez-Eppler, Karen. "Temperance in the Bed of a Child: Incest and Social Order in Nineteenth-Century America." *American Quarterly* 47, no. 1 (March 1995): 1–33.

Schneider, Rebecca. "Performance Remains." *Performance Research* 6, no. 2 (2001): 100–108.

Schneider, Rebecca. *Performing Remains: Art and War in Times of Theatrical Reenactment.* New York: Routledge, 2011.

Scull, Andrew T. "Madness and Segregative Control: The Rise of the Insane Asylum." *Social Problems* 24, no. 3 (February 1977): 337–51.

Sedgwick, Eve Kosofsky. *Touching Feeling: Affect, Pedagogy, Performativity.* Durham: Duke University Press, 2003.

Sedgwick, Eve Kosofsky, and Adam Frank, eds. *Shame and Its Sisters: A Silvan Tomkins Reader.* Durham: Duke University Press, 1995.

Sekora, John. "'Mr. Editor, If You Please': Frederick Douglass, *My Bondage and My Freedom,* and the End of the Abolitionist Imprint." *Callaloo* 17, no. 2 (Spring 1994): 608–26.

Semonin, Paul. "Monsters in the Marketplace: The Exhibition of Human Oddities in Early Modern England." In *Freakery: Cultural Spectacles of the Extraordinary Body,* edited by Rosemarie Garland Thomson, 69–81. New York: New York University Press, 1996.

Shaffer, Jason. *Performing Patriotism: National Identity in the Colonial and Revolutionary American Theater.* Philadelphia: University of Pennsylvania Press, 2007.

Silverman, Joan L. "'I'll Never Touch Another Drop': Images of Alcoholism and Temperance in American Popular Culture, 1874–1919." PhD diss., New York University, 1979.

Singer, Ben. *Melodrama and Modernity: Early Sensational Cinema and Its Contexts.* New York: Columbia University Press, 2001.

Skinner, Maud, and Otis Skinner. *One Man in His Time: The Adventures of H. Watkins, Strolling Player, 1845–63, from His Journal.* Philadelphia: University of Pennsylvania Press, 1938.

Skocpol, Theda. *Protecting Soldiers and Mothers: The Political Origins of Social Policy in the United States.* Cambridge: Belknap Press of Harvard University Press, 1992.

Smith, Susan Harris. *American Drama: The Bastard Art.* Cambridge: Cambridge University Press, 1997.

Snyder, R. Claire. *Citizen-Soldiers and Manly Warriors: Military Service and Gender in the Civic Republic Tradition.* Lanham, MD: Rowman & Littlefield, 1999.

Sofer, Andrew. *The Stage Life of Props.* Ann Arbor: University of Michigan Press, 2003.

Sorisio, Carolyn. *Fleshing Out America: Race, Gender, and the Politics of the Body in American Literature, 1833–1879.* Athens: University of Georgia Press, 2002.

Spero, Patrick. "The Revolution in Popular Publications: The Almanac and *New England Primer,* 1750–1800." *Early American Studies: An Interdisciplinary Journal* 8, no. 1 (Winter 2010): 41–74.

States, Bert O. *Great Reckonings in Little Rooms: On the Phenomenology of Theater.* Berkeley: University of California Press, 1985.

Stevenson, Louise L. "Virtue Displayed: The Tie-Ins of *Uncle Tom's Cabin,*" 2007. Available at Stephen Railton, ed., *Uncle Tom's Cabin and American Culture,* online archive, University of Virginia, http://www.iath.virginia.edu/utc/interpret/exhibits/stevenson/stevenson.html.

Strang, Lewis C. *Players and Plays of the Last Quarter Century.* Boston: L. C. Page, 1902.

Swift, Mary Grace. "Dancers in Flames." *Dance Chronicle* 5, no. 1 (1982): 1–10.

Tanner, Tony. *Scenes of Nature, Signs of Men.* Cambridge: Cambridge University Press, 1987.

Taylor, Diana. *The Archive and the Repertoire: Performing Cultural Memory in the Americas.* Durham: Duke University Press, 2003.

Thompson, William F[letcher, Jr]. *The Image of War: The Pictorial Reporting of the American Civil War.* 1960. Reprint, Baton Rouge: Louisiana State University Press, 1994.

Thompson, William F[letcher, Jr]. "Pictorial Images of the Negro during the Civil War." *Wisconsin Magazine of History* 48, no. 4 (Summer 1965): 282–94.

Thompson, William F[letcher, Jr]. "Pictorial Propaganda and the Civil War." *Wisconsin Magazine of History* 46, no. 1 (Autumn 1962): 21–31.

Thurman, Howard. *Deep River: Reflections on the Religious Insight of Certain of the Negro Spirituals.* Port Washington, NY: Kennikat Press, 1969.

Toll, Robert C. *Blacking Up: The Minstrel Show in Nineteenth-Century America.* New York: Oxford University Press, 1974.

Tomkins, Silvan S. "The Quest for Primary Motives: Biography and Autobiography of an Idea." *Journal of Personality and Social Psychology* 41, no. 2 (1981): 306–29.

Tomlinson, Stephen. *Head Masters: Phrenology, Secular Education, and Nineteenth-Century Social Thought.* Tuscaloosa: University of Alabama Press, 2005.

Tompkins, Jane. *Sensational Designs: The Cultural Work of American Fiction, 1790–1860.* New York: Oxford University Press, 1985.

Turner, Patricia A. *Crafted Lives: Stories and Studies of African American Quilters.* Jackson: University Press of Mississippi, 2009.

Turner, Patricia A. "The Rise and Fall of Eliza Harris: From Novel to Tom Shows to Quilts." 2007. Available at Stephen Railton, ed., *Uncle Tom's Cabin and American Culture,* online archive, University of Virginia, http://utc.iath.virginia.edu/interpret/exhibits/turner/turner.html.

Tyrrell, Ian R. *Sobering Up: From Temperance to Prohibition in Antebellum America, 1800–1860.* Westport, CT: Greenwood Press, 1979.

Tyrrell, Ian R. "Women and Temperance in Antebellum America, 1830–1860." *Civil War History* 28, no. 2 (June 1982): 128–52.

Vacca, Carolyn Summers. *A Reform against Nature: Woman Suffrage and the Rethinking of American Citizenship, 1840–1920.* New York: Peter Lang, 2004.

Van Wyhe, John. *Phrenology and the Origins of Victorian Scientific Naturalism.* Aldershot, England: Ashgate, 2004.

Venet, Wendy Hamand. *Neither Ballots nor Bullets: Women Abolitionists and the Civil War.* Charlottesville: University Press of Virginia, 1991.

Voskuil, Lynn M. *Acting Naturally: Victorian Theatricality and Authenticity.* Charlottesville: University of Virginia Press, 2004.

Wallach, Alan. "Thomas Cole's *River in the Catskills* as Antipastoral." *Art Bulletin* 84, no. 2 (June 2002): 334–50.

Warder, Graham. "Selling Sobriety: How Temperance Reshaped Culture in Antebellum America." PhD diss., University of Massachusetts-Amherst, 2000.

Warner, Jessica, and Janine Riviere. "Why Abstinence Matters to Americans." *Addiction* 102, no. 4 (April 2007): 502–5.

Welter, Barbara. "The Cult of True Womanhood, 1820–1860." *American Quarterly* 18 (Summer 1966): 151–74.

Whites, LeeAnn. "The Civil War as a Crisis in Gender." In *Divided Houses: Gender and the Civil War,* edited by Catherine Clinton and Nina Silber, 3–21. New York: Oxford University Press, 1992.

Whitney, Lisa. "In the Shadow of *Uncle Tom's Cabin:* Stowe's Vision of Slavery from the Great Dismal Swamp." *New England Quarterly* 66, no. 4 (December 1993): 552–69.

Williams, Judith. "*Uncle Tom's* Women." In *African American Performance and Theater History: A Critical Reader,* edited by Harry J. Elam and David Krasner, 19–39. New York: Oxford University Press, 2001.

Williams, Linda. *Playing the Race Card: Melodramas of Black and White from Uncle Tom to O. J. Simpson.* Princeton: Princeton University Press, 2002.

Wilson, Dudley. *Signs and Portents: Monstrous Births from the Middle Ages to the Enlightenment.* London: Routledge, 1993.

Winter, William. *The Jeffersons.* Boston: James R. Osgood, 1881.

Wren, René. "Players Who Died Acting." *Theatre Magazine* 30, no. 9 (1919): 166.

Wyatt-Brown, Bertram. "Modernizing Southern Slavery: The Proslavery Argument Reinterpreted." In *Region, Race, and Reconstruction: Essays in Honor of C. Vann Woodward,* edited by J. Morgan Krousser and James M. McPherson, 27–49. New York: Oxford University Press, 1982.

Young, Harvey. *Embodying Black Experience: Stillness, Critical Memory, and the Black Body.* Ann Arbor: University of Michigan Press, 2010.

Newspapers, Television, Blogs, and Websites Cited

CNNMoney.com (http://www.cnnmoney.com)

Dateline (NBC)

MediaBistro.com (http://www.mediabistro.com)

MSNBC.com (http://www.msnbc.com)

New York Daily News

New York Times

PressThink (http://archive.pressthink.org)

Pretty on the Outside (http://prettyontheoutside.typepad.com)

The Scoop (http://scoop.today.com)

Today (NBC)

Washington Post (Washington, DC)

Washington Times (Washington, DC)

Index

Page references in italics indicate an illustration.